RACE, IQ AND JENSEN

I approach the doctrine of Forms with reluctance
because it was brought into philosophy by friends of
mine; but surely for a philosopher ... an even better
friend must be the truth.

Aristotle

RACE, IQ AND JENSEN

DISCARDED

JAMES R. FLYNN
Professor of Political Studies

University of Otago

Routledge & Kegan Paul

London, Boston and Henley

TO NATALIE

First published in 1980
by Routledge & Kegan Paul Ltd
39 Store Street,
London WC1E 7DD,
9 Park Street,
Boston, Mass. 02108, USA and
Broadway House,
Newtown Road,
Henley-on-Thames,
Oxon RG9 1EN
Printed and bound in Great Britain by
Thomson Litho Ltd,
East Kilbride

British Library Cataloguing in Publication Data

Flynn, James Robert
  Race, IQ and Jensen.
  1. Intellect
  2. Ethnopsychology
  I. Title
  153.9'2   BF432.A1   80-49972

ISBN 0 7100 0651 9

CONTENTS

PREFACE AND
ACKNOWLEDGMENTS

This book deals with areas in which research and publications accumulate swiftly. The reader has a right to know
the cut-off date of the author's research: the author
stopped reading books on race and IQ, with some pleasure,
on 1 January 1980 and published research, with a few exceptions, on about the same date. No doubt I have missed
something of significance and of course I have not used
everything read.

As for thanking others for their help, I owe much to
many but will limit myself to expressing my gratitude to
those whom I bothered the most: Prof. John C. Loehlin,
Department of Psychology, University of Texas; Dr G.F.
Liddell, Mr J.A. Harraway, and Mr B.F.J. Manly, Department
of Mathematics, University of Otago; and Mr F.W. Pernell
of the National Archives and Records Service, Suitland,
Maryland. Prof. Loehlin read a complete draft of the
manuscript and I owe him a particular debt for saving me
from a number of mistakes and omissions.

Arthur R. Jensen was generous enough to grant me access
to material from his own most recent book, 'Bias in Mental
Testing', prior to its publication. Both Sandra Scarr
and Jensen extended the same courtesy by sending me drafts
of material to be included in her forthcoming book, 'IQ:
Race, Social Class, and Individual Differences'.
vi

Chapter 1

THE RACIST AND HIS NEED FOR EVIDENCE

Before we get to Jensen and race and IQ, some philosophy
and some history. The racist must choose between two
options: that people of a certain colour (say black) or
appearance ('looks' Jewish) are to be despised or feared
or exploited or rejected simply because of their colour or
appearance; that they merit such treatment because their
colour or appearance is correlated with certain personal
traits. Philosophical analysis shows that the first
option is non-viable; history shows that every racist
ideologue of any sophistication has seen this and chosen
the second. The second option forces him to assert pro-
positions which can be falsified by evidence - and thus
engenders a powerful need for evidence he can use in his
own defence.

Philosophers have argued that whenever a man claims to
hold a principle or ideal, we can ask him to universalize
it. This sounds very profound, but for our purposes we
can treat it as meaning no more than that whenever people
use words or make judgments they must do so with logical
consistency. This is true not just when we talk ethics
but also of everyday life. If someone picks up a copy of
the London 'Times' and says 'the newspaper has come' and
then, the next day says 'the cat is on the mat', he had

better explain himself.   Unless he does, says something
like 'the "Times" is so catty in its editorials that I
have a special name for it', he pays the price of confus-
ing whoever hears him.   If a man tells his fiancé that he
loves steak and then turns up his nose when she cooks it
for him, he too had better have an explanation, perhaps
that he is feeling ill or is too upset to eat.   Then we
understand: to like steak one day and not like it the
next seemed inconsistent, but now his criteria for liking
steak have been elaborated - 'I like it when I am in good
health, have not already had it for lunch, it is cooked to
my taste, and so forth.'   Now that his criteria have been
spelled out, his judgments are at least logically consistent and we can understand him, which is a prerequisite
for deciding whether or not we agree with him.

When a racist makes judgments, we can use logic as a
powerful weapon to force him to make his ideals clear.
When he says black men deserve to be excluded or kept in
their place or exterminated, we can ask him whether this
is true simply because they are black.   For example, if
it were a Nazi talking we might say this: assume that
through industrial pollution a chemical got in the water
supply which turned the skins of all Germans permanently
black;   would they then deserve to be exploited or exterminated?   He can of course answer in the affirmative with
complete logical consistency but this merely shows that
while logic is important, it is not everything.   The
reason a Nazi could not answer as above has nothing to do
with logic but with the fact that such an answer carries
with it an unacceptable price.

It is important to be clear about that price.   It is
not that only a 'fanatic' could bear to imagine the people
he admires dying.   Our Nazi might well be proud to see

every last German die in the service of his ideals, let us
say to avoid being dominated by an 'inferior' race.   The
real price he would pay is that of denying the universal
experience of mankind, including himself and his fellow
Germans, about what is important in relations between
human beings, namely, such things as intelligence, character and personal traits.   When we interact with people,
we do so in terms of whether they are honest or dishonest,
generous or miserly, courageous or cowardly, witty or
boring.   Our Nazi admires his fellow Germans not simply
because they are white but because they are the 'master
race', they are (he thinks) more creative, courageous,
regal, etc., than the rest of us.   In this he is like
everyone else: everyone reacts to people in terms of personal traits;   and to deny that these are relevant to our
judgments about the merits of men, to say that colour uncorrelated with personal traits is our criterion, is to
treat as unimportant what everyone finds to be important
in his everyday experience.

There is of course no such thing as an absolute price
and there are no logical limits on human psychology.   We
may someday find a racist who says that colour uncorrelated with personal traits is his criterion of merit.   Let
him: his 'ideology' is logically flawless but he has rendered it completely non-viable.   A man who tries to build
an ideology on a distaste for colour has put himself in
the same position as a book reviewer who tells us that his
criterion for judging books is the colour of the binding.
You cannot build an ideology on a brute psychological
fact.   Booth Tarkington speaks of a Frenchman who went
beserk every time he heard the word 'camel'.   Interesting
psychologically but it does not have much ideological
potential.   I hope no one thinks I am denying any of the

facts of racist psychology.   The racist may well hate
people simply because they are black and want to see them
go under simply because they are black;   that is not unusual but quite common among racists.   However, this complex of emotions adds to my thesis rather than the reverse: they virtually impel the racist to claim that
blackness is correlated with unlovely personal traits.
The more he hates black men the more he finds it impossible to say, 'I hate them with all my soul, but they are
wiser, stronger, more courageous, more generous than we
are.'   Hatred of colour for its own sake tends to liqui-
date itself as a criterion of human worth.

    As a matter of historical record, there has never been
a racist ideologue who merely asserted that he hated a
particular colour or race.   Whether we read Drumont,
Gobineau and Treitschke in the nineteenth century, or
Chamberlain, Rosenberg and Hitler in the twentieth, their
books are full of the connection between race and personal
traits.   To take Hitler as an example, we find that Jews
are selfish, filthy, dishonest, cowardly (1) - also
greedy, heartless, and unscrupulous. (2)   They tend to be
bow-legged and have a distinctive body odour repugnant to
Gentiles, although they often conceal this with per-
fumes. (3)   They take a special delight in raping Gentile
girls so as to defile the race. (4)   The Jew can accomplish this last because his traits are genetic rather than
environmental: 'He has certain traits which Nature has
given him and he can never rid himself of these traits.'
The Jew cannot become a German at heart because of his
blood and character. (5)   Hitler did not neglect blacks
or their IQ or their genetic potential.   The interbreed-
ing of black and white produces inferior offspring and he
is not impressed by the fact that a few blacks can be edu-

cated to practise a profession.   They are born half-apes
and the same effort expended on the intelligent races
would bring all of the latter to the same achievements a
thousand times sooner. (6)

An ideologue who wishes to stake a claim to serious
consideration does not of course stop at warning us of a
threat, he must have a theory of history and social
change.   Hitler explained most of world history in terms
of race, for example, the inherent characteristics of the
Jews illuminate the defeat of Germany in the First World
War, the Russian revolution, the Bolshevik domination of
Russia. (7)   Once one sees that Nordics are born rulers,
Alpines perfect slaves, Irish childish and unstable, Slavs
beings who think with the spinal cord rather than the
brain, Jews no more than Alpine Slavs, much becomes clear.
These views, by the way, were all expressed by American
intellectuals in the present century and America has not
lacked for those who wrote history as a story of Anglo-
Saxon superiority.   We need only note such works as E.A.
Freeman, 'Comparative Politics' (1874), J.K. Hosmer,
'Short History of Anglo-Saxon Freedom' (1890), J.W. Bur-
gess, 'Political Science and Comparative Constitutional
Law' (1890), and even Theodore Roosevelt, 'The Winning of
the West'. (8)

I have no wish to dwell on this dreary material but I
did want to show that racism has never been (and can never
be) simply a set of ejaculatory utterances, a complex of
emotions, or an aesthetic quirk about certain colours.
It is a full-blown ideology which asserts empirical hypotheses at every turn.   Moreover, we have added to our
knowledge: the racist not only asserts a connection between race or colour and personal traits; he also asserts
that the connection is genetic rather than environmental

and he associates a genetic connection with something that is necessary or permanent.   First, his psychology demands it: his hatred of blacks is such that he does not want to allow for the possibility of redemption and he fears that environmentalism will offer the 'inferior' individual a chance of such.   Second, the core of his ideology is warning an audience of a threat and the pollution of the genetic pool is irreplaceable in its rhetorical impact. Third, there is his claim to intellectual eminence, that only he really understands history.   Unless the connection between race and culture has remained constant, at least for the duration of historical time, and unless that connection is causal, the causal lines running from race to culture rather than the reverse, history becomes a complex interaction of peoples and cultures and race loses its explanatory force.   This means something the racist cannot tolerate: his kind of history becomes too much like anyone else's history and he has nothing unique to contribute.   All of the hypotheses he finds so essential are of course falsifiable by evidence, and therefore the many works I have cited, including Hitler's, grasp at every conceivable piece of evidence which could add plausability to their claims.

We are all aware of the mountain of evidence under which racist ideology has been buried in our own time. Modern genetics complicates things for the racist.   There may be a rough correspondence between different races as socially defined and different gene pools; gene pools may differ in the frequencies of many genes; and therefore, human populations may differ on certain personal traits at least in statistical terms, e.g. differing frequencies could account for differences in mean IQ.   However, these differences come about because, thanks to geographic and social isolation, natural selection operates within different environmental contexts.   If conditions alter, natural selection can alter the gene frequencies within various breeding groups and an advantage in terms of personal traits can be lost.   There is nothing immutable or eternal about human gene pools, although large changes may take a considerable period of time.   Anthropology has also made a contribution.   Pioneers such as Franz Boas and Ruth Benedict showed repeatedly that peoples closely related in terms of 'race' often had very different cultural patterns (and personal traits), while peoples less closely related were part of the same cultural complex.

The advance of historical scholarship may have left us with much bad history but at least it is about the birth, rise and decline of civilizations rather than races. Personal experience with other races has helped to educate people: a recurrent tragedy in frontier America was the recovery of a son taken captive by Indians as an infant; these young men were found to be fully acculturated Sioux or Cherokee or whatever and the consequences can be imagined.   In the South, those who attempted to defend slavery (like Hitler) simply denied that blacks could ever really be scholars, creative artists or scientists.   When Frederick Law Olmstead travelled through the ante-bellum South, he continually heard laws against educating blacks defended on the grounds that they were no more capable of learning than animals or maniacs.   Olmstead asked why there were no laws to prevent animals and maniacs from being educated.(9)

Today no one who wishes to claim even a minimal regard for reason or evidence can espouse racist ideology as it was in its heyday, a system as comprehensive as Marxism and to

some clearly equally as satisfying.   However, thanks to
Jensen and Eysenck and Shockley, the racist can cling to
the periphery of his ideology; for example, he can provide a reasoned defence of his position on certain issues
such as immigration and foreign policy.   I do not wish to
minimize the ground he has lost: the retreat from world
history to little more than immigration quotas is a great
defeat for the racist and a great source of satisfaction
for all of his opponents.   I am quite convinced that the
refutation of racism in the light of reason is almost complete (the effort to eradicate it as a social force is a
different matter and may never be fully accomplished).
However, the last stand of the racist is not without importance, something I will attempt to demonstrate by
giving a racist ideologue his say.

A colleague of mine recently dined with an intellectual
who supports the National Front and who stated his case as
follows: 'The Front has good reasons for opposing Asian
immigration to Britain but these reasons are primarily
social and economic.   I am equally concerned with black
immigration because it holds a threat which goes well
beyond the usual considerations.   You liberals and radi-
cals like to treat us as if we were all Neanderthals, but
some of us read you know, I at least have read both Jensen
and a fair sample of those who have tried to answer him.
Jensen himself possesses neither our courage nor our
ideals and therefore, he refuses to follow his research
through to its logical conclusion.   Nevertheless he has
shown something of the greatest importance: that while
the issue is not settled (what scientific issue ever is
settled?), we have every right to hypothesize that most of
the 15-point IQ gap between black and white is genetic
rather than environmental; indeed, that hypothesis is

more reasonable in the light of the evidence than any
alternative hypothesis.   I know of course that Jensen's
analysis applies in a strict sense only to US blacks, but
why should we take a chance on the blacks who want to come
to Britain until the former are shown to be atypical?

'Jensen's critics have a great deal to say about IQ
tests being culturally biased, namely, that they test only
for a kind of abstract thinking valued within Western
civilization and which is not valued within non-industria-
lized or simpler or more bucolic cultures.   So be it!
They do not seem to realize that they have conceded exactly what we have always contended: that blacks are genetically unsuited to carry on the work of our civilization
- and I have no objection to emphasizing that it is "merely" ours, the civilization we Britons helped to build,
cherish, and want to sustain.   Our culture may be unusual
in that it sets a value on physicists and engineers and
surveyors, a pity that and a dreadful cultural bias on our
part, but there it is: we want to comprehend the heavens,
build highways and bridges, and so forth.   If blacks are
genetically less capable of abstract thought than whites,
less capable of learning higher mathematics for example,
they will provide a disproportionately small number of the
minds who can sustain and advance our civilization.   They
will also provide a disproportionate number of those who
carry on the least demanding roles including those who
become a burden on the public.   I doubt we would ever be
mad enough to allow a black majority to develop in Britain
but if we did, we have every reason to believe that it
would mean a debased version of our civilization, one
skewed towards stupidity, a mere shadow of its former
self.   And let me say this: we must help our brothers in
Rhodesia and South Africa who are doing everything they
can to escape just such a fate.

'Then there are those who attack IQ tests on the
grounds that they are not particularly useful as diagnos-
tic instruments.   They contend that a battery of tests
designed for the purpose do a much better job of revealing
just where school children are deficient.   Again I am
happy to assent to this because it misses the point: I
value IQ tests not because of their pedagogical utility,
but because they have warned us of a threat.   They are
quick, easy to administer, and reveal the lack of something which, while not identical to a capacity for academic excellence, is highly correlated with it.   As for
the threat, I know it is unpopular to be honest about it
these days, but do we not have a right to a legitimate
concern not only about our civilization but also, on a
deeply personal level, about the nature of our grandchildren?   Young people marry for romantic reasons, good
looks, who can dance this or that, who seems "cool" -
nothing is more certain than that many of our children
will marry blacks and that many of our grandchildren will
have less genetic potential than we might desire.

'After the educators come the sociologists.   Some ex-
pend much energy trying to show that blacks score at white
norms on IQ tests if we select out those few who match
middle-class whites on certain "modal characteristics",
mainly things that have to do with socio-economic status
such as home ownership, father's occupation, parent's education.   Or they try to show that the gap between black
and white disappears entirely if they take into account
not only SES but also aspirations (believing one can
achieve success through one's own efforts) and anxiety
(fear of taking tests, making mistakes, not being promo-
ted).   These studies are useless thanks to the fact that
IQ is correlated with academic success and that the latter

is correlated with career opportunity. Assuming that IQ
is dictated largely by the genes, such correlations mean
that the blacks in question achieved high socio-economic
status partially because of their innate intelligence -
they are an elite within the black population genetically
as well as in terms of SES. Jensen calls such studies
examples of the "sociologist's fallacy" and his guess that
once we have made a proper allowance for environmental
factors, something like a 10-point gap between black and
white will remain seems reasonable. Concerning the busi-
ness about aspirations and anxiety, this is so absurd it
calls for little comment. If someone has low intelligence, it is only natural to believe that luck rather than
ability determines a man's fate and only realistic to fear
tests and failure. To use these factors to explain low
IQ is like explaining my limitations as a weight-lifter by
my aspirations and fears. Given my size and musculature,
I long ago put unrealist hopes aside and I would certainly
fear failure if forced to compete.

'The geneticists have done even less to shake me in my
convictions. I accept the fact that human gene pools are
not immutable and that natural selection can cancel an advantage that one people have over another. But the fact
that blacks might in the distant future have equal genotypes for IQ does nothing to remove the immediate threat
to our gene pool, namely, the threat of lowering its quality by the addition of a large number of people whose
genotypes happen to be inferior. Assuming that natural
selection was responsible for rendering blacks inferior as
a separate breeding group, this may well have happened
before the dawn of historical time. Jensen himself hypothesizes that black Africans and Europeans may have been
unequal in terms of genetic pools for intelligence long

before black slaves were brought to America early in the
seventeenth century.   He seems to concede that under
normal conditions of genetic selection, 200 years would be
insufficient to bring about the gap which exists between
black and white today, which implies that 200 years would
not be enough to close it.   No doubt some systematic, co-
ercive programme of eugenics might work more quickly but
let us then wait for someone to put such a programme into
effect.

'Geneticists talk a great deal about "genotype X environment interaction" which is a way of saying that a group
whose genes are an advantage in one environment are at a
disadvantage in another.   We hear about species of plants
within which one group grows taller if trace elements are
at a certain level, while another group does better if the
level is doubled.   We are told of two strains of inbred
mice: group A lagged behind group B in solving a maze in
a standard environment but then forged far ahead when both
were given an enriched environment.   It appears that similar fluctuations in performance were observed in rats who
had been bred for ability at solving mazes.   The problem
with all of this is that we must decide whether we are
talking about changes in man's environment that lie upon
the spectrum of anything which has happened thus far in
human history - or about some radical change which is a
matter of sheer speculation.   No enrichment of environment within the range which exists at present within Western civilization shows any signs of allowing black performance on IQ tests to forge "far ahead" of whites exposed to that same environment.

'In view of this, the geneticists should spell out just
what they have in mind, just what new environmental conditions might interact in a radically beneficial way with

the genes of blacks or in a radically detrimental way with
the genes of whites.   Perhaps something like food proces-
sing putting a non-detectable trace of an amino acid in
our diet, an amino acid which the genes of blacks allow
them to convert but which accumulates in whites so that
mild brain damage results.   Or perhaps it will be discov-
ered that putting expectant mothers in oxygen tents will
increase the supply of oxygen to the brain of a black
foetus (to a beneficial degree) while a white foetus, because of some organic difference, does not benefit.   This
sort of speculation seems to me to be pointless.   It
amounts to what I call the Irish Sweepstakes defence of
racial equality - the hope that blacks just might have
bought (without knowing it of course) a winning ticket in
the evolutionary lottery.   I am more than happy to have
my opponents rest their case for equality on something
like that.

'Finally the educationists have an argument which has
much of the flavour of the above, although it does not
posit genotype X environment interaction or some altoge-
ther novel environmental change.   They speculate that if
all black children were given the best of the environmental conditions we know today, then their mean IQ would
rise from 85 to 100;   and they argue that even if a 10-
point gap persists (thanks to all white children enjoying
an enriched environment as well), it would make no difference - if blacks could perform as well as whites do today,
why be concerned about the IQ gap?   Perhaps the educationists are correct in this, perhaps blacks would reach
the present white norm given an environment several standard deviations above what we can hope for in the forsee-
able future.   But if that happens, and if whites also improve up to a norm of say 110, who knows how much higher

we will set our goals in terms of cultural achievement?
Why have an anchor dragging us down below whatever level
of civilization we hope to attain: we might want to build
an Athens in England's green and pleasant land.

'I am no madman who goes berserk whenever he sees the
colour black.   The Front is unrealistic when it advocates
sending home the blacks already in Britain, that is, any
attempt at coercion would be both unjust and ineffective.
The blacks here must be treated as individuals: a few of
them will make outstanding contributions and must be re-
warded for such; thanks to Jensen we now know that most
of them will not, but they have become too interwoven with
the fabric of our society to tear them out.   All the more
reason to take a stand now and allow no more blacks to im-
migrate.   You may ask why not treat prospective immigrants as individuals and give them an IQ test?   In
reply, this would be neither practical nor desirable.
The masses of those who want to come to Britain from
Africa or the West Indies are doomed to do badly, and
faced with massive failure rates black nations, under-
standably enough, will not welcome the humiliation of
their nationals that testing would entail.   As for the
elite who would do well, these are mainly the professional
classes, small in number, an elite these under-developed
countries have produced after much effort.   It is hardly
a service to them to strip them of their very best.   If
there is someone truly outstanding that we need, let him
come but let us be clear that we are behaving selfishly
rather than morally in such cases.   As for large-scale
immigration, we must ask ourselves this: does Britain
really want to add thousands to its population who lack
the genetic potential for abstract thought?   Does anyone
really believe that Britain needs even more people who
find logic and clear thinking difficult?'

The author wishes to make clear that even if we were to
concede the hypothesis on which the racist builds his
case, we would not be at a loss in terms of argument.
The hypothesis is that a 10-point gap would persist between black and white even though both enjoyed an environment of the same quality, say the full range of environments which exist in white America or white Britain today.
Even if that were true, we could raise a number of points
a racist ideologue would find troublesome.   However reluctant he may be to admit it, his whole line of argument
implies that it makes sense to rank men on the basis of
their intelligence rather than their race.   If IQ is his
real concern, he should welcome the notion of mental tests
for prospective migrants, accepting those who earn a pass
irrespective of race.   He of course argues that such
testing is unworkable and he may be correct.   But we have
every reason to suspect his sincerity, suspect him of
wanting testing to be unworkable and of being unwilling to
accept it even if black nations were to do so.   Moreover,
our racist ideologue places an extraordinary emphasis on
the intellectual virtues in general and abstract thought
in particular.   If we take him seriously, he has a very
limited notion of what might enrich British culture.
When we reflect on what blacks have added to American culture, their contribution to America's vocabulary, humour,
entertainment, cuisine and sport, the fact that they have
almost single-handedly given America its only claim to
artistic originality (I refer to music and the development
of original modes of expression such as jazz, the Negro
spiritual, rock and rock opera), the fact that they have
produced perhaps the only convincing existentialist literature in America (Richard Wright and Ralph Ellison), we
can appreciate the point.

Despite all of this, it is not clear that we can rout
him completely.   Even if we got him to swallow testing
prospective migrants, however demoralizing this would be
for him, we would find it almost equally repulsive, naturally for very different reasons.   And his case against
black rule in Africa would be more difficult to answer,
that is, more difficult to answer within its own terms.
For here, as far as a particular country is concerned, the
choice really may lie between rule by black and rule by
white, with rule by the 'best' without regard to race just
not a realistic alternative.   At any rate, whatever our
ability to embarrass him in argument, this much is certain: Jensen strips us of our most direct and most satisfying refutation of the racist, namely, that he is simply
wrong about his facts.   By offering him the thesis that
it is a reasonable hypothesis (the most reasonable hypothesis) that blacks are genetically inferior in terms of
IQ, we offer him a last chance at viability in the light
of reason and evidence.   We offer him the first piece of
evidence he can use in his own defence that he has had in
a long, long time.

I think that I have shown why so many of us find Jensen's publications so disturbing.   Jensen himself is
aware of our distress and tries to alleviate it by digging
an unbridgable gulf between facts and values.   He asserts
that racist ideology does not follow 'logically' from a
recognition of genetic differences - and that the absence
of group differences is not a prerequisite for belief in
equal rights.   In his own words: 'Equality of rights is
a moral axiom: it does not follow from any set of scientific data.' (10)   These assertions are quite true and
quite misleading.   At least they are true if one under-
scores the word 'logically': recognition of an important

genetic difference between black and white does not coerce
us towards racist value judgments by way of deductive
logic;   recognition of lack of important differences does
not coerce us into accepting humane values.   But they are
misleading nonetheless and we can see this if we stop
talking about going from facts to values and focus on
going from values to facts.

Take two men, one of whom has a proclivity for treating
all men humanely and seeking the welfare of all despite
their differences, the other of whom has a proclivity to
rank men in a value hierarchy and favour the better (the
superior) over the worse (the inferior).   Neither of
these proclivities is in any way an operational ideology
or code of ethics until it has something to assess, a set
of facts about the real world including the men who live
in it.   Unless a man possesses a set of facts he has
nothing to use his 'values' on, he can make no judgments
and therefore no recommendations of any sort.   Take our
nascent humanist: he wants to seek the welfare of all
men, but if all blacks were deficient in rationality to
the degree Aristotle thought 'natural slaves' were, the
only way to promote their welfare would be to substitute
our reason for theirs.   Take our nascent racist: he may
want to rank the races hierarchically and favour some over
others, but if there exist no racial differences which can
be plausibly assessed in terms of inferior-superior, he
cannot do so.

Every set of values that becomes operational becomes
tied, not through deductive logic but through assessment,
to a set of facts about human beings.   As I have been at
some pains to show, the values of the racist are such that
genetic differences between the races assume a central
place in his ideology and therefore, evidence which shows

the lack of such can totally destroy his viability.
Jensen implicitly grants the relevance of facts to values
when he emphasizes that racists usually propagate the myth
that genetic differences between the races are immutable,
while in fact they can be altered by natural selection. (11)   As we have seen, racists indeed find this a
bitter pill to swallow and someone like Hitler could not
possibly do so - it would mean revising his ideology in
ways too painful to accept.   But a more sophisticated
racist will swallow it if he must, just so long as the
pace of change is glacial and the 'inferior race' is
likely to remain inferior for a very long time. (12)

To put the point as simply as possible: if the evidence shows that black and white do not differ genetically
in terms of significant personal traits, humanism is
viable and racism is not; if the evidence were to show
that black and white did differ genetically in terms of a
whole range of traits, both humanism (as amended) and
racism would be viable; if the genetic difference is 10
IQ points, humanism is certainly viable - and racism very
much on the defensive but still capable of a troublesome
last stand in terms of viability.

Jensen focuses too much on the fact that we can defend
humanism despite the recognition of the sort of genetic
differences he has in mind.   He quite rightly says that
we can still endorse equality before the law, equality of
political and civil rights, equality of opportunity in
education and employment. (13)   But all of us want more
than that, none of us want to concede that both racism and
humanism are viable!   Faced with an ideological opponent,
we want to show that however appealing his ideology may be
in the imperfect world in which we live, however much he
may best us in the realm of rhetoric, he is at our mercy

in the perfect world of ideal debate, a world in which
reason and evidence count and the goal is the search for
truth.   The more we loathe his ideology, the more pas-
sionately we hope to strip him of any rational viability.
Jensen's contention, the contention that the IQ gap is
probably more genetic than environmental, can hardly make
our task easier - it can only make it more difficult.   I
apologise for taking so much space to demonstrate what is
painfully obvious, but the point has been denied so often
it simply had to be said. (14)   Our intellectual who supports the National Front is only one illustration of this.
I could just as easily have chosen someone who uses the
hypothesis of genetic differences to argue against affirmative action (programmes designed to increase the percentage of blacks in the professions and other elite work
roles) or someone who uses it to argue in favour of the
pass laws in South Africa.

Jensen grants that his scientific research may be misused, and therefore may seem to have anticipated my
point. (15)   However, the illustrations he gives, e.g.
the possible misuse of atomic energy, show that he has
not.   There are two very different things humane men can
lament in the use of a scientific discovery.   The first
is when an anti-humane man uses it as an instrument to
accomplish cruel ends, as when a knife is used to commit a
murder.   Virtually any scientific discovery can be used
in that way and, as Jensen says, if that were the source
of my anxiety, I would have to be frightened of any and
every scientific advance.   The second is when an anti-
humane ideologue uses a scientific discovery to give his
ideology epistemological respectability, when he finds he
can use it to defend his vicious ideology against rational
critique.   Most scientific hypotheses cannot be used in

that way, indeed Jensen's is one of the few that can, and
therefore it is a special source of anxiety.   I have con-
veyed to the reader, I hope, that my concern is over the
epistemological consequences of Jensen's work, not its
possible instrumental abuse.   If ethical systems really
were 'axioms' by their very nature impervious to rational
critique, then of course nothing would be lost, but we
have shown this to be a philosophical mistake.   Moreover,
men in the real world of ideological debate do not treat
principles as non-debatable axioms: even if the racist
ideologue would lose an ideal debate after prolonged and
subtle argument, he can use Jensen's hypothesis to give
his ideology the appearance of viability in the eyes of
ordinary men.   In terms of rhetoric as well as epistem-
ology, it is far more useful to the racist than the
humanist and therefore, it differs from a discovery of
purely instrumental value which would be there to be used
by both.

Having said the above, I also want to say that this
book will criticize Jensen's analysis and conclusions
(tentative conclusions) and not Jensen the man.   Jensen
has been acting as a scientist and testing a hypothesis,
the hypothesis that the IQ gap between black and white is
largely genetic in character.   If he really believes that
the evidence thus far renders that hypothesis more probably than any other, and it is clear that he does, what
choice does he have - to pretend that he believes something else?   After all, if we came to agree with him
about the evidence, what choice would we have - to join in
some sort of conspiracy to conceal the truth?   It is very
painful to face up to a truth which gives our ideological
opponents pleasure, but we would have to do it: if we did
not value the truth so much, we would not wish so passion-

ately to have it on our side.   In this event, the racist
and ourselves would agree about the facts.   The difference between us would lie in our reaction to those facts,
his being to treat them as all-important, ours being to
give them low priority compared to other human traits and
continue to seek the welfare of all.

I have no sympathy (to put it mildly) with those who
have attempted to deny Jensen an opportunity to present
his views, (16) those who have called him a racist or
racial ideologue, (17) and those who have questioned his
professional competence or ethics. (18)   Jensen's reaction to a putative genetic gap is thoroughly humane rather
than racist, as is attested by passage after passage in
his works. (19)   If any reader has doubts about Jensen, I
urge him to read the five-page section entitled 'Extending
the spectrum of measured abilities' and tell us if he can
just how it could be bettered as a humane response.
Everything is there: he totally rejects the notion that
capacity for abstract thought should constitute an all-
important criterion of human worth; he endorses the goal
of the welfare of all as his principal concern; more spe-
cifically, he exhibits a real passion for giving every
child (black or white) the best possible education and for
giving blacks increased access to occupations and all
other aspects of American life denied them at present. (20)   It is worth remembering that Jensen began to
investigate race and IQ because of his concern for the
plight of black children falsely classified as retarded
because of the misuse of IQ tests as a criterion of
such. (21)

Concerning Jensen's professional competence, like
Lavoisier vis-à-vis his contemporaries, he strikes one as
a professional surrounded by amateurs.   He also raises

all the important issues, which is why I decided to focus on his views rather than those of Shockley or Eysenck (these three, by the way, differ among themselves in significant respects).   Concerning his professional ethics, he is scrupulous in his attitude towards evidence, even bringing forward evidence he knows to be antagonistic to his own position, a habit not as common among social scientists as one might desire.

A few more points about the remainder of this book: it is about race and IQ and not about the immigration issue. There are a multitude of considerations relevant to the issue of black immigration into Britain which have not been discussed and will not be discussed.   I can think of humane reasons for more immigration, limited immigration, and even some (but not many) for a virtual ban on immigration.   My concern, although in this book only, of course, is not with particular issues but with reasons, with the kind of debate which is likely to go on about a whole range of racial issues.   My concern is this: reasonable men for the first time in a generation must consider a complication they thought they had banished, the possibility that blacks are genetically inferior to whites in terms of a significant personal trait.   There are a whole host of issues that are sensitive enough without throwing that particular weight in the scales.   It is likely to make issues like immigration so embittered, so insulting to blacks, so devisive for whites that reason will have a harder time than usual against its ancient enemies.

In order to outline the structure of the remainder of this book, I must describe the bare bones of Jensen's argument.   He begins by arguing for high h^2 or heritability estimates.   These estimates attempt to measure the extent

to which genetic and environmental factors explain differential performance on IQ tests: the higher the h^2 estimate, the more role for genes and the less role for environment.   For example, an h^2 of .80 (the figure Jensen
favours for white Americans) means that 80 per cent of
variance in IQ within a given population is genetic and 20
per cent (or less) environmental.   Using these estimates,
he has fashioned a powerful argument in two steps: first,
most of the IQ variance within white America is due to
genetic factors and most of IQ variance within black
America may be, although here the evidence is just beginning to come in; second, we can falsify every current
hypothesis which attempts to explain the gap between black
and white in environmental terms.   Therefore, we have
good reason to suspect that most of the gap between black
and white is genetic.

   Stated thus Jensen's argument looks vulnerable, at
least to a professional geneticist, and many of his
critics think they have a simple reply which constitutes a
devastating refutation.   In this they are mistaken.   The
only way to refute Jensen is to face up to his challenge
and undertake a series of complex tasks.   We must argue
either that h^2 estimates are unfounded or that they should
be put lower than Jensen believes, we must show that there
actually is evidence that the gap between black and white
is environmental, we must attempt to isolate the specific
environmental variables which explain the above gap, and
so forth.   To anticipate: Chapter 2 will defend Jensen
against his critics; Chapter 3 will present evidence that
the gap between black and white has some environmental explanation - but without putting forward specific hypotheses to explain it; Chapter 4 will argue for lower h^2
estimates than are commonly accepted; Chapter 5 will sug-

gest places we might look for specific environmental hypotheses, hypotheses which render explicit the variables
that handicap blacks on IQ tests;   Chapter 6 will be a re-
capitulation, a very brief reminder of the chief critical
points I want to make about the debate on race and IQ.

Finally, I have had to add two appendices.   Appendix A
contains data and calculations necessary to support some
of the assertions made in Chapter 3 and Appendix B comments on an exchange between Jensen and Sandra Scarr.
This last was published while this book was in press but
since it presents Jensen's objections to some of the evidence I use in Chapter 3, it was too important to be
omitted.

Chapter 2

JENSEN AND HIS CRITICS

Jensen estimates the IQ gap between black and white Americans at 15 points, positing a white mean of 100 (with a standard deviation of 15) and a black mean of 85 (with an SD of 13). (1) He bases these estimates on Audrey Shuey's review of 382 studies, the majority of which tested school children and high-school students and involved over 100,000 blacks, and I will accept them as accurate throughout this book. (2) Jensen states his conclusions about the IQ gap as follows:

> In view of all the most relevant evidence which I have examined, the most tenable hypothesis, in my judgment, is that genetic, as well as environmental, differences are involved in the average disparity between American Negroes and whites in intelligence and educability, as here defined. All the major facts would seem to be comprehended quite well by the hypothesis that something between one-half and three-fourths of the average IQ difference ... is attributable to genetic factors, and the remainder to environmental factors and their interaction with the genetic differences. (3)

In terms of IQ points, this means that approximately 8 to 11 points of the gap are genetic and would remain even if the environments of black and white were rendered equivalent.

The above poses two questions: why does Jensen think
the IQ gap is so important, which raises the question of
why he believes IQ scores are important; and why does he
think that the gap is largely genetic rather than environmental?   Throughout the sections to follow, I will sometimes dispense with repeated and tedious references to
Jensen or use of the third person, but the reader should
assume that the views presented are his (or at least my
attempt to present his views) and not necessarily my own.

On one level, Jensen defends the importance of IQ scores
by simply saying that they correlate with 'the good things
in life', that is, what most men desire who live in a
modern industrial society.   IQ exhibits the following
correlations: .80 with scholastic achievement; from .50
to .70 with occupational status; .50 with speed and ease
of training for whatever job one gets; from .20 to .25
with ratings of actual performance on the job; and .35
with income.   As for the individual, an extra 15 points
added to an IQ of 70 may mean self-sufficiency in terms of
work, added to an IQ of 100 it may mean success at college, and it may mean (assuming high heritability of IQ)
an extra 7 points on the IQs of one's children.   The
latter is significant in that if we compare siblings, the
child with the higher score tends to move above his parents in terms of socio-economic status and the child with
the lower score tends to go down.   Jensen often cites
Terman's study as evidence of the benefits of having an
exceptionally high IQ.   Terman selected a group of gifted
children in elementary school, children with IQs over 140,
and followed up 1,528 of them into middle age.   As
adults, they were far above the average in terms of education, income, prestigious occupations, entries in 'Who's

Who', the intelligence of their spouses, and the intelligence of their children (their mean IQ was 133); they had better physical and mental health than the average, a lower suicide rate, a lower mortality rate, and a lower divorce rate.   Jensen concludes that 'these results should leave no doubt that IQ is related to socially valued criteria.'

On another level, Jensen goes beyond what men desire to what society needs.   He argues that IQ scores measure an important personal trait, our ability to think abstractly, an ability which is essential for acquiring a whole range of skills needed in a modern industrial society.   He divides intelligence (without claiming that he is in any way exhausting all kinds of intelligence) into Level I and Level II.   Level I intelligence or 'associative learning ability' is what we use in rote learning, short-term memory, tasks which are 'a kind of recording and playback on cue'; children whose ability is primarily on this level may do well in subjects characterized by repetition such as penmanship, spelling, mechanical arithmetic, memorizing the words of songs, but they encounter frustration as school subjects make greater conceptual and abstract demands.   Level II intelligence or 'cognitive ability' has to do with reasoning abstractly, with the ability to generalize from particulars, solve complex problems, conceptualize, perceive relationships and correlates, perceive abstract similarities and differences; it is used when we master skills like reading comprehension, scientific method, algebra and higher mathematics, when we write computer programmes, achieve scientific or technological innovations, invent something new.   Level I intelligence is a prerequisite for doing well on IQ tests but it is not a sufficient condition; the most recent tests in particu-

lar are heavily loaded with items testing for Level
II. (4)

Jensen does not go so far as to say that a drop of 15
points (or even 25 points) would put an end to our civilization.   It would strip us of most of the 1 or 2 per cent
of gifted individuals who were needed to create our civilization, but it takes less intelligence to perpetrate the
advances men of genius made.   Without men like Leibniz or
Newton, calculus might not have been invented, but those
of us who are merely above average can learn and use it.
On the other hand, if we wished to improve on our civilization rather than merely perpetuate it, we would have
little hope of doing so: if the past is any guide, there
would be no real progress in science, mathematics, philosophy, industry, law, politics and the arts.   When dis-
cussing the 15-point gap which separates black and white,
Jensen emphasizes the greater number of blacks with IQs
below 70:   'If as many as one-sixth to one-fourth of the
members of a community have IQs below 70, it is difficult
to imagine that the quality of the environment would not
be adversely affected.'   He says that we cannot pass this
off lightly as a cultural difference because 'the behavioral correlates of an IQ below 70 are probably a handicap
in any modern culture.'   He predicts that as modern industrial society becomes more complex, needs people who
can write a computer programme rather than merely operate
an adding machine, those with IQs of 85 (the black mean)
will find it increasingly difficult to do any job that
needs doing in such a society. (5)

As an educator concerned with the welfare of all,
Jensen is not prepared to write off those with IQs below
85 or even those with IQs below 70.   He believes that we
should survey a variety of occupations to see if we are

demanding qualifications which are irrelevant to actual
performance on the job.   He also wants radical changes in
formal education.   Jensen divides low-IQ children into
those who are low in terms of both levels of intelligence
and those who are adequate on Level I and low only on
Level II.   He emphasizes that genetic differences between
various classes and races for Level I intelligence may be
relatively small and advocates an ambitious programme of
research, a programme designed to discover teaching methods that will improve the scholastic performance and vocational prospects of children with mainly Level I abilities.   We would attempt to match modes of instruction
with the learning processes of such children, taking as a
guide the sort of tests on which they do well, tests involving memory span, serial learning, paired-associate
learning, and free recall.   As to what goals seem realistic, there is little doubt that some educational and occupational skills are too abstract or cognitive for those
whose strengths are confined to Level I, presumably creative roles in academic disciplines and occupations requiring higher mathematics.   On the other hand, Jensen suspects that all children with normal Level I learning
ability can master basic skills such as those which are
the subject matter of elementary school.   Concerning
skills which lie between these two extremes, we do not
know how much can be done and we should experiment with a
variety of school subjects.   However, Jensen holds out
little hope that those who lack Level II intelligence will
ever master 'the more academic aspects of the curriculum,
especially at the advanced levels'. (6)
    In his famous article, published in 1969 in the 'Har-
vard Educational Review', Jensen gave his critics an
opportunity to claim that he was defending the importance

of IQ scores on the basis of a crude operationalism, a
philosophical doctrine which holds that the meaning of a
concept is given by a set of operations, in this case primarily by the process of measurement.   For example, in
one passage, he says that 'intelligence, by definition, is
what intelligence tests measure'; (7)   and as we have
seen, he sometimes speaks as if it makes little difference
what IQ tests measure, just so long as the scores correlate with things men desire (such as scholastic achievement and so forth). (8)   Philosophers have subjected this
sort of doctrine to devastating critique.   It poses problems such as: if intelligence is literally what a particular IQ test measures, then we could never improve on that
IQ test;   if IQ scores are valuable simply because they
correlate with scholastic success, then it makes no difference why they do so - if bribing teachers came to have
the same degree of correlation with scholastic success, we
would not make a distinction between the two correlations.

However, a careful reading of Jensen reveals that he
was never as naive as this.   Right from the beginning of
the IQ controversy he has claimed that IQ tests measure
something beyond performance on the tests themselves,
namely, the ability to reason abstractly.   A few para-
graphs after the very passage in which he gives his opera-
tionalist 'definition' of intelligence, he cites the defi-
nitions offered by certain thinkers, those of Spearman
(the ability to educe relations and correlates) and
Aquinas (the ability to combine and separate). (9)   Moreover, when he defends the importance of IQ scores, he
goes beyond stating correlations to argue that what IQ
tests measure contributes to the 'common good', at least
within the context of modern industrial societies;   he
argues that they measure a problem-solving ability which

is a causal prerequisite for playing certain roles society needs, an ability that is functionally related to being, say, a good scientist or a good mathematician.

Thinkers such as Block and Dworkin have attacked Jensen for making such claims. They argue that Jensen cannot defend the importance he places on IQ tests unless he can give us an adequate theory of intelligence. They take him up on his example of the thermometer, as an effective measuring device, and note that we have confidence in the thermometer because we know how it works. The implication seems to be that in order to defend IQ tests we would have to possess a coherent concept of intelligence, precise enough so that we can clearly recognize its operations independently of the tests, and a theory which makes explicit just how the tests measure intelligence. (10)

I do not doubt the desirability of an adequate theory of intelligence, but here I must side with Jensen against his critics. First, even if we did not know how a thermometer works, we would have a certain level of confidence in it because of what we experience when we interact with it: when we get a high reading, we feel hot, when we get a low reading, we feel very cold. I do not think we can ignore the actual experiences we have when we take IQ tests. Unless the reader is very different from myself, when he does IQ tests he often finds that he is doing some thinking or reasoning of some sort. Take tests like Raven's Progressive Matrices or Catell's Culture-Fair Tests: when we do them, they just seem very like a mathematics test with the need to have mastered specific areas of mathematics or its symbols removed. These tests have considerable predictive value in terms of selecting out children who will do well at mathematics. By far the most plausible explanation is that the connection is

causal rather than contingent, that is, that the tests do
a reasonably good job of telling us which children have,
say at the age of 6, learned to reason mathematically even
though they as yet know almost no mathematics.   If the
connection is contingent, it seems odd that we cannot find
large numbers of men who are outstanding scientists or
mathematicians and yet do poorly on IQ tests.   If the
connection is contingent, we should be able to show that
performance on IQ tests is correlated with something
clearly distinct in functional terms from the ability to
reason abstractly, e.g. things like race of the tester,
tests written in an unfamiliar vocabulary, items which are
not culturally fair.   But clearly this line of attack
collapses into the debate about what accounts for variable
performance on IQ tests, and therefore it is not a distinct critical point.

   An analogy may be of some use.   Someone claims that a
test of speed, running a 100-yard dash at school in less
than 10 seconds, is a causal prerequisite to developing an
occupational skill, not being caught from behind in professional football (gridiron).   If we wanted to refute
such a claim, we would try to find players who have the
skill but ran worse than 10 seconds at school, perhaps
showing that maturation is important or that manoeuvrabil-
ity is more important than sheer speed.   Or we might
argue that such tests are part of a system which arbitra-
rily eliminates people who could have developed the occupational skill.   This would mean showing that good performance on the test is correlated with something clearly
distinct in functional terms from speed, e.g. race of
officials who run school sports, whether children are
familiar with the starter's commands, whether children
have been taught to use starting blocks and a proper

sprint start.   The resemblance between running on a track
and running on a football field is so obvious that we must
stretch the analogy a bit to illustrate our other point,
the importance of what we experience when we take an IQ
test.   But let us do so: when we run at school sports,
we experience an activity appropriately labelled 'running
as fast as I can';   if we experienced being thrust through
the air by powerful forces, we would take them less seriously as evidence of running ability, although they would
raise some interesting scientific and theological problems.

I have emphasized our experiences when taking IQ tests,
at least some IQ tests, mainly as an appeal to the common
sense of the general reader.   Jensen himself has answered
his critics on this point and his answers are very convincing.   In his recent publications, Jensen has stressed
the concept of 'g'.   The symbol 'g' refers to the factor
that emerges when we analyse the performance of people on
an IQ test as a whole rather than their performance item
by item.   If you take a particular item on an IQ test, it
may test for something very specific, say memory or vocabulary or general information;   therefore, when one person
gets that particular item correct and another gets it
wrong, there is little significance in that and we could
go through the whole test and say much the same for many
items, each taken in isolation.   However, if we take the
performance of a group of people on the test as a whole,
or preferably on a whole battery of tests, a different
picture emerges.   Using factor analysis, we can show that
performance on the various items and tests, including
those which run from the very specific to the very abstract, is highly intercorrelated.   To paraphrase Jensen:
any single test item measures something peculiar to itself

more than what it has in common with other items; but
when we compose a test of a large number of items, those
examined differ in their overall performance primarily in
terms of the common factor, rather than the 'background
noise' which is specific to each item.   In other words,
although this is to oversimplify a bit, what separates
those with high IQ from those with low IQ in terms of
their overall score is a general performance factor; and
this is the crucial differentiating factor between people
on all of the test items taken collectively, even though
it is not dominant on any given item.   Therefore, it
appears that IQ tests are measuring what deserves to be
called a 'general mental ability' - hence the name 'g'.
And since 80 to 90 per cent of variable performance on
most IQ tests is attributable to 'g', we can essentially
identify it with tested IQ.

Jensen then calls attention to a series of correlations
of great significance, correlations between IQ and learning ability.   IQ is most highly correlated with learning
ability when: (1) the task calls for conscious mental
effort rather than simple repetition;   (2) the students
are given time to think about the task rather than forced
to respond at once;   (3) the material is hierarchical in
the sense that mastering later tasks is dependent on mastering earlier ones;   (4) the material learned has to be
related to knowledge or experience already possessed by
the student;   (5) the material involves catching on to a
new concept;   (6) the material is of moderate difficulty
or complexity rather than so difficult that all students
are reduced to trial-and-error.   As Jensen says, in the
light of these correlations, it is hard to deny that IQ
plays a causal role at least in school learning or academic achievement.   There is also evidence that IQ plays a

role in activities unconnected with school and the academic life: a study of US Army cooks on-the-job revealed
that making jelly-rolls was more 'g'-loaded than preparing
scrambled eggs. Presumably the former, as compared to
the latter, involved more of the kind of activity that
brings out 'g' on mental tests, a greater degree of complexity, uncertainty, mental manipulation, and retrieval
of relevant information from memory.

Jensen is fully aware that factor analysis and the correlations it engenders have not given us either an adequate definition or an adequate theory of intelligence.
He believes that all the speculations about the nature of
'g' thus far have failed to generate testable hypotheses,
the essential prerequisite to constructing a theory. He
suspects that trying to relate 'g' to an analysis of the
mental tasks we perform when we do 'g'-loaded tests is a
blind alley - and that before we can make further progress, we need to know more about anatomical, histologi-
cal, physiological, biochemical and electro-chemical
underpinnings of 'g'. (11) In sum, Jensen concedes we
have no adequate theory of intelligence but contends that
nonetheless, we have good reason to believe that IQ tests
measure something significant, a general mental ability
which plays an important causal role. I agree: it is
logically possible that when we develop an adequate theory
of intelligence, it will discredit all present-day IQ
tests, but I would hate to bet on that outcome. Let us
therefore, go on to examine Jensen's account of the roles
heredity and environment play in the determination of IQ.

The old sterile debate about whether heredity or environment was more important in the development of human
beings, sometimes likened to a debate over whether bricks

or mortar was more important in constructing a building,
has been over for many years.   No one denies that genes
are important and that environment is important and that
if an infant were left to languish in a darkened room it
would develop no IQ at all.   When Jensen assesses the
roles of genes and environmental factors, he is talking
about h^2 or heritability estimates: these purport to
measure the extent to which variance of IQ within a given
population is correlated with genetic variance within that
population, the remainder of IQ variance being due to
measurement error and differences in environment.   Let me
oversimplify to make a start at explanation.   Assume that
the extent to which the IQ scores of individuals resemble
one another (within America today) matches the extent to
which those individuals have genes in common, for example:
assume that the IQ scores of identical twins who have 100
per cent of their genes in common are virtually the same,
even when the members of a twin-pair are separated and
raised in different environments;   and assume that unrelated children who are raised by the same family show no
significant correlation in their IQ scores.   Under those
conditions, we would be inclined to say that the degree to
which people vary in terms of genes shared accounts for
most of the difference in their IQs, also that the degree
to which their environments are shared counts for little.
It is very unlikely we would ever conclude that genes
account for all the IQ variance within a given population
but, depending on the data, we might set our h^2 estimate
at .80, which means that 80 per cent of variance is due to
genetic factors and only 20 per cent is due to environment.

In other words, an h^2 estimate is a population statis-
tic, it applies to a given population with a given range

of environments at a given time.   It allows us to say
nothing whatsoever about mankind or human beings in general.   Indeed, it tells us very little about the individuals who make up the population to which it refers.   We
can use an h^2 estimate to generalize about an individual
but only as an anonymous member of the population, not as
a particular individual with his own unique genetic make-
up and his own unique environment;   for example, any particular individual could be that infant kept in a darkened
room for whom environment counts for everything.   When an
insurance company gives me a mortality rate for Americans
of my age, I can use it to generalize about my life expectancy but the generalization must be qualified by considerations such as the current state of my health.   And
just as the mortality rate for a population as a whole
need not apply to a subpopulation, just as the mortality
rate for Americans in general is not the same as the rate
for black Americans, so may black and white Americans have
different values for h^2 or heritability of IQ.   For example, assume that black and white Americans are roughly
similar in terms of genes for IQ;   if blacks experience a
wider range of environments than whites, that in itself
would cause environment to account for a higher percentage
of their IQ variance, assuming of course that environment
counts for anything at all.

To get a better understanding of h^2 estimates, we will
have to define some terms.   There are a variety of ways
in which we could mathematically describe the range of
scores within a population on IQ tests, but the accepted
way is to calculate what statisticians call the 'variance'.
This is simply a matter of finding the difference between
each score and the population mean, squaring each of those
differences, adding together all of the squared differen-

ces, and dividing the total by the number of scores.   If
those with a dash of statistics wish to be convinced that
the variance is a meaningful measure of variable performance, they may be reassured to know that it is essentially the standard deviation squared.   As we have seen, h^2
estimates aim at telling us what percentage of variance is
due to genetic factors and what percentage is due to environmental factors; the mathematical technique was developed by the great British mathematician Sir Ronald
Fisher.

When we use h^2 estimates to generalize about populations or individuals, we might say something like 'black
and white Americans differ in regard to IQ both in terms
of phenotype and genotype'.   This would mean that black
and white differ not only in terms of the scores they make
on IQ tests, but also in terms of their genetic make-up.
Just to spell this out, an individual's 'genotype' is his
genetic make-up which was established at the moment of
conception, when the genes contributed by his father and
mother respectively joined in certain combinations.   A
'phenotype' (in this context) is a piece or pattern of behaviour: the phenotype we are interested in is performance on IQ tests, particularly the score attained, say an
IQ of 120.   An individual's 'genotype for IQ' is that
portion of his genetic make-up which is most relevant to
his IQ test performance, e.g. gene combinations which contribute to the development of his brain may be more relevant than those which make other contributions.   His IQ
is the product of the causal interaction of his genotype
for IQ with the experiences and influences provided by his
environment.   When the individual himself becomes a
parent he of course transmits to his children, not his
genotype for IQ, but rather the relevant genes which combine with those of his spouse to form the child's genotype.

In Chapter 4, we will analyse in some detail the methods by which h^2 estimates are derived.   For now, the
reader will have to be content with the information that
Jensen arrived at his figure of .80 (80 per cent of IQ
variance due to genetic factors) on the basis of his reading of an extensive body of data, studies of IQ correlations among subjects with varying percentages of their
genes in common, for example: identical twins with 100
per cent of their genes in common, fraternal twins with 50
per cent (plus a bit more thanks to assortive mating),
parent and child with 50 per cent (minus a bit), siblings
with 50 per cent (plus a bit), unrelated children reared
together with 0 per cent, and so forth. (12)   The above
estimate of h^2 is by no means universally accepted, but
just as no one today believes that genes account for all
of IQ variance within any population, no one (with the
possible exception of Leon Kamin) thinks that environmental factors are all that count.   Despite this, I will use
terms like 'hereditarian' and 'environmentalist'; it must
be understood that they are being used to distinguish
scholars at opposite ends of a spectrum, e.g. to distinguish those who accept a high h^2 estimate for America
today (say .80 or above) from those who accept a relatively low one (say .50 or below).   And in some contexts,
I will use those terms as a short-hand to distinguish
those who accept a mainly genetic hypothesis about the IQ
gap between black and white from those who accept an environmental hypothesis.

Jensen is confident of his h^2 estimate as applied to
the population of white America; however, heritability
studies of American blacks are just beginning to be done
and we cannot generalize from white data to the black population.   The question of the value of h^2 for blacks is

significant in that if most whites have an adequate environment and if blacks are divided between those with adequate and those with inadequate environments, we would expect blacks to have a lower h^2.   Jensen himself has obtained IQ correlations for a large number of black sibling pairs and on that basis, he anticipates that values for h^2 will be roughly the same for white and black.   But he emphasizes that such a prediction must be tentative until full-fledged heritability studies are done on blacks. His interpretation of the few studies already done, none of which are statistically adequate for strong inference, suggests to him that his prediction will turn out to have been correct. (13)

Thanks to high h^2 estimates, Jensen believes that genetic factors are far more important than environmental factors within both the black and white populations of America today and he believes that this renders a genetic hypothesis about the IQ gap between the races probable.   He does not believe that h^2 estimates alone can decide the issue of genetic versus environmental hypotheses.   However, he argues that the probability of a genetic hypothesis will be much enhanced if, in addition to evidencing high h^2 estimates, we find we can falsify literally every plausible environmental hypothesis one by one.   He challenges social scientists who believe in an environmental explanation of the IQ gap between the races to bring their hypotheses forward.   Given his competence and the present state of the social sciences, the result is something of a massacre.

1 Hypothesis: The IQ gap is an artifact of the tests themselves.   Jensen: This contention is usually supported by a number of arguments, ranging from the claim that

the content of the tests is culturally biased through
assertions that blacks would do better if the tests were
written in ghetto dialect and administered by blacks.
The latter have simply been shown to be false: when the
Stanford-Binet was translated into ghetto dialect, black
children who took the revised test scored less than one
point above a control group; the race of the examiner has
little or no effect on performance.   Shuey surveyed 2,360
black school children tested by blacks, compared them to
30,000 black children most of whom were tested by whites,
and found a difference of .3 of an IQ point.   A review of
thirty studies designed to detect the effect of the race
of the examiner revealed mainly non-significant and negligible effects.

The claim that the tests are culturally baised is more
complex, but now at last it can be rejected on the basis
of overwhelming evidence.   There are culturally loaded
items on IQ tests, items referring to exotic animals,
fairy tales and musical instruments, and blacks do worse
on them than whites.   But they do worse still on the
items that seem the least culturally loaded, for example,
the Block Design subtest of the Wechsler.   The gap between black and white is more a function of an item's complexity than of its rarity or culture-loading and this is
true whether the item involves verbal, numerical or spa-
cial content.   The fact that a test is culturally loaded
does not necessarily mean that it is culturally biased.
The Peabody Picture Vocabulary Test is highly culturally
loaded, and yet the rank-order of item difficulty is the
same for black and white; if the test were biased,
surely some items would reflect this fact to a greater
degree than others!   Indeed, item-analysis of a whole
range of IQ tests confirms that the same items prove more

difficult for both white and black and moreover, that even
the degree of difficulty is much the same. That is, although blacks get a lower average score overall, the percentages of those getting the various items correct bear
the same ratios to one another for both black and white.
We do find minor race X item interactions but actually,
these allow us to offer the most devastating possible
refutation of the cultural bias hypothesis. We can simulate the racial differences merely by dividing the population of white children into two groups, each group entirely composed of white children and differing from one
another merely in terms of age (an average difference of
about two years). Certainly this implies that the only
'bias' of the tests is that they test for mental maturity.

Despite many attempts, no one has been able to devise a
mental test which can both eliminate the gap between the
races and meet the basic criteria necessary to validate a
test.   These are that the test include items of reasonable complexity and that it correlate with things like
educational and occupational success.

2 Hypothesis: The IQ gap has no larger significance -
the tests measure nothing save how good blacks are at
taking IQ tests.   Jensen: The predictive validity of the
tests for good performance in various areas, ranging from
university, to armed forces training programmes, to a
whole list of skilled and semi-skilled occupations, is
much the same for black and white.   When there is a
racial difference, the tests tend to over-estimate future
black performance, which is to say that their bias is in
favour of blacks.   Given a white applicant and a black
applicant, the scores may predict a better performance for
the black and get him accepted, when in fact both would do
equally well. (14)

3 Hypothesis: Black children are less motivated than
white children on IQ tests.   Jensen: If so, why are the
races equally motivated on other kinds of tests, that is,
tests which do not require the child to reason abstractly?
Psychologists have devised a series of tests designed to
separate motivational factors from cognitive abilities,
namely: the Making Xs Test which indicates whether the
subject is willing to comply with instructions in a test
situation and work with speed and persistence;   the
Listening-Attention Test which measures whether the subject suffers from inattention, distractability, careless-
ness, inability to follow directions;   and the free recall
tests, the FRU and the FRC, which are designed to discover
whether perceiving that a test is or is not an intelligence test makes a difference (the FRC is a disguised IQ
test).   All of these show that black and white children
do not differ significantly in terms of motivational factors, indeed blacks had a slight advantage in making Xs,
and differ primarily in terms of cognitive processes.

4 Hypothesis: Black children have an unfavourable
self-concept or low self-esteem which adversely affects
their performance.   Jensen: The testee's self-esteem may
affect his test performance, the evidence being ambiguous
with approximately a dozen studies divided for and
against.   However, it remains to be shown that black
children really do have lower self-esteem and if so, that
this correlates with lower IQ or scholastic achievement.
Even if such a correlation does exist, there is a problem
of cause and effect: does the child do poorly because of
low self-esteem or is his low rating of himself a realistic appraisal based on his awareness that he does not
measure up to his schoolmates?   Many questions which purport to measure self-esteem really leave the causal prob-

lem hopelessly confused, questions like: 'do you feel you
can learn?' - 'how do you compare in ability with your
friends?'

5 Hypothesis: The notion of competing with whites
awakens crippling emotions in blacks, fear, anger, expec-
tation of failure or humiliation, and IQ tests engender
these emotions.   Jensen: It is mistakenly believed that
the research of Irwin Katz supports this kind of hypothesis.   Katz's research is important in its own right but
he achieved his results on tests other than IQ tests and
under experimental conditions, e.g. using hostile examiners and external threats, which are quite atypical of
ordinary intelligence testing.

6 Hypothesis: Teachers expect black children to perform at a lower level than whites and this affects their
scores on IQ tests.   Jensen: In 'Pygmalion in the Classroom', Rosenthal and Jacobson reported research done in
San Francisco.   In each class they compiled a list of
children at random, presented it to the teacher, and told
the teacher that those listed had done best on an earlier
IQ test; they concluded that teacher expectations affected subsequent test performance.   In fact, the expectancy
effect shows up in only two of the seven grades tested and
the methodology is too bizarre to be taken seriously, for
example, in one of these two the control group had a mean
IQ of 31 (barely at the imbecile level).   Nine attempts
to replicate the results of Rosenthal and Jacobson have
failed.   Teacher expectations affect a variety of things
in the classroom, perhaps even academic achievement, but
they do not appear to influence IQ.

7 Hypothesis: Black children receive less verbal stimulation from their parents and their parents often use an
atypical and ungrammatical dialect - the result is a lang-

uage deprivation which handicaps them on IQ tests.
Jensen: IQ tests are divided into verbal and non-verbal
or performance subtests, e.g. the Wechsler has 6 verbal
and 5 performance subtests.   If language deprivation
plays the dominant role, black children should have their
poorest scores on the verbal subtests but in fact the reverse is true.   Also Entwistle has shown that lower-class
black children are actually ahead of middle-class white
children in language development at the age of six and
fall behind at about the age of eight.   Entwistle gives
an environmental interpretation of the relative decline of
black children, but it may be an example of a fundamental
biological principle which holds both across and within
species: the more prolonged the infancy the greater the
cognitive development at maturity, which is to say that
the rapid early development of black children may be
linked with lesser cognitive ability later on because of
innate factors.   Children who are born totally deaf, certainly the most verbally deprived of children, reverse the
pattern we find among blacks.   They do badly on verbal
tests but match the IQ level of hearing subjects on non-
verbal performance tests of intelligence.

8 Hypothesis: Because of poverty, because of poor
health, poor pre-natal care, higher rates of venereal disease and drug addiction, black women provide a less adequate pre-natal environment for the developing foetus.
Jensen: It is clear that blacks have higher rates of
foetal loss, complications of pregnancy, labour and
delivery, and infant mortality; and it is clear that
these are associated with mental retardation and brain
damage.   However, higher rates of reproductive casualty
may be caused by either environmental or genetic factors.
The rates are higher for blacks than for whites of even

the lowest socio-economic status;   whites in turn had
higher rates than Orientals and Jews at a time when the
latter were immigrants living in poverty.   All of this
suggests a genetic hypothesis.   There is some evidence
that higher rates of reproductive casualty has to do with
too much diversity of ancestry and the ancestry of US
blacks may well be genetically more diverse than that of
US whites.

9 Hypothesis: Poor nutrition, whether pre-natal or
post-natal, affects black intellectual development.
Jensen: Severe malnutrition causes a cognitive deficit
but emphasis must be on the word 'severe'.   In order to
find cases, researchers are usually forced to go to parts
of Africa, Asia and Latin America in which children suffer
from the most extreme poverty and protein deficiency.
There is no reason to believe that an appreciable number
of American blacks suffer from malnutrition to this
degree, for example, they do not show signs of stunted
physical growth, below-normal performance on infant tests
of sensori-motor development, or deficit in memory ability.   When Carter et al. studied the poorest families of
Nashville, Tennessee, they found no children with the
emotional or physical symptoms associated with poor nutrition in developing countries.   But let us assume that 9
per cent of US blacks suffer an IQ deficit of 20 points
(the largest reported in the overseas literature) - such a
deficit would have depressed the black mean by less than
two points.   Harrell et al., in one study though not in
another, found a gain of 5 to 8 points in four-year-olds
whose mothers had been given dietary supplements during
pregnancy (maternity clinics in Norfolk, Virginia).   However, we do not know whether these effects would have per-
sisted into adolescence.   Towards the end of the Second

World War thousands of children were conceived, gestated and born during a severe famine in the Netherlands (duration 6 months); when tested as adults, their IQ scores were normal.   Some suggest that lowered IQ can result from poor nutrition which goes back to previous generations but this is unproven in humans.   Note that many of the ancestors of the whites now resident in Europe and North America themselves suffered from countless generations of rural poverty. (15)

10 Hypothesis: American blacks are clearly below whites in socioeconomic status (SES) and this, given all the environmental handicaps it entails, is sufficient to account for the IQ gap.   Jensen: When black and white Americans are matched for the usual SES variables, this merely reduces the IQ gap from 15 points to 10 or 11 points.   However, even this exaggerates the significance of SES as a causal factor: if we match blacks whose SES is at the white mean or above with the corresponding whites, we are matching the upper 13 per cent of blacks with the upper 50 per cent of whites;   and if we match whites whose SES is at the black mean or below with the corresponding blacks, we are matching the lower 10 per cent of whites with the lower 50 per cent of blacks (circa 1960).   If SES is positively correlated not only with favorable environmental variables but also with superior genes for IQ, both of these comparisons favour blacks: the first compares a small black elite in genetic terms with the upper half of whites;   the second compares a very low group of whites in genetic terms with the lower half of blacks.   That there is a positive correlation between genotype for IQ and SES is beyond dispute.   All we need do is show that IQ (which has a large genetic component) is a causal factor in social mobility which operates inde-

pendently of correlated environmental factors.   The evidence: there is a much lower correlation between IQ and the SES in which people are reared than between IQ and the SES they attain as adults; and within families, siblings whose IQs are above the family average tend to move up in SES and those below the family average tend to move down. (16)

In sum, a person's genotype for IQ is to some degree a cause of both his score on an IQ test (his phenotype) and his SES - SES is not just a causal factor of IQ but to some degree an effect as well.   The notion of treating SES as a purely causal factor is simply a fallacy, indeed, it has been given a name the 'sociologist's fallacy'. Finally, those who emphasize SES to explain away the gap between black and white must face up to some embarrassing facts when they compare blacks to other US minority groups: Indians and Mexicans are above blacks on IQ tests despite being below them in SES; Chinese and Japanese at least match whites on IQ tests despite lagging behind them in SES.   It is difficult to see how socioeconomic status can be used to equate various social groups in terms of their genotypes for IQ. (17)

11 Hypothesis: Although each environmental variable may have a relatively small impact on IQ, all of them work to the disadvantage of blacks and there is reason to believe that collectively they explain the IQ gap. Jensen: We cannot allow a few points for the fact that blacks have a lower SES, and then add a few points for a worse pre-natal environment, and then add a few for worse nutrition, hoping to reach a total of 15 points.   To do so would be to ignore the problem of overlap: the allowance for low SES already includes most of the influence of a poor pre-natal environment, and the allowance for a poor

pre-natal environment already includes much of the influence of poor nutrition, and so forth.   In other words, if we simply add together the proportions of the IQ variance (between the races) that each of the above environmental variables accounts for, we ignore the fact that they are not independent sources of variance.   The proper way to calculate the total impact of a list of environmental variables is to use a multiple regression equation, so that the contribution to IQ variance of each environmental factor is added in only after removing whatever contribution it has in common with all the previous factors which have been added in.   When we use such equations and when we begin by calculating the proportion of variance explained by SES, it is surprising how little additional variables contribute to the total portion of explained variance.

In fact, even the use of multiple regression equations can be deceptive.   If we add in a long enough list of variables which are correlated with IQ, we may well eventually succeed in 'explaining' the total IQ gap between black and white.   Recently both Jane Mercer and George W. Mayeske have used such methods and have claimed that racial differences in intelligence and scholastic achievement can be explained entirely in terms of the environmental effects of the lower socio-economic status of blacks. The fallacy in this is that described earlier, the 'sociologist's fallacy': all they have shown is that if someone chooses his 'environmental' factors carefully enough, he can eventually include the full contribution that genetic factors make to the IQ gap between the races.   For example, the educational level of the parents is often included as an environmental factor as if it were simply a cause of IQ variance.   But as we have seen, someone with

a superior genotype for IQ is likely to go farther in
school and he is also likely to produce children with
superior genotype for IQ: the correlation between the
educational level of the parents and the child's IQ is,
therefore, partially a result of the genetic inheritance
that has passed from parent to child.   Most of the 'environmental' variables which are potent in accounting for
IQ variance are subject to a similar analysis. (18)

   12 Hypothesis (really an excuse, an assertion, and a
deduction): Social science is in its infancy and we cannot as yet isolate the environmental variables which
affect IQ; but we can raise the mean IQ of deprived
groups as much as 30 points by altering their environment;
and this shows that the hereditarians must be mistaken.
Jensen: The assertion that we can raise the IQ of deprived children by 20 to 30 points is correct.   However,
they must be deprived to a degree well beyond the scale of
environments in which almost all Americans, whether black
or white, live.   As for the deduction that an h^2 estimate
of .80 must be mistaken, the findings of three studies are
usually cited in support of this but in fact all three are
consistent with such an estimate.   First, Skodak and
Skeels (1949) studied 100 children who were born to
mothers with a mean IQ of 85.7, who were adopted into exceptionally good, upper middle-class families, and who
(when tested in adolescence) attained a mean IQ of 107.
Before drawing any conclusions, we must compare that
result with what a genetic model using an h^2 of .80 would
predict: assuming the children had been raised in a
random sample of homes in the general population, their
predicted IQ would be 96, only 11 points below the actual
result.   Our genetic model also predicts that an environment 1.6 standard deviations above the average would raise

IQ by 11 points and there is every reason to believe the adoptive homes were superior to that degree.   Finally, it is doubtful that the children adopted were a random sample of the offspring of the low IQ mothers: the brighter children had a much better chance of being put out for adoption than the less bright and those judged defective. (19)

Second, Skeels and Dye (1939) studied orphanage children who gained in IQ from an average of 64 (at 19 months of age) to an average of 96 (at age 6) as a result of extra attention and eventual placement in good homes. But the children were living in conditions of extreme environmental deprivation, they suffered not just from lack of middle-class amenities but from little sensory stimulation and little contact with adults.   Our h^2 estimates apply essentially to those who live in the normal range of environments existent in America, not to those so deprived or privileged that we would have to put them in the lower or upper fraction of 1 per cent.   Third, Dr Rick Heber has recently found differences of 20 to 30 IQ points between a group of children reared experimentally and a control group left in what may well be the lowest 1 or 2 per cent of environmental conditions.   But once again, we are dealing with gains achieved in the most mentally stimulating environment psychologists know how to devise, an environment beyond the scale of normally occurring environments. (20)   None of these results, however worthwhile in themselves, give the slightest indication of what would occur if we eliminated the environmental differences between black and white which exist in America today.

The last section attempts to present Jensen's case as convincingly as possible and recall, it attempts to stick to

the text of Jensen as closely as possible.   I do not mean
to imply that everything Jensen says is accurate.   Nor do
I mean to imply that Jensen so overwhelmed his opponents
that they simply gave up and made no attempt to answer him
back.   Thomas Sowell has pointed out that the ghetto environment may well discourage reasoning abstractly even
more than it retards language development; (21)   Vera John
has argued that the Indian children who show up in test
results may be an elite, thanks to the failure of brain
damaged children to survive on reservations and the failure of many to attend state schools; (22)   Sandra Scarr
claims to have evidence which indicates that blacks score
relatively worse on tests that are culturally loaded than
on tests which are more culturally fair, evidence contrary
to that cited by Jensen. (23)   And I want to say something about how Jensen squares the findings of Skodak and
Skeels with his h^2 estimate of .80.

I believe that his analysis involves both a mistake and
a questionable assumption.   Given that Jensen is calculating the difference between the adopted children being
raised in an average family environment and being raised
in the superior family environment of their adoptive
homes, he should use his value for between families environment in calculating the IQ gain per standard deviation
of environmental effects (a value of .12).   Instead he
uses his value for all environmental factors which includes both between and within family environment (a value
of .20).   He assumes that the natural mothers whose mean
IQ was 85.7 mated with men whose average was the population mean of 100;   it would be normal to assume that the
fathers' average was half way between the mothers' mean
and the population mean, that is, 92.9.   The effect of
all this is as follows: Jensen can put the environment of

the adoptive homes at only 1.6 standard deviations above
the average home which is the 95th percentile and is
plausible; when the above corrections are made, we must
put the adoptive environments at 2.8 standard deviations
above the average which is the 99.74th percentile and is
not plausible.

Formula: $\bar{O} = \bar{M} + h_N^2 (\bar{P} - \bar{M})$.   Jensen's estimate of
$h_N^2 = .71$. (24)

Calculations:

(1) $\bar{P} = (85.7 + 92.9) \div 2 = 89.3$; $\bar{M} = 100$.

(2) $(89.3 - 100) \times .71 = -7.6$.

(3) $\bar{O} = 100 - 7.6 = 92.4$ as predicted IQ.

Actual IQ of children = 107.   Jensen's estimate of
between families environment = .12. (25)

Calculations:

(1) $107 - 92.4 = 14.6$.

(2) $15^2 \times .12 = 27$; $\sqrt{27} = 5.2$.

(3) $14.6 \div 5.2 = 2.8$ standard deviations above the
      average family environment.

However, I must add that I am scoring mainly a debating
point: Jensen is correct in saying that the less intelligent children of the mothers in question may not have been
adopted.   If we allow for this, the findings of Skodak
and Skeels are compatible with a range of h^2 estimates
whose upper limit would be .70 and if valid, that figure
would be almost as awkward as Jensen's estimate of .80.
Moreover Jensen has doubts about the methodology of Skodak
and Skeels.

As the above shows, we must not be content to score
points off Jensen here and there but must attempt to shake
the core of his position and on the face of it, his position rests on a foundation of great strength.   At the
very least, we can say that Jensen's work landed like a

bomb-shell in the midst of the environmentalist camp.
Most of us, particularly those in the social sciences, had
come to look upon an environmentalist hypothesis about the
IQ gap between black and white as virtually self-evident,
with only the triumphant accumulation of more and more
evidence in its favour to come.   By simply demanding
actually to see some evidence and subjecting it to the
most minimal criteria one would normally apply to the
social sciences, Jensen showed that many of the most cher-
ished environmental hypotheses were sheer speculation
without one piece of coherent research in their favour.
Thanks to Jensen, the day is past when the environmentalist can say with any pretence of respectability: 'well,
we all know the many ways in which blacks are disadvantaged and certainly, these just must be enough to explain
the gap between black and white.'

Far too many of Jensen's critics have not taken up the
challenge to refute him in any serious way, rather they
have elected for various forms of escape, the most popular
of which has been to seize on an argument put forward by
the distinguished Harvard geneticist Richard C. Lewontin.
Lewontin pointed out that black and white Americans may
well constitute two distinct populations as far as h^2
estimates are concerned, it being sufficient to assume
that they exist in environments which differ significantly
in terms of factors relevant to IQ test performance.   If
so, Jensen's h^2 estimates are estimates which refer only
to the heritability of IQ within white America and within
black America respectively.   He then cited an axiom of
elementary genetics: it is erroneous to assume that high
h^2 estimates for a particular trait *within* each of two
distinct populations shows that a difference *between* those

two populations is heritable;   despite high h^2 estimates
the between population difference (e.g. a 15-point difference in mean IQ) may be caused by either genetic or environmental factors.

Lewontin gave an example which made a powerful impression.   I have taken a few liberties with it for purposes
of clarification, but the gist is as follows: (1) we have
a sack containing seed of an open-pollinated variety of
corn, a variety with lots of genetic variation in it;   (2)
we take two random samples of seed from the sack - there
will be considerable genetic variation within each sample
but let us assume we have been fortunate enough to get two
perfectly matched samples, so that there is no difference
between them in genetic terms;   (3) batch A is grown in an
artificial standardized environment, so that every seed
has an identical environment, and its soil is enriched
with a full allotment of nitrates and trace elements of
zinc salt;   (4) batch B is also grown in a standard environment but its soil is impoverished by getting half the
necessary nitrates and no zinc salt.   As to the results
of the experiment, after several weeks we measure the
height of the plants: (1) all of the variation within
batch A is due to genetic differences - after all we
allowed for no environmental differences within the batch,
and therefore the h^2 estimate is 100 per cent or 1.00;
(2) all of the variation within batch B is genetic in
origin and the h^2 estimate is 1.00 for the same reason;
(3) however, all of the difference in mean height between
the two batches is environmental in origin - after all the
two batches were matched in genetic terms, and the difference in nutrients was solely responsible for the better
growth of A as compared to B.   As Lewontin says: 'Thus,
we have a case where heritability within populations is

complete, yet the difference between populations is entirely environmental!' (26)

It is easy to understand the appeal of Lewontin's argument.   To deny that black and white may be separate populations due to significant environmental differences is to
beg the whole question of race and IQ.   As for h^2 estimates, they are relative to the population being measured:
there can be no such thing as an 'absolute' h^2 estimate
any more than there can be an 'absolute' infant mortality
rate;   we can only measure the respective contributions
of genes and environment in a given population at a given
time, just as we only make predictions about infant mortality in a given population at a given time.   Which is
to say that h^2 estimates do not necessarily measure the
importance of heredity and environment, they may measure
no more than the relative uniformity of environmental factors: remember that h^2 estimates give us correlations between variance on IQ tests (how much performance varies
from person to person) and variance in environmental factors (how much those factors vary from person to person).
However potent an environmental factor in stunting intellectual development, if all members of a population are
affected by it equally, it cannot account for variable
performance and will not show up in h^2 estimates.   Note
Lewontin's example of a plant having too few nutrients:
this was potent enough to stunt the growth of the whole of
population B;   but since the degree of deprivation did not
vary within the population, it had no impact on the h^2
estimate for height.

Let us take another example closer to the human situation.   Imagine we collect a group of excellent chess
players all about to begin their careers in tournament
play.   Using random selection we divide them into two

groups.   We allow group A to play in tournaments unhin-
dered, while group B is forced to play blindfolded.
Looking at between-group differences in performance, the
members of group A will undoubtedly have a much better
average won-lost record than the members of group B, due
of course almost entirely to an environmental factor, the
absence or presence of blindfolds.   But within each of
the groups, the blindfold factor will have zero influence
on differential performance: all within group A lack
them, all within group B have them;   you cannot measure
the impact on performance of non-existent differences.
Which is to say, if we made h^2 estimates of the relative
influence of genes and environment on ability at chess,
the within-group estimates would entirely miss the influence of the blindfolds: they would entirely miss the
whole explanation of the between-group differences.   How
then can within-white and within-black h^2 estimates for IQ
shed any light on between-group differences?   How could
Jensen have been so blind?

The range of scholars who have used some version of the
above argument against Jensen is quite extraordinary (they
differ of course in the degree of importance they attach
to it).   I am sure the following is incomplete but it
contains a fair number of them listed in chronological
order: J.F. Crow (1969), Gregg and Sanday (1971), Sandra
Scarr (1971), W.F. Bodmer (1972), Howard F. Taylor (1973,
1976), S.J. Gould (1975), Glenys Thomson (1975), David
Lazar (1976), Block and Dworkin (1976), and Ehrlich and
Feldman (1977). (27)   For some, Lewontin's argument is so
self-evident and so significant that whether or not a
scholar accepts it is the measure of whether he has anything worthwhile to say about race and IQ!   When review-
ing the superb book by Loehlin et al. on the subject,

Glenys Thomson found that her initial enthusiasm vanished when she realized that: 'They still subscribe to the belief that a knowledge of the heritability of a trait within a population can tell us something about between-group differences.' She herself knew that this was just not so and she laments that the authors 'do not seem to have grasped that fact'. (28)   Ehrlich and Feldman take the same line and clearly believe that Jensen's notions about the relevance of h^2 is based on sheer ignorance of the science of genetics. (29)

After reading these scholars, it comes as something of a shock to realize that Lewontin's example does not at all show the irrelevance of high h^2 estimates to finding an explanation of between-population differences.   Indeed, in Lewontin's example, the h^2 estimates of 1.00 set the whole context of what we must look for if we are to explain the between-population difference in terms of environmental factors.   Remember just what the plant example says: if there is a significant difference between two groups in terms of the level of an important nutrient; and, far more rare, if the high level of that nutrient is perfectly uniform throughout population A; and if the low level is perfectly uniform throughout population B; then we can explain a between population difference in environmental terms despite h^2 estimates of 1.00.   And remember just what the chess example says: if we have reason to believe that almost everyone in one group has a blindfold and that almost everyone in another group has none, then we can explain a between-population difference despite high h^2 estimates.   In other words, the real message of Lewontin's example is that we can ignore high h^2 estimates only if there exists a highly specific and highly unusual set of circumstances.   Therefore, it is absurd to say

that high h^2 estimates within black and white respectively
are irrelevant.   Their relevance consists precisely of
this: they force us to look for a plausible candidate for
the role of blindfold.   They force us to look for an environmental factor or factors which can satisfy these criteria: it must handicap the IQ test performance of blacks
or discourage the development of the skills tested;   it
must be largely confined to the black population;   it must
be pretty uniform within that population with very little
variance from person to person;   and if we accept Jensen
on SES not qualifying as a plausible candidate, it must
function largely independent of SES.

There is no doubt that high h^2 estimates force environmentalists to find a factor or factors that are relatively
uniform in their presence within the black population -
and within the white population as well if they operate
there.   After all, if an environmental factor is potent
enough to account for the 15-point performance gap between
black and white, and if it varies much from person to
person within the black population, it would be extremely
odd if it accounted for none of the variable performance
within the black population!   And if it did, it would of
course increase the role of environmental factors in explaining IQ variance and thus lower the h^2 estimate for
blacks.   There is also no doubt that this criterion, the
criterion of uniform presence, is the most crippling of
those the environmentalist is forced to accept.   If we
seize on SES as a between-population explanation, who can
deny that there are large differences in SES within black
America;   if we seize on education, who can deny that
blacks differ significantly in terms of quality of education?   The usual candidate brought forward for the role
of blindfold is racism: after all every black suffers

from racial bias, and no white suffers from at least that
kind of handicap, and racism is very potent.   But this
too is simply an escape from hard thinking and hard research.   Racism is not some magic force that operates
without a chain of causality.   Racism harms people because of its effects and when we list those effects, lack
of confidence, low self-image, emasculation of the male,
the welfare mother home, poverty, it seems absurd to claim
that any one of them does not vary significantly within
both black and white America.   Certainly there are some
blacks who have self-confidence, enjoy a stable home, a
reasonable income, good housing; and certainly we all
know whites who have a poor self-image, suffer from emasculation, or suffer from poverty.

It may be said that the above underestimates the extent
to which certain environmental factors are peculiar to
blacks, or at least affect blacks to such a degree as to
set them off from whites as a group.   It is here that
Jensen's attempt to falsify all of the environmental hypotheses on his list comes into its own.   For what he is
doing in effect is attempting to show that there is no
plausible candidate for the role of blindfold.   If we say
'let us assume reaction to the race of the examiner separates black and white, let us assume self-image sets apart
black and white, let us assume dialect separates black and
white', Jensen has his answer ready: 'Even if that is so,
there is no evidence that these factors operate as potent
handicaps on black performance on IQ tests.'   Once again:
it is easy to forget that the positing of a blindfold is a
logical prerequisite to the contention that high h^2 estimates are irrelevant.   Jensen uses high h^2 estimates to
force us to look for blindfolds; and then uses his list
to systematically strip us of our leading candidates for

the role.   That is why I say that he makes his case in
two parts.   The two parts together have tremendous force:
they have a potency that each of them lacks in isolation.

   In sum, that Jensen attempts to falsify all environmental hypotheses is bad enough.   But he uses his high h^2
estimates to cast an implication of absurdity over the
whole environmentalist position: when we look at variables like SES which vary within the black community, we
are left wondering how a variable that makes so little
difference there could make so much difference between
black and white;   when we look at variables like reaction
to race of the examiner which might be uniform, we are
left with a strong suspicion that they are probably pretty
trivial.   I see nothing in Lewontin's example to encourage optimism.   We environmentalists have always known
that we had to find environmental factors that handicapped
blacks.   To be told that those factors must be uniform
within black and white, like a nutrient artificially doled
out during a controlled scientific experiment, is not much
help.   The whole notion of something playing the role of
our blindfold seems scarcely plausible.

Jensen may have encouraged the excesses of his critics in
that his explicit reply to Lewontin is too cryptic to be
convincing. (30)   But his books tell a different story
and show that he is fully aware of the relativity of heritability estimates, the axioms of genetics, and the existence of plant examples which suggest environmental differences between populations despite 100 per cent h^2 estimates within those populations. (31)   His books also show
that his two-step argument has an impressive flexibility:
it is hard to tell whether it is more potent when the h^2
estimates come first and the attack on candidates for the

role of blindfold second, or when the steps come in reverse order.

He usually begins with his first step. He concedes
that high **heritability** estimates do not in themselves constitute a case for a genetic hypothesis about group differences, rather such estimates merely set the stage for
evidence which renders such a hypothesis highly probable.
They set the stage of course by driving the environmentalist to posit what I have called a blindfold and what
Jensen calls a factor X: a factor 'which is present in
one population and not in the other and which affects all
individuals in one population and none in the other'; and
which must have 'an equal or constant effect on all members of the population in which it is present'. And once
we have falsified every specific environmental hypothesis
which puts forward a candidate for the role of factor X, a
genetic hypothesis is highly probable; it cannot be certain because the dogmatic environmentalist can always
assume the existence of an unknown X, so unknown we cannot
test for it. But this last is not very impressive. To
illustrate his point, Jensen considers motivation as a
candidate for factor X and asks how plausible it is to
assume that all blacks differ from all whites by a constant amount in terms of motivation. (32)

At other times, he reverses the order and begins with
his second step. He asks us to set aside the implausible
concept of a factor X and he emphasizes that environmentalists themselves usually turn to something more prosaic
when they want to explain racial differences in IQ,
namely, factors correlated with SES or income. This
means that environmentalists are assuming in effect that
the factors which differentiate individuals within each
racial population are also the principal factors which en-

courage IQ differences between the two racial groups.
Once this assumption is made, Jensen can use his h^2 estimates as a powerful weapon.   Using an h^2 for both black
and white of .85 and a between-families environmental component of .05, he calculates that a strictly environmental
hypothesis about the 15-point IQ gap between black and
white must assume the following: the average white family
and the average black family would have to differ by 4.5
standard deviations in terms of systematic environmental
effects; or to put the point more dramatically, the
'average Negro environment is ... something below the
0.003 percentile of systematic environmental effects on IQ
in the white population.'   This does seem implausible, it
seems most implausible that most of black America suffers
from an environment so bad that it falls virtually off the
bottom end of the scale of environmental effects in the
white population.   Jensen challenges environmentalists to
find any significant environmental factor on which the gap
between black and white is even close to 4.5 standard deviations.   He provides a series of estimates: the gap for
SES is about 1.24 SDs, for income .80 SDs, for unemployment rates .33 SDs, and so forth. (33)

I do not want, even at this early stage in my analysis,
to surround Jensen with an aura of infallibility.   When
he gets away from the two steps which constitute the core
of his case, his arguments are sometimes less impressive.
I cannot cover them all, but will select out two for comment.   These two arguments have the following in common:
first, both had a considerable impact at the time Jensen
put them forward; next, after careful analysis, both were
found to be irrelevant or at least of only tangential
relevance; and finally, unless I am mistaken, Jensen has
begun to acknowledge their limitations and has signalled

that he is now ready to withdraw them from the race and IQ
debate.

In his early works, there are a number of passages in
which Jensen focuses on the phenomenon called 'regression
to the mean' and emphasizes that while whites tend to regress to their population mean of 100, blacks tend to regress to their own population mean, namely, an IQ of 85.
For example: if we take a group of whites with an average
IQ of 120, their offspring (or siblings) may have an average IQ of 110 (half way between 120 and 100); while if we
take a group of blacks with an IQ of 120, their offspring
(or siblings) may have an average IQ of 100 (about half
way between 120 and 85).   The implication is not entirely
clear but it seems to be that this stands as evidence that
the population means have some sort of genetic component,
so that it would be difficult to explain the gap between
black and white in environmental terms.   This was the
interpretation espoused by Sandra Scarr and Jensen quotes
her with approval. (34)   J.M. Thoday tells us that initially, he believed that the above clearly counted against
an environmental hypothesis. (35)

If we understand why regression to the mean occurs, we
will see that this argument, as it stands, has no relevance.   The reason for regression to the mean is purely
statistical: when we select out an atypical group using
the criterion of IQ, another group selected out in terms
of criteria which merely correlate with IQ is not likely
to be as atypical as they.   There is of course a correlation between being someone's child and having his genes
for intelligence but the correlation is not perfect -
there are genetic differences between parent and child;
and there is no doubt a correlation between the environment that conditions a child's IQ and that which influen-

ced his parent's IQ, but again the correlation will not be perfect.   This means that the children of a group who are atypical in terms of IQ will be more like their parents than the average person would be, the ties of parenthood in terms of heredity and environment count for something, but they will not be as atypical as their parents.   On the average, they will have gone some distance away from the parents' mean towards the population mean - hence the term 'regression to the mean'.   (The reader need not fear that every generation will be bunched up around the population mean to a greater degree than its predecessor with both high and low IQ types tending to disappear.   If we go back to our sample of persons with an average IQ of 120, their parents would have a lower IQ for the very same reason their children do.   Again, regression to the mean has to do with samples selected according to different criteria, not with changes over time.)

Now take our samples of whites and blacks each of which have an average IQ of 120.   The reason that the children of the blacks regress to a lower IQ than the children of the whites is not because the genes of blacks have created a 'black mean' which is inferior to the 'white mean' created by the genes of whites.   It is simply because a group of blacks with an IQ of 120 are a more atypical sample of their own population than are a group of whites with an IQ of 120.   It is the greater degree of atypicality that dictates the greater regression of their children: the more atypical a sample, the greater the divergence of another sample selected by criteria which merely correlate with the original criterion.   The only way in which the population means are relevant is that they serve as a measure of the relevant atypicality: clearly a black with an IQ of 120 who is 35 points above his population mean

(85) is more atypical than a white of 120 who is merely 20 points above his population mean (100).   In sum, blacks must regress to the black population mean and whites to the white population mean.   The fact that black and white regress to different means signifies no more than that they have different means.   It leaves the central question of providing a causal explanation of why they have different means untouched.

Jensen's most recent statement of the argument appears to concede the above.   In an article published in 1975 and republished in 1977, he says that despite the existence of the regression phenomenon, 'the difference between the populations ... could be all environmental, or all genetic, or anything in between.'   He does not abandon the argument entirely but now, he claims for it only a very limited role in the race and IQ controversy, namely: that the degree of regression to the mean seems similar for white and black; and that the most parsimonious explanation of this is that both races have the same, very high heritability of IQ. (36)   In effect, this collapses the regression argument into his original two-step argument, the former being significant only as evidence for high h^2 estimates.   And if that is its principal significance, twin data (whatever its defects) is acknowledged as providing evidence of far superior quality and we would do better to focus our attention on it.   Before we leave the regression argument behind us, I wish to add that there may be one version of it which has merit, but only because hidden behind the language of regression to the mean there is a real substantive point.   Jensen asserts that thanks to regression, black children raised by black parents of upper socio-economic status develop lower IQs than white children raised by white parents of low SES. (37)   This data certainly does pose a problem for environmentalists but the problem derives from the fact that black children seem to profit so little from what appears to be a good environment - what appears to be an environment equivalent in quality to an above average white environment.   The fact that compared to their parents they are regressing to the black mean adds nothing.   As for an answer to Jensen's substantive point, the best road for an environmentalist to take is to look at what happens to black children who are actually raised in a white environment, something which will be done in the next chapter.

The second argument I have chosen for critique at this point has to do with the connection between heritability within groups and heritability between groups.   At the very beginning of the controversy, Jensen began to use it to refute those who, reasoning on the basis of Lewontin's plant example, denied the existence of any such connection.   He set out an equation which states the formal relationship between the two kinds of heritability and used it to generate certain calculations.   These calculations show that 'between group heritability is a monotomically increasing function of within group heritability', which is to say the greater our h^2 estimates within black and white America respectively, the greater the heritable or genetic component in the difference between the mean IQs of the two populations.   And he presented graphs which show the heritability of the gap between black and white reaching 100 per cent for certain values of the 'within group genetic correlation for the trait in question' (which measures the extent to which classifying people as black renders them more alike in terms of genes for IQ).

In works published during 1972 and 1973, Jensen refers to the above equation on four occasions. (38)   On two of

these occasions he adds that since we do not as yet have a
value for the above 'within group correlation', the formula is at present of no practical use in determining the
heritability of the difference between the mean IQs of
black and white. (39)   And he always emphasizes that the
formula does not render a genetic gap between black and
white certain, rather it gives mathematical expression to
a probable relationship between high h^2 estimates and a
genetic gap.   However, all in all, the reader who confined himself to Jensen's books could be forgiven if he
feels shaken.   Up to now, he has thought that even if
Jensen proved correct in his speculations about h^2 estimates for both black and white, there were two possibilities: a blindfold might exist which would explain the
black/white IQ gap environmentally;   there might be a huge
gap in terms of non-blindfold type environmental factors
which could supply such an explanation.   Neither of these
looked very promising, but now are environmentalists to be
pressed even closer to the wall?   Does the above equation
allow for a sort of 'end-run' around these possibilities?
This would be true if the equation meant that, rather than
having to falsify such environmental hypotheses, we could
merely: collect more data in favour of high within group
h^2 estimates;   collect more data about the degree of genetic similarity between black and white;   and then calculate that blacks fall so many IQ points below whites because of genetic differences.

The fears described are groundless but this can only be
seen by a careful reading of Jensen and I think I have
shown that this is desirable.   Let us go back to the
equation in question and note the exchange which occurred
between Professors Jensen, Fuller, and DeFries concerning
its applicability.

Formula for the relationship between heritability between group means (h_B^2) and heritability within groups
(h_W^2):

$$h_B^2 \simeq h_W^2 \frac{(1 - t)r}{(1 - r)t}$$

h_B^2 is the heritability between group means;

h_W^2 is the average heritability within groups;

t is the intraclass correlation among phenotypes
   within groups (or the square of the point biserial
   correlation between the quantized racial dichotomy
   and the trait measurement);

r is the intraclass correlation among genotypes within
   groups, i.e., the within-group genetic correlation
   for the trait in question.

Note: Sometimes Jensen states this equation with a
different notation, that is, he substitutes r for t
above and substitutes p for r above.   Unless the
reader is careful, he may mistake what r refers to.
It was DeFries who originally took the equation out of the
realm of quantitative genetics and applied it to racial
differences.   In his derivation of it, he makes clear
that he is setting aside the possibility that 'certain
genotypes are forced to live in inferior environments'; (40) and that, for simplicity's sake, he has
assumed the absence of a 'significant genotype-environment
correlation'. (41)   What this means is that DeFries was
assuming the following: that when black and white are
equal in genetic value for IQ, they are also equal in
terms of quality of environment.   Naturally, no environmentalist will concede such an assumption: the environmentalist must argue that despite possessing a genetic
value equal to whites, blacks are worse off environmentally; otherwise how could the IQ gap have an environmental
explanation?   DeFries emphasizes that if we reject his

simplifying assumption, we need more data to put his equation to work, namely, data which tells us the extent to
which there is a negative correlation between black genes
for IQ and quality of environment.   As he says, if the
correlation were both negative and large, the genetic
value of blacks might actually exceed the genetic value of
whites.

It is difficult to see how we would get the necessary
data without using research designs which would in themselves settle the debate about race and IQ.   Ideally, we
would study a situation in which blacks we knew to be
typical genetically lived in an environment we knew to be
equivalent to the average white environment.   Jensen himself arrived at a similar conclusion, namely, that we must
be able to calculate r (the genetic intraclass correlation) in order to actually use the above equation; and
that 'if we knew r, we would already know what we really
wanted to know in the first place'. (42)   DeFries adds
that his formula would still be useful, presumably by
giving us an estimate of the actual number of IQ points
that separate black and white because of genetic differences. (43)   I would like to add that the research designs
which are a prerequisite for using DeFries's formula
would, in all probability, already have given us an excellent estimate.   In view of some of the illustrations various scholars have given about how the equation in question might be used, it is also important to note that in
computing r, we cannot use data on the genetic similarity
between black and white based on things like the distribution of genes for blood groups.   It is quite possible
that differences between races in terms of genes for IQ do
not match differences between races for other kinds of
genes.   So in order to compute the relevant genetic simi-

larity between black and white, we would have to be able
to actually identify the genes for IQ.   Needless to say,
we cannot do this at present, save for cases of obvious
genetic abnormality such as children who suffer from
Mongolism or phenylketonuria. (44)

The exchange with DeFries has had a clear effect on
Jensen's most recent publications.   In articles published
in 1975 (originally) and 1978, he mentions the equation in
question but spends all his space rehearsing its limitations. (45)   I think it is fair to say that it can now be
given a decent burial, as far as the debate on race and IQ
is concerned.   This is much to be desired: it has caused
far more confusion than it is worth.

The ancillary arguments examined above add little or
nothing to the core of Jensen's case; neither do they detract.   Jensen's case stands or falls on the merits of
his two-step argument and these are considerable: he has
drawn upon an impressive range of evidence from many
areas, population genetics, human genetics, twin studies,
sociology, educational psychology, special education, nutrition, tests and measurement; and he has integrated
this evidence into a coherent conceptual system.   Jensen
has forged a steel chain of ideas, the key links in which
are heritability estimates and the absurdity of the concept of a blindfold or a factor X, and that steel chain of
ideas leaves the environmentalist with almost no freedom
of manoeuvre.   And yet, as we shall see, this conceptual
system and this mass of evidence apparently so secure lead
to some very puzzling problems.

Chapter 3

DIRECT EVIDENCE
AND INDIRECT

Jensen has argued for a genetic gap between black and
white of 8 to 11 IQ points.   For the time being, I will
set aside the task of trying to pose problems for Jensen
and take a more positive approach.   I want to develop a
case of my own in favour of genetic equality.   In this
chapter, we will examine a body of evidence, all of which
appears in the literature in one place or another, but
which has not received sufficient emphasis or analysis.
In my opinion this evidence taken collectively allows a
reasonable man to conclude that an environmental hypothesis about the gap between black and white is more probable
than a genetic hypothesis.

     This is not to say that a reasonable man can cherish a
dogmatic commitment to the proposition that all races of
mankind are absolutely equal in terms of genotypes for IQ;
Jensen is correct in asserting that natural selection
could produce such differences and differences may well
exist at a particular point in time.   The question that
is really central is the magnitude of the differences: a
genetic gap of say ten points allows a racist to make a
last stand in defence of the epistemological viability of
his ideology;   while if white and black differ genotypically by five points or less, setting aside whether such a

difference favours white or black, the racist ideologue
has no real foundation for his defence.   Five points is
the gap which consistently favours singletons over twins,
but no one has in recent years become alarmed over that
fact.   The 'dilution' of the gene pool by a 10 per cent
minority five points below the mean would make an overall
difference of only one-half of an IQ point.   As for a
difference of two or three points, there is some evidence
that New Zealand school children enjoy such an advantage
over American school children.   England may have some
preference in favour of New Zealand immigrants but she
does not seem to have taken the possibility of a superior
genotype for IQ into account.   If our racist ideologue
were to attempt to put a strong emphasis on such differences, he would have to draw distinctions within the world's
white population which he would not find congenial.

   The content of the remainder of this chapter is dictated by a distinction, a distinction between two kinds of
evidence.   What after all is the whole debate about race
and IQ about?   Essentially this: what would happen to
the mean IQ of American blacks if they found themselves
distributed among the range of environments existent in
contemporary white America in the same proportions as
whites; and, a less pleasant prospect, what would happen
to the mean IQ of American whites if they were to find
themselves in the context of the American black environment.   An overwhelming proportion of the evidence presented on race and IQ has the purpose of attempting to simulate such circumstances or to predict what would occur in
such circumstances.   But there exists evidence of another
sort, namely, evidence concerning groups who are actually
in the above circumstances at the present time, groups who
have actually experienced such an exchange of environments.

I will call the latter sort of evidence 'direct' and
the former 'indirect' and define those terms as follows.
Direct evidence refers to evidence as to how black and
white genes function when they are actually taken out of
their usual environmental context, for example, when both
are put into a neutral environment, or when white genes
are put into a black environment, or vice versa.   The
major instances of this are when US black and white troops
father children abroad, or when whites sexually interact
with blacks in America and the offspring are absorbed into
the black community, or when black children are adopted by
white parents.   Indirect evidence refers to everything we
have covered thus far, attempts to predict what would
happen if black and white genes exchanged environments,
whether this is done by weighing the influence of specific
environmental factors (e.g. calculating correlations between IQ and SES, and attitudes, and maternal attitudes,
and so forth) or by weighing the influence of environment
in general against genetic factors in general (through h^2
estimates).   There are even those (not Jensen) who try to
make studies of identical twins raised apart an autonomous
basis of prediction: they speculate on whether the difference between the environments of the separated twins
matches the difference between black and white environments and then calculate whether, in those cases, a gap of
15 IQ points emerges or does not emerge.

I am going to argue that direct evidence takes priority
over indirect evidence however extensive for one reason
which seems to me sufficient: evidence which tells us
what actually happens in a given situation must be given
priority over evidence which predicts what must or should
or would happen in that situation.   If direct evidence
accumulates which shows that black and white Americans

have similar genotypes for IQ, all of the twin studies, h^2 estimates, path analyses, multiple regression equations, assertion and falsification of specific environmental hypotheses will have to give way.   Direct evidence has another great advantage.   It transcends all the debate about whether IQ tests are fair, whether the content, race of the examiner, wording of the directions, motivational situation favour black or white.   It would be surprising if children fathered by black soldiers in occupied Germany, raised entirely by German mothers, never having any real contact with their black fathers, carried over US black vocabulary, culture or attitudes.   Racial prejudice might affect them but the total impact of the American black environment would not.   It would be surprising if blacks who are 25 per cent white in terms of their genealogy but whose white ancestors date back in time and whose parents were, thanks to racial bias, designated as 'black' and socialized in the black community carry over the advantage of white vocabulary and attitudes.   They might benefit from a bias in favour of light skin within the black community itself, but they are much more a part of that community than any other.   It can still be argued that IQ tests do not measure anything significant, of course; but if direct evidence is available, we can tell which groups (if any) have the best genotypes for whatever it is that they measure.

We will begin with evidence on how white genes function when put in a black environment.   Thanks to sexual interaction throughout American history, there are plenty of white genes within the population Americans classify as 'black'.   It is estimated that as of today US blacks have from 20 per cent to 30 per cent white ancestry and these

estimates are derived from evidence ranging from genealog-
ical surveys to analysis of blood groups. The latter is
based on these facts: the European population from which
America's whites came has a certain distribution of blood
types, while the African population from which America's
blacks came has a very different distribution; for example, one blood group present in over 40 per cent of Cau-
casians is virtually absent in West Africans. By analysing the distribution of blood types among US blacks, we
can estimate the 'distance' they have gone from their original distribution towards a white distribution.   If
whites enjoy a genetic advantage for IQ over blacks, the
IQ of US blacks should rise in proportion to the degree of
white ancestry; William Shockley has estimated that 'for
low IQ populations, each 1 per cent of Caucasian ancestry
raises average IQ by one point', (1) although we should
note that few advocates of a genetic hypothesis would go
so far.

Virtually all scholars agree that most of the studies
done prior to 1965 are of little value. Audrey Shuey
surveyed sixteen such studies and concluded that, while
racial hybrids had an advantage over darker blacks, the
advantages were not typically large and that 'these
studies make no important contribution to the problem of
race differences in intelligence'. (2)   Most of these
studies attempted to correlate skin colour with IQ and, as
Jensen has pointed out, light skin is also correlated with
higher socioeconomic status and may even have been the
basis of assortive mating within the black population.
This last would bring about a correlation between light
skin and above-average IQ quite independent of the degree
of white ancestry. When a visible characteristic is
valued within a population, whether it be height, small

noses (among Eskimos), or light skin colour, it becomes
correlated with other valuable characteristics: just as
intelligent people mating with other intelligent people
will produce a group higher above the mean than when there
is no such assortive mating, so if high-status (and therefore more intelligent) blacks mated disproportionately
with light-skinned blacks, this would move light-skinned
blacks to a position above the mean IQ.   Jensen concludes
that correlations between skin colour and IQ may have
nothing to do with sexual interaction with whites. (3)

In 1972, Jensen suggested that we abandon skin colour
(a visible characteristic which can be socially valued) in
favour of blood groups (an invisible characteristic) in
our efforts to establish meaningful correlations between
IQ and white ancestry.   The following year Loehlin, Vandenberg and Osborne published an analysis of a sample of
40 black adolescents (20 twin pairs) from Atlanta, Georgia, and a sample of 44 black adolescents (22 twin pairs)
from Louisville, Kentucky.   They ranked 16 blood-group
genes in terms of their greater frequencies within white
samples as compared to the black samples.   They then
ranked the same 16 in terms of the extent to which each
gene was predictive of good performance among blacks as
measured by a battery of 19 cognitive tests.   The authors
asked whether the blood genes characteristic of whites
were also the genes predictive of good performance and
calculated a rank-order correlation: the Atlanta data
showed that the correlation was actually negative (-.38)
and the Louisville data that it was virtually nil
(+.01). (4)   In 1977 Scarr et al. published results based
on 288 young blacks (144 twin pairs) aged 10 to 16, a
sample drawn mainly from the state schools of Philadelphia, Pennsylvania.   They ranked their subjects according

to their degree of resemblance to an equally large white
sample, that is, in terms of 12 blood-group genes which
differentiated the black and white samples.   They also
ranked their subjects according to their performance on
four cognitive tests, using the first principal component
of these tests as a measure;   the authors believe that
this gave them a reliable measure of intellectual skills
and something analogous to 'g' ('g' = general intelligence).   In this case, the correlation between good performance and white blood-genes was positive but very low
(+.05) and when SES and skin colour were partialed out the
correlation fell away to virtually nil. (5)

None of the above correlations attained statistical
significance and on the face of it, the results seem to
show that white ancestry confers neither an advantage nor
a disadvantage within the American black population.
However, Loehlin has raised a troublesome point: whether
given independent gene assortment over many generations,
the blood-genes from the white ancestors of US blacks are
still associated with IQ-genes from those ancestors.   If
not, there might still be a correlation between blacks
having white ancestry and high IQ despite the lack of a
correlation between their having white blood-genes and
high IQ.   Loehlin argued that if white blood-genes were
still associated with white IQ-genes within the American
black population, then the various blood-genes should
still be associated with one another;   after all, if the
blood-genes from white ancestors have drifted apart, why
should they not have drifted apart from white IQ genes?
He found that they were not still associated with one
another. (6)   Scarr did find a correlation between one
set of three blood-genes and another set of nine plus a
correlation between these sets and skin colour;   but the

correlations were in the .10 to .20 range which is not
very impressive. (7)

Once again, studies of racial admixture do not seem to
promise very much.   However, there is one exception: one
study stands out as of considerable significance, a study
done by Witty and Jenkins in Chicago in 1934.   Note the
two problems we have encountered: how to detect the presence of white genes for intelligence within the US black
population; how to detect IQ differences, which may be
slight, between subpopulations of US blacks who possess.
different amounts of such genes.   Witty and Jenkins
attacked these problems by focusing on certain fundamen-
tals.   First, blacks who have white genes for intelligence are by and large simply those who have white ancestors.   Witty and Jenkins, rather than seeking correlations with skin colour or blood types, decided to ask
blacks what they knew about their ancestors, which of them
were reputed to be white or partially white.   Second,
they capitalized on the mathematical properties of a normal curve.   IQ scores fall into the pattern of a normal
curve and one of its properties is this: take two populations or subpopulations; differences which are slight and
difficult to ascertain by comparing the means of the two
populations become great, and therefore readily apparent,
at a level several standard deviations above the mean.

For example, assume we had two black populations who
differed by 30 per cent in their degree of white ancestry; assume that the mean IQs of these two populations are
84 and 87 respectively, a difference of only three points.
If we chose a score four or five standard deviations above
their means, say an IQ of 140, we would find of course
that only a few from either population could attain that
score or better.   But the important point is that the two

populations would no longer appear to be relatively equal:
thanks to the pattern of a normal distribution, within the
class with IQs above 140, the population with a slight advantage at the means would be overrepresented by a ratio
of two or three to one.   We now have a testable hypothesis: if white ancestry has been of advantage to American
blacks, then those blacks with a large degree of white ancestry should be overrepresented at high IQ levels.

Using Terman's method, Witty and Jenkins did a systematic survey of over 8,000 black children in 7 state elementary schools in Chicago;   they identified 63 children
with IQs of 125 or above, 28 of whom were 140 or
above. (8)   A few years earlier (primarily in 1925-6),
Herskovits had obtained geneological information from over
1,500 black adults whose geographical distribution (in
terms of birth place) was a reasonable approximation of US
blacks in general including recent migrants from the West
Indies.   Herskovits classified them as unmixed Negro (N),
more Negro than white (NNW), about equal (NW), and more
white than Negro (NWW) on the basis of what they reported
concerning known ancestors, being impressed by their ad-
missions of ignorance (e.g. of 40 per cent of their grand-
parents) and their unsolicited mention of Indian ancestors. (9)   Witty and Jenkins secured geneological information from the parents of their high-IQ children, used
the same mode of classification as Herskovits, and compared their high-IQ children to the larger US black population as described by Herskovits. (10)   The results are
shown in Table 3.1:   the match in terms of degree of white
admixture between the high-IQ black children and blacks in
general is remarkable;   there is no sign of overrepresen-
tation of those with a large degree of white ancestry.
As Loehlin et al. point out, the data best fits a hypothe-

sis of 'no average genetic difference' between the Caucasian and African ancestral populations of US blacks. (11)

TABLE 3.1   White admixture of black children with high IQs, compared to the black population in general

Class	Black pop. %	No.	Above 125 %	No.	Above 140 %	No.
N	28.3	(439)	22.2	(14)	21.4	(6)
NNW	31.6	(490)	46.0	(29)	42.9	(12)
NW	25.3	(393)	15.9	(10)	21.4	(6)
NWW	14.8	(229)	15.9	(10)	14.3	(4)

Witty and Jenkins's results carry another implication of great interest, namely, that a reasonably representative sample of the original black population has interacted sexually with American whites.   If the blacks who mated with whites were markedly superior (in terms of genotype for IQ), this in itself would give blacks with white ancestry an advantage;   if they were inferior, this would put the latter at a disadvantage.   Juggling combinations of atypical blacks plus atypical whites does not eliminate all differences for all degrees of racial admixture.   The only possibility left open is that the whites who interacted sexually with American blacks were atypical.   If this were so, the lack of a genetic gap between blacks and this subpopulation of whites would not entail lack of a gap between blacks and the white population in general.   Indeed, if blacks were equivalent to a group of whites say 15 points below the white mean, we would tend to put the black-white gap at 15 points.

We have no hard historical data which would tell us whether whites who have mated with blacks over the last 300 years were above or below their population mean. However, if we consider just what the selective mechanism

would be and the magnitude of its likely effects, it
appears that a large genetic gap (between whites who mated
with blacks and whites in general) is very improbable.
First, the sexual partners involved did not screen each
other by giving IQ tests.   The selective mechanism would
have to be something like social class or occupation;   for
example, let us assume that, throughout all of American
history, whites who mated with blacks have been mainly
from the working class.   In 1930, when unskilled and
slightly skilled workers, both urban and rural, plus far-
mers comprised 45 per cent of the American population,
Terman found that their mean IQ was at least 95. (12)
This is 5 points below the mean in terms of phenotypic IQ,
but we would expect the genetic gap to be less, something
like 3 points.   The reason for this will be made clear a
bit later, but it comes down to the fact that a group
below the population mean suffers on the average from a
substandard environment and this expands the gap which
would be caused by genes alone.   In order to get a group
with a genetic gap of 5 points, we would have to assume
that sexual interaction with blacks was exclusively confined to some below-average fraction of unskilled white
workers, at least we would have to assume this in contemporary America.

Which suggests a second point: as Jensen has pointed
out, the correlation between IQ and class was almost certainly weaker throughout most of American history than it
is today.   Modern technology has had a number of effects:
it has eliminated much of the need for manual labour thus
making unskilled workers a much smaller proportion of the
population than formerly;   it emphasizes skills which have
tended to select out of the lower classes those who excel
at abstract thinking;   and it encourages academic prereq-

uisites (for middle-class jobs) which have the same
effect.   All in all, it would be very difficult to defend
a genetic gap of more than 5 points; indeed, I believe
that 3 or 4 points is about the highest figure which could
be defended with plausibility.

We have been exploring the hypothesis of negative selection, but positive selection is an alternative hypothesis.   It has been argued that the direction of selection
may well have fluctuated during American history, perhaps
having been positive (skewed towards higher-status slave-
owning whites) at one time, then perhaps negative (under
Jim Crow), and now perhaps neutral (as interracial mar-
riage and sexual contact become more common among college
students).

Witty and Jenkins must be replicated if we are to accumulate a solid body of evidence in this area.   Moreover
it must be replicated with at least one alteration in the
research methodology, namely: a random sample must be
taken of the local population (say 10,000 school children
in Boston) from which the high-IQ group is drawn; and
they too must be surveyed as to their geneology, their
degree of white ancestry.   The rationale for this should
be clear enough.   Herskovits collected his data in the
1920s, and despite his best efforts he could not take
samples which were fully representative of the US black
population even at that time.   Also as each study is done
in a particular locale, we must eliminate the possibility
that the local population is atypical of the US black population in general.   Witty and Jenkins do give us two
samples, children with IQs over 125 and children with IQs
over 140; these are both drawn from the parent population
and they tally pretty well.   But this is no substitute
for a comparison between the local high-IQ blacks and the
local population from which they are drawn.

Even the best methodology cannot solve all of the problems associated with studies of racial admixture among American blacks.   As we have seen, assortive mating may give blacks with light skin colour an irrelevant advantage in terms of IQ.   If that is so, then in so far as there is a correlation (estimated at .35) between having a light skin and having white ancestors, assortive mating would also give an irrelevant advantage to blacks with white ancestors, although the effect would be much diminished of course.   And recall that light-skinned blacks tend to be brought up in a more favourable environment (homes with a higher SES);   once again this would give blacks with white ancestors an advantage in IQ that had nothing to do with white genes for IQ.   However, all these factors work to distort results in one direction: away from evidencing black-white equality.   And therefore, results which supported a hypothesis of equality would be all the more significant.

We now turn to another class of direct evidence, how black genes function when put into a white environment.   Let us imagine what would constitute an ideal test of whether the IQ gap between black and white is environmental.   Imagine that: a random selection of black men from America were transported to Germany, fathered children with a random sample of German women, and then were removed from the environment entirely;   and a random sample of white men from America fathered children under exactly the same conditions.   If the offspring of the black fathers and the offspring of the white fathers were found to have the same mean IQ, this would constitute powerful evidence for an environmental hypothesis.

This brings us to Eyferth's study of the offspring of

black and white occupation forces in Germany after the
Second World War, his study of occupation children born
from late 1945 up through 1953.   Eyferth had official
data on the approximately 4,000 children of black fathers
born during this period and he attempted to secure a representative sample of 5 per cent. (13)   He matched the
sample with the larger population in terms of age, sex,
socioeconomic status of the mother or foster parents,
number of siblings, number of black children in the
locale, type of schooling, and skin colour. (14)   His
sample of black children numbered 181, almost all of whom
were illegitimate and most of whom were from the lower
class.   He then selected a control group of 83 white
occupation children, taking one white child for every two
black children in a particular locale and very often finding white and black in the same classroom, thus control-
ling for educational experience as well. (15)   He also
attempted to control for relevant variables, particularly
the socioeconomic circumstances of the mother and home.
When he checked his black sample and white control group
against one another, he found that they matched on all of
the variables listed above plus family circumstances such
as the proportions living in state homes, foster families,
and solo-mother households.   He also found that his white
children were representative of their larger population,
just as his black children were representative of theirs;
in fact the larger populations of black and white occupation children were so similar that they could be considered one. (16)

   Eyferth ignored the British zone of occupation because
so few black children were born there and selected his
subjects from the American and French zones. (17)   He
asserts that 75 to 80 per cent of the black children were

American in origin, an assertion which tallies with my own
calculations based on locale;   the remainder were fathered
for the most part by troops from the French North African
corps. (18)   Given that the members of the control group
were selected from the same locales, the white children
would have been fathered by American and French troops in
much the same proportions.   Eyferth could get little information about the fathers because their identity was
often unknown and, where known, they had no real contact
with the children although some did send occasional sums
of money.   However, he supplies considerable detail concerning the German mothers.   They were mainly (although
not exclusively) from the lower classes, tended to be
young, many of them were illegitimate themselves, and some
had been pushed into relations with soldiers by their own
mothers.   Only a few were genuine prostitutes, however,
the situation of many having been desperate particularly
in the early days of the occupation. (19)

As for the environment in which the occupation children
were being raised, the minority of mothers from the middle
class were often totally rejected by their parents after
the illegitimate child was born, particularly if it was
black.   Some of these mothers were themselves in homes
for problem youths.   The parents of mothers from the
working class tended to be more accepting, but most of
them were raising their children under difficult conditions.   Their incomes were low and most lived in substandard neighbourhoods, many in 1960 were still living in
barracks, housing for the unemployed or state housing.
Many were living with their own parents with much over-
crowding, for example, the children almost never had a
room of their own. (20)   The children also suffered from
less tangible handicaps.   Eyferth found that Germans had

strong feelings against illegitimate children and those whose mothers had been 'American-lovers' and had had affairs with the enemy.   He hypothesizes that the black children may have had their own problems because their skin colour advertized their position so clearly. (21) From sources other than Eyferth, we know that there was prejudice against black children, for example, Wolff has described German attitudes all too familiar to those of us who are Americans. (22)

Eyferth tested his black and white children with a German version of the Wechsler Intelligence Scale for Children and found the following: white boys had a mean IQ of 101 and white girls an IQ of 93 - which gives an overall mean of 97.2; black boys had a mean IQ of 97 and black girls an IQ of 96 - which gives an overall mean of 96.5.   In other words, it made little difference whether the father was white or black: the mean IQs of the two groups of children were virtually identical. (23)

We have found that Eyferth's results are the same as those we posited in our description of an ideal experiment.   However, the experimental situation falls short of our ideal on several important points, namely: the mothers were not a random sample of German women; a minority of the fathers were of French rather than American origin; and the American fathers were not a random sample of American whites and blacks respectively, thanks to the fact that the US armed forces had screened its accessions by giving them a mental test.   The failure rate for blacks on this test was considerably higher than for whites, which would have closed the IQ gap between black and white to some degree.   Fortunately, the first of these differences, while we must take it into account later on, is not of primary importance; the German

mothers were almost certainly below the norm in terms of
mean IQ, but Eyferth made every effort to match them for
the black and white children in terms of relevant variables - so that whatever their IQs it would not have a
differential impact on the races.

In order to deal with the other differences, I am going
to argue for several hypotheses: (1) that the presence of
the French fathers makes little or no difference; (2)
that armed forces testing had a limited effect on US black
troops in Germany - and therefore, at least 80 per cent of
the usual IQ gap between black and white Americans was
left intact; (3) that a pretty random sample of US black
troops fathered occupation children - if anything they
were slightly below the prevailing mean and not above.

To begin with my first hypothesis, the white fathers who
were of French origin can be dealt with quickly. It is
unlikely that the mean IQ of white troops in any affluent
industrialized nation, whether America, France or Britain,
differs substantially from the mean of the larger white
population. In time of war you have a mass army; in
time of peace you may be more selective but the percentage of the general population excluded are usually balan-
ced by failure to attract men from high IQ professions.
We have data on the mental test performance of the US
armed forces during the relevant period, extensive data,
some of it for the armed forces in general but much of it
actually referring to the occupation troops in Germany.
It shows that the mean IQ of the American contingent of
white occupation troops was no higher than 101, one point
above the population mean. The reader should consult
Appendix A for the data and calculations on which this
estimate is based, plus all other assertions I make about

the mean IQs of US black and white troops. The French
army of the occupation does not appear to have compiled
similar data, but we do have their rates for those treated
or discharged because of mental subnormality or retardation and these run at less than 3 men per 1,000. (24)
These rates are so low as to demonstrate that the usual
selective mechanisms were at work. However, even if we
accept the possibility that the mean IQ of French white
troops might have ranged anywhere from 99 to 103, the
outer limits of speculation, their presence could not possibly have made an appreciable difference.

The black fathers of French origin merit more attention. Underprivileged or unacculturated racial minori-
ties find it much more difficult to meet armed forces
mental test standards. America used several screening
devices during the relevant period but the principal one
was the Army General Classification Test (AGCT) and a high
percentage of blacks failed to qualify; the effectiveness
of this test is open to dispute but if we give it the
benefit of the doubt, it raised the mean IQ by approximately 6.5 points, from 85 to 91.5. Again this is based
on US armed forces data which tells us the distribution of
black troops in terms of their performance on the AGCT.
By comparing this distribution to that of black Americans
(in the relevant age group) in general on the AGCT, we can
estimate the rise in IQ. In theory, the French blacks
could have been relatively unselected or more highly selected than US blacks (the French kept no differential
records), that is, their mean IQ may have ranged from say
85 up to 95. The latter figure, given that the French
supplied 25 per cent of the fathers at most, would raise
the mean IQ of black occupation troops in toto by less
than one point - by .88 points to be exact. I emphasize

the possibility that the French raised the black mean because that, the possibility of their being an elite group,
is the only one which poses a problem for an environmental
hypothesis.   (There may seem to be an obvious objection
to my arithmetic: what if French blacks do not suffer
from any genetic or environmental disadvantage and would
score approximately 100 on IQ tests?   Actually this would
make no difference in that when I posit some scenarios to
interpret Eyferth's data, I set the genotypic IQ of American blacks at scores from 96 to 104.   That is, I hypothesize that if the American blacks suffered from no environmental disadvantage they would score 100 ± 4 points.)

A rise of .88 points would not make much difference,
but I am reluctant to rest my case on arithmetic alone.
We know that in February 1946 all soldiers originating
from French West Africa were ordered to assemble at
Frejus, presumably for disembarkation.   Records for the
French occupation forces in Germany which list 'colonial
autochthons' (indigenous or aboriginal colonial troops)
separately begin in 1949 by which time all such troops had
departed. (25)   We can make use of these facts in con-
junction with Eyferth's chronology.   He divided his
children into five groups by age and each of these groups
was conceived within its own nineteen-month period. (26)
He also supplies graphs which allow us to follow fluctuations in the scores of the occupation children over
time. (27)   When we look at Table 3.2, we see that it is
unimportant whether the French blacks departed in early
1946 or whether the bulk of them were gone by, say, mid-
1948.   The earlier date precedes a 7-point drop in the
scores of black girls but a 7-point rise in the scores of
black boys;   the later date would signal a 12.5 rise in
the scores of the girls and a 13-point drop in the scores

TABLE 3.2 Occupation children: trends over time

Chronology	Black girls	Black boys	White girls	White boys
Feb 45-Aug 46	96.5 (36)	95.0 (37)	88.5 (15)	108.0 (16)
Sep 46-Mar 48	89.5 (20)	102.0 (21)	97.0 (7)	103.0 (7)
Apr 48-Oct 49	102.0 (19)	89.0 (13)	88.5 (6)	90.0 (7)
Nov 49-May 51	97.0 (10)	92.0 (4)	85.0 (4)	97.0 (6)
Jun 51-Dec 52	79.0 (5)	96.0 (6)	- (1)	- (1)

Note: The author has altered the presentation of Eyferth's data as follows:
(1) chronology substituted for classification of children by age - the chronology refers to time of conception;   (2) the scores are approximations based
on a reading of calibrations in Eyferth's graphs - they are not IQ scores and
must be adjusted for age (usually by about three points) to convert to IQ;
(3) the numbers within the brackets are also approximations based on the percentage of Eyferth's total sample represented in his graphs (90.5 per cent).

of the boys.   There are fluctuations of a similar magnitude thereafter which can of course have had nothing to do
with the presence or absence of French blacks.   Eyferth
himself believes that the above fluctuations were partially the result of age at the time of testing.

My second hypothesis asserts that at least 80 per cent
of the usual IQ gap between black and white was present
among US troops in Germany.   I base this assertion on the
fact that at most, armed forces testing raised the mean
phenotypic IQ of blacks to 91.5 and the mean genotypic IQ
of blacks to 88.6.   I will try to clarify these two
terms.   It is not enough to have an estimate of how black
troops in Germany would perform on IQ tests, what is
usually called IQ and what I have called phenotypic IQ.
We are interested in these men as fathers.   They may be
6.5 points above black Americans in general in terms of
test performance, but we want to know how much of that advantage is genetically transmissible to their children.
They cannot pass the whole of their advantage to their
children because, like any elite group, some of it is due
to the fact that on the average they had better luck than
most blacks in terms of environment.   It might seem that
all we need do is use an h^2 or heritability estimate, the
sort of estimate which tells us what proportion of IQ
variance is due to genetic factors.   But actually, we
must use a special kind of h^2 estimate, called h^2 narrow.
This is because the genetic make-up of a person includes
random or chance factors having to do with how genes combine in terms of dominance and epistasis.   Our elite
blacks cannot transmit good luck in gene combinations any
more than good luck in environment.

The estimates of h^2 narrow will of course be smaller
than estimates of h^2 broad.   A range of h^2 broad esti-

mates running from .45 through .63 to .80 would correspond
to h^2 narrow estimates of .40 and .55 and .70, a range
going from a low estimate to a very high one.   My estimate of the genotypic IQ of black soldiers in Germany is
based on .55, not because I accept it (as the reader will
see) but because it is generally accepted and I want to
carry my colleagues with me.   Therefore, in order to calculate how much of their 6.5-point advantage our elite
blacks would tend to pass on to their children, we multiply 6.5 IQ points by .55 which gives 3.6 points - add this
to the black population mean of 85 and we get 88.6 as the
genotypic IQ of our black troops.   We can now define the
term in question.   The genotypic IQ of a group provides
an estimate of the mean IQ of their children, assuming
that their spouses have the same genotypic IQ and that
their children have average luck on environment and gene
combinations.   Where the genotypic IQs of the fathers and
mothers differ we would of course take the average as our
estimate.   (The term 'genotypic IQ' is a misnomer in that
we transmit genes to our offspring and not genotypes.
But I find a term like 'genetically transmissible IQ'
awkward and 'breeding IQ' even worse;   moreover the latter
might be confused with the existent term 'breeding value'.
I hope the purist will forgive me now that the term has
been defined.)

Given that there is a controversy over h^2 estimates,
particularly in regard to blacks, I want to emphasize how
little difference it makes whether we use .40 or .55 or
.70.   When we apply our low, medium and high figures in
turn, we get estimates of 87.6, 88.6, and 89.6 for the
genotypic IQ of US black troops.   I consider an estimate
of 88.6, particularly when rounded off to 89, a maximum
estimate.   If the reader consults Appendix A, he will

find that far more important than h^2 estimates is the
question of whether or not the armed forces test (the
AGCT) had a significant correlation with IQ when administered to black Americans.   I believe that the generally
accepted correlation is much inflated and that the most
realistic estimate of the genotypic IQ of our black troops
would be approximately 87.   However, I will use the maximum estimate most of the time so as to be as generous to
the hereditarian as possible.   The estimate for white
troops is straightforward enough (here the correlations
are valid) and gives an estimate of 100.7 rounded off to
101.   There is of course a 12-point gap between 89 and
101, which is why I say that, from a genetic point of
view, at least 80 per cent of the 15-point IQ gap between
black and white survived among US troops in Germany.

My third hypothesis asserts that a pretty random sample
of black troops fathered occupation children in Germany
and that, if anything, they were below the prevailing
mean.   There is a large amount of anecdotal evidence from
US military officers that it is the low AGCT score blacks
who are getting into trouble, not just committing assaults
and robberies, but going AWOL (absent without leave) and
becoming repeated venereal disease offenders. (28)   Certainly these last two sins must have a high correlation
with sexual contact with German women and the fathering of
children.   However, thanks to a Colonel Chase we have
something better than anecdotal evidence.   In 1947 he
conducted a study of the relationship between the AGCT
scores of black troops in Germany and their commission of
serious offences (including contracting venereal disease).
He found that men whose AGCT scores ranged between 70 and
78 were the worst offenders, while those with scores below
70 and over 100 were the least involved (29)   Thanks to

extensive armed forces data, we can calculate the mean
AGCT score of black troops during the period of the German
occupation - it was approximately 78.   If those going
AWOL and contracting venereal disease repeatedly were in
the range between 70 and 78, they were hardly a group
above the black mean.

As for US troops in general, both white and black,
Harold Zink (former Chief Historian, US High Commissioner
for Germany) tells us that 'no American with even faint
eyesight could ignore the widespread sexual relations between American males and German women' - and that 'particularly during the early period of the occupation all ages
and all ranks of Americans from generals down to privates
... engaged in sexual relations with Germans.'   It has
sometimes been claimed that officers were less active than
enlisted men, but Zink asserts that 'the sexual antics of
some colonels and a larger number of lower officers who
belonged to the age group over forty must have served to
reduce the respect of some Germans for the American military government personnel almost to the point of ridi-
cule.' (30)   Zink stops short of supplying names, but
once more we do not have to depend entirely on anecdotal
evidence.   Studies were done which indicated that about
eight out of ten young US soldiers dated German girls
'more or less frequently'. (31)

Having argued for my three hypotheses, I am ready to interpret Eyferth's results.   The most obvious interpretation is that whatever IQ gap existed between the black and
white fathers was absent in the offspring and was therefore environmental.   I have put this gap at 12 points in
terms of genotypic IQ, which would leave the real genotypic gap between black and white at 3 points - a negli-

gible amount, and even that might be environmental in
origin if black children in occupied Germany suffered because of their race.

However, I do not wish to pretend that only one interpretation of Eyferth's results is conceivable.   Let us
offer a few scenarios concerning his study based on our
estimates.   The key estimates have to do with the genotypic IQs of the parents and now only one of these is
missing, namely an estimate for the German mothers.
Looking back to Eyferth's description of them, they seem
to have come predominantly from an unusually demoralized
sector of the working class.   Data from five large-scale
studies from both America and Britain suggest a mean for
workers in general (depending how the class is defined) at
somewhere between 95 and 97, which would yield a genotypic
IQ of about 97 or 98. (32)   Our estimates for the white
and black fathers respectively were 101 and 89.   The
estimate for the black fathers is by far the most important; as the scenarios will show, varying the other estimates does not make too much difference.   Other than our
key estimates, we should keep in mind Eyferth on the fact
that he matched the mothers of black and white on relevant
variables, Eyferth on the substandard environment of the
occupation children, and Eyferth and Wolff on the unusual
problems of the black children.

SCENARIO I - white occupation children
Genotypic IQ of German mothers: 97
Genotypic IQ of white fathers: 101
Putative (phenotypic) IQ of children: 99
Actual (phenotypic) IQ of children: 97
Comment: The putative figure of 99 is the mean one
would expect in terms of performance on IQ tests if the
children were in an environment of average quality.

The actual figure of 97 which Eyferth's tests yielded
is assumed to be the result of a two-point decrement -
due to the occupation children's substandard environment.

SCENARIO I - black occupation children
Genotypic IQ of German mothers: 97
Genotypic IQ of black fathers: 89 = 104
Putative (phenotypic) IQ of children: 100.5
Actual (phenotypic) IQ of children: 96.5
Comment: This scenario assumes that there is no real
genotypic gap between black and white, that we must add
15 points to a black IQ to get a white equivalent, thus
89 + 15 = 104.   The difference between the putative IQ
of the children (100.5) and the actual IQ (96.5) is
assumed to be the result of: a two-point decrement for
occupation children; another two-point decrement for
being black occupation children with unusual environmental problems.

SCENARIO II - white occupation children
Genotypic IQ of German mothers: 98
Genotypic IQ of white fathers: 100
Putative (phenotypic) IQ of children: 99
Actual (phenotypic) IQ of children: 97
Comment: The only change from our first scenario is
minor alterations in the estimates for the mothers and
the white soldier fathers.   As long as we allow for
some environmental decrement, such minor shifts are
seen to make little difference.

SCENARIO II - black occupation children
Genotypic IQ of German mothers: 98
Genotypic IQ of black fathers: 89 = 99
Putative (phenotypic) IQ of children: 98.5

Actual (phenotypic) IQ of children: 96.5

Comment: Here the scenario assumes that 10 points of the gap separating black and white is environmental (89 + 10 = 99) and that 5 points are genetic in origin. As above, the shift from our first scenario in the estimate for the German mothers is inconsequential, the real difference being this: an allowance for environmental decrement has been made for being occupation children, but no allowance has been made for being black.

SCENARIO III - white occupation children

Genotypic IQ of German mothers: 97

Genotypic IQ of white fathers: 97

Putative (phenotypic) IQ of children: 97

Actual (phenotypic) IQ of children: 97

Comment: The estimate for the mothers is unchanged from our first scenario, but the estimate for the white fathers has been dropped by a full four points. This alteration is a consequence of assuming no environmental decrement for occupation children.

SCENARIO III - black occupation children

Genotypic IQ of German mothers: 97

Genotypic IQ of black fathers: 91 = 96

Putative (phenotypic) IQ of children: 96.5

Actual (phenotypic) IQ of children: 96.5

Comment: A scenario which assumes that only 5 points of the gap between black and white is environmental (91 + 5 = 96) and that 10 points is genetic. In order to make that assumption we have had to boost the black genotypic IQ by two points - plus make no allowances (in terms of environmental decrement) for either being occupation children or being black.

As for evaluating the above scenarios, I believe that
the first, which assumes that all 15 points of the gap between black and white is environmental, is the most probable.   Allowing for a small environmental decrement on
behalf of the occupation children seems almost mandatory
and allowing a point or two extra for being black seems
reasonable enough.   (These environmental decrements
entail the following assumptions.   Using Jensen's estimate that between-family environmental differences account
for .12 of IQ variance: the allowance for occupation
children assumes that their environment was at the 35th
percentile of systematic environmental effects in the
German population;   the total allowance for black occupation children assumes the 22nd percentile.)   The key
estimates for the genotypic IQs of the parents are in line
with all of the evidence I have seen with one exception:
the genotypic IQ of the black fathers may well have been
lower than I have assumed (87 rather than 89).   If we
used 87 in our first scenario, we would conclude that
blacks were genetically superior to whites by a margin of
2 points.   A critic of our first scenario would probably
attack the allowance of a decrement for being black as its
weakest point: although the existence of some racial bias
against blacks appears undeniable, such bias does not
result in an IQ decrement in every cultural setting (wit-
ness the achievements of the Jews in Germany).   If we
were both to eliminate this decrement and use the most
realistic estimate of the genotypic IQ of the black
fathers, we would conclude that whites were genetically
superior to blacks by 2 points.   In sum, it is the
author's view of Eyferth's results that they count in
favour of a rough equality between the races, equality
within a range of plus or minus 2 points.

Moving on to the second scenario, I would call it possible rather than probable.   Let us look at its assumptions in turn: it uses an estimate for the German mothers (98 rather than 97) that is certainly defensible but seems a bit high; it assumes that the white troops who fathered children were a bit below the prevailing mean (100 rather than 101); it makes no similar assumption about the black troops; in addition, it uses an estimate for the black troops that is definitely a maximum estimate (89 rather than 87); and the elimination of any decrement for being black is plausible enough but by no means certain.   In other words, while each of its assumptions can be defended one by one, collectively they mean that we must give the hereditarian some sort of concession on virtually every point.   Whatever the plausibility of our second scenario, it would still leave the genetic gap between black and white at only 5 points - and this, as we have seen, can be of little comfort to any racist ideologue.

The third scenario is a different matter in that it posits a genetic gap of 10 points.   However, when we examine each of its assumptions in turn, we find we must make not merely a minor concession on each point but rather a major concession.   The estimate for the genotypic IQ of the black fathers (91 rather than 89) assumes: either standards of armed forces selection far above what we know to have been the case; or that a group above the prevailing mean was sexually active, which contradicts the available evidence; or that the minority of black fathers who were of French origin were of extraordinary quality, that is, superior genotypically to any *white* troops of which we know.   As for its other two assumptions, these simply go beyond the bounds of plausibility: that no allowance is to be made for the substandard environment of

the occupation children - recall Eyferth on their environmental circumstances; and that the genotypic IQ of the
white soldiers who fathered children was 97, a full 4
points below the prevailing mean - this would be 6 points
in phenotypic terms!   All in all, our third scenario
appears very, very improbable.

The hereditarian can of course entertain a suspicion
that Eyferth made mistakes in the execution of his study
or that he had bad luck in his subjects despite scrupulous
execution.   The best way to prove such a point would be
to attempt to replicate the study, a development to be
welcomed.   No one has done a similar study of the US
occupation of Japan or Korea or Vietnam, presumably because they lack indigenous scholars obsessed with IQ and
because Oriental languages are not often part of an American social scientist's education.

This is a pity because studies like Eyferth plus
studies like Witty and Jenkins have a value collectively
beyond that which they have separately.   For example, it
has been suggested that the offspring of racially mixed
matings may suffer some sort of special reproductive
stress and that this could have an adverse effect on
IQ. (33)   The evidence for this is weak but if it were
proven, such a factor would affect the results of studies
like Witty and Jenkins by 'pulling down' the IQ of blacks
with a large amount of white ancestry.   There would
still be countervailing factors 'pulling up' their IQs,
i.e. assortive mating, higher than average SES, and so
forth.   However, my main point is this: whatever such a
hypothesis would detract from Witty and Jenkins, it would
add to Eyferth.   If the offspring of interracial mating
are handicapped by special reproductive stress, the children of the black troops in Germany were so handicapped and

we would have to build this factor into our scenarios,
thus enhancing Eyferth as evidence in favour of an environmental explanation of the IQ gap between black and
white.

In October 1976 Sandra Scarr and Richard Weinberg published a study of 101 families resident in the state of
Minnesota who collectively had 321 children four years of
age and older: 145 natural children and 176 adopted children.   All the adoptive parents were white and all had
adopted at least one non-white child.   Using the records
of the State Department of Public Welfare, they established the race of 143 of the adopted children: 25 were
white; 68 were black-white (in all but two cases a white
mother and a black father); 29 were black-black; and 21
were other non-white, mostly Asian and North American
Indian.   They used the Stanford-Binet, the Wechsler for
children, and the Wechsler for adults to obtain IQ data
for the adoptive parents and their children, both their
adopted children and their natural children.   They also
collected data on the natural parents of both the black-
white and black-black adopted children; they could not
obtain IQ scores but were successful in some cases in
establishing the educational level (years of school completed) for the natural parents, which they compared to
the appropriate norms for both the North Central states
and the Minneapolis-St Paul (Minnesota) area.   This data
plus some other relevant data concerning the adoptive history of the children is contained in Table 3.3. (34)
     The aim of course was to assess what happened to the
IQs of black children when they were raised in white home
environments rather than black.   Therefore, this study
falls within our category of direct evidence on race and

TABLE 3.3   Data from Scarr and Weinberg

I   Comparison of adopted children by race

Race	Number	IQ	Age at adoption	Time in adoptive home
Black-black	29	96.8	32.3	42.2
Asian and Indian	21	99.9	60.7	63.8
Black-white	68	109.0	8.9	60.6
White-white	25	111.5	19.0	104.2

Note: ages and times given in months

II   Natural parents of black children, compared to their respective populations

Race	Number	Parent's education	Population education	Pop. IQ
Black M of BB	22	10.9	12.0	90
Black F of BB	15	12.1	12.0	90
White M of BW	66	12.4	12.5	105*
Black F of BW	20	12.5	12.0	90

Note: educational level given in years of schooling.
* Author's estimate - not from Scarr and Weinberg.

III   Adoptive parents and their natural children

	Father	Mother	Parental average	Natural children
Mean IQ	120.8	118.2	119.5	116.7

IQ although we must remember that it cannot simulate a total shift of environments for a variety of reasons: the pre-natal environment remains black for all children with black mothers;   children are rarely adopted at birth and often not until they are three or four or even five years

of age; being a black child with white parents may engender certain stresses; a black child in a white home does
not necessarily escape whatever racism exists in the
larger environment outside the home.   We can contrast
such studies with Eyferth's in which the first and second
of the above problems were absent, although not the remainder.

Let us look initially at the performance of the black-
black adopted children.   As we can see from the tables,
the educational level of their natural fathers is almost
exactly the average for black males in the Minnesota area;
however, their natural mothers are a full year below the
mean for black women.   Since the mean IQ for blacks in
Minnesota is 90, we would anticipate that these children,
if raised in the average black environment in that state,
would develop an IQ of about 89.   The fact that they
attained a mean of approximately 97 when raised in white
homes signals a significant gain and stands as evidence
that the typical black home environment, even in a relatively prosperous northern industrial state like Minnesota (with a black minority of less than 1 per cent), has
a negative effect on IQ.   However, the question arises as
to why the gain was not greater still, particularly why
the all black children did not do as well as the black-
white children who rose from a predicted 90 (in a black
environment) to a mean of 109.   These results stand out
in contrast to our blood-group studies and Witty and Jenkins, studies which suggested that socially classified
blacks did not benefit from a large degree of white ancestry.

By way of explanation the environmentalist can point to
a number of factors, but two stand out.   First, every
other piece of direct evidence we have encountered thus

far has controlled for the pre-natal environment: in
Witty and Jenkins the groups compared all had a black pre-
natal environment; in Eyferth both groups had a white
pre-natal environment.   In this study, although the
mothers of the black-black children were of course black,
the mothers of the black-white children were white with
only two exceptions.   The question of whether differences
in the pre-natal environment are significant, within the
range of environments existent in America, is much dispu-
ted.   The major piece of evidence in favour is the research done by Harrell, Woodyard and Gates.   They gave
dietary supplements during pregnancy to welfare mothers in
Norfolk, Virginia, of whom 80 per cent were black: at age
four, children whose mothers had received mixed vitamins
were 8.1 IQ points above the placebo group.   They found
no similar results among whites in Leslie County, Kentucky, women who were poor but whose diet is described as
more adequate and as including a significantly higher intake of ascorbic acid, vitamin A, and vitamins of the B
complex. (35)   Concerning Minnesota we can say only two
things: it is a much more prosperous state than either
Virginia or Kentucky; on the other hand, nation-wide
evidence indicates that pregnant women from the bottom 25
per cent (of residential districts) within high-income
states are even worse off nutritionally than they are in
low-income states. (36)   The pre-natal environment may
well be significant and it involves factors that go beyond
the quality of the mother's diet.

A second factor has to do with the adoption histories
of our black-black and black-white children.   The latter
were adopted at a mean age of nine months and had spent an
average of five years in their white adoptive home at time
of testing; the former were adopted at almost three years

of age (32.3 months) and spent an average of three and a
half years in their adoptive homes.   Given the importance
of the first three years of a child's life, the environmentalist will question whether the black-black children
really experienced an environment equivalent in quality to
the white average in Minnesota.   In passing, the Asian
plus Indian group of adoptees, who were not adopted until
five years of age and had spent five years in their adoptive home, also performed at a relatively low level
(99.9);   some data suggests that these ethnic groups are
marginally superior to whites in terms of genotype for IQ.
Scarr and Weinberg prefer to take into account the full
range of post-natal factors which separate the black-black
and black-white children (age at adoption, number and
quality of placements before adoption, quality of adoptive
homes, and so forth);   using part correlations, they calculated that the race of the mother accounted for only 3
per cent of the IQ variance within the whole group of
children socially classified as black.

Those who hold a genetic hypothesis about the races
will not find the above convincing.   They will question
the significance of the pre-natal environment, note that
the quality of temporary homes in which Minnesota places
its children is good, and emphasize the fact that the
adoptive homes are above average.   All in all, those of
us who hold an environmental hypothesis can give an explanation of the performance of Scarr and Weinberg's
black-black children;   but it is one piece of direct evidence which does force us to search for explanations.

The case of the black-white children does not pose the
same sort of problem.   Given the match between the educational levels of their natural parents and the relevant
population means, we would predict an IQ of 90 if they had

been raised in the average Minnesota black environment;
the result of 109 signals a gain of 19 points, four points
above the 15-point gap which separates black and white.
This raises the question of the quality of the environment
in their adoptive homes. We know that it was above the
Minnesota white average in that the adoptive parents had
(in 1975) a mean income of approximately $US16,000, were
above average in level of education, and had a mean IQ of
120, the usual figure given for US college graduates. (37)
One method of assessing the quality of the environment
these parents provided is to focus on their natural children, predict the IQ the latter would have in the average
Minnesota white environment, and then subtract this from
the actual IQ of their natural children.   Using Jensen's
estimate of .7 for h^2 narrow (and assuming an average IQ
of 105 for whites in Minnesota), we would predict a mean
of 115.2; their actual mean is 116.7.   This would put
the worth of the adoptive homes at only 1.5 points above
the average for white homes in Minnesota.   This figure
seems too low and if we were to use a value for h^2 narrow
of .55, we would get a result of 3.7 points which is
rather more plausible.

Another method, if we focus on the group of all white
adoptees and assume that they are genotypically average
for Minnesota whites, we get a higher estimate: actual IQ
of 111.5 minus the state average of 105.0 gives a figure
of 6.5 points.   However, whether we put the above-average
worth of the adoptive homes at 2 points or 4 points or 6
points does not make much difference.   Recall the natural
parents of our black-white children: both the black
parent and the white parent were at about the average for
their respective area populations.   And recall that the
black-white children achieved a mean IQ of 109, four

points above the average for Minnesota whites.   Assigning
a 4-point environmental increment to their adoptive homes
would imply that their natural parents were equivalent to
one another in terms of genotype for IQ.   If we had only
the results of the black-white adoptees from Scarr and
Weinberg, we would conclude that their results tallied
with those which support the relative equality of black
and white.

Our last case of blacks being taken out of their usual
environmental setting transports us from America to England.   Most blacks in England are from the West Indies
and this means we cannot generalize the results without
reservation to US blacks.   But the change of locale has
several advantages, posing an interesting hypothesis about
the black pre-natal environment in America, challenging
some of the assumptions about child care US professionals
tend to make, and it of course takes us closer to home as
far as our adherent of the National Front is concerned.

   In the early 1970s Barbara Tizard and her colleagues
did a number of studies of long-stay residential nurseries
in England.   They were sceptical of the hypothesis that
an institutional environment is necessarily deleterious
for intellectual development, and incidentally they collected comparative data on children of different racial
groups.   The first group tested were all children in 11
residential nurseries who met the following criteria:
aged from 24 to 59 months;   resident in the nursery at
least six months;   medical record showed them to be healthy, full-term babies;   their doctors did not consider
them handicapped.   They did not screen out children whose
families had a history of epilepsy, psychopathy or depression.   The children numbered 85, were all illegitimate,

and most had been admitted to the residential nursery as
infants, 70 per cent before 12 months, 86 per cent before
24 months. (38)   The second group tested were all available children aged 4.5 years who had been admitted to any
of the residential nurseries of three voluntary societies
by the age of four months and remained there until at
least the age of 2 years.   These numbered 64, and at the
time of testing 25 were still resident in the nurseries,
24 had been adopted, and 15 restored to their natural
mothers.   As for the tests, they used the Reynell for
children from 2 to 5, the Minnesota non-verbal for children 3 to 5, and the Wechsler for the group aged $4\frac{1}{2}$;   they
obtained the results shown in Table 3.4. (39)

The results are consistent from test to test in showing
a better performance of both black-white and black-black
children as compared to white.   It should be stressed
that the number of children in each cell is limited and
only the black advantage on the Minnesota non-verbal
attains statistical significance.   However, I have taken
the liberty of pooling the results for the 149 children
involved (ignoring the possibility of some overlap) of
whom 75 are white-white, 43 are black-white and 31 are
black-black.   Setting the white performance at 100, this
gives the following means: white-white = 100; black-
white = 104.8; and black-black = 103.1.   Taking the
children socially classified as black as one group, they
would have a mean of 104.1.   Since the standard deviation
on some of the tests used was 10, the advantage of black
over white is really .33 SD units or the equivalent of
approximately 5 IQ points.

The major difficulty in assessing these results is the
lack of data about the natural parents of the children
concerned.   There is no substitute for full and relevant

TABLE 3.4   Data from Barbara Tizard

I Children in residential nurseries

	Reynell comprehension		Reynell expression		Minnesota non-verbal	
	No.	Mean	No.	Mean	No.	Mean
White-white	39	102.6	39	98.5	24	101.3
Black-white	24	105.7	24	99.3	15	109.8
Black-black	22	106.9	22	97.8	15	105.7

Ages: from 2 years 0 months to 4 years 11 months.
Institutional history: 70 per cent admitted before 12
months, 86 per cent admitted before 24 months.

II Children in residential nurseries up to age 2 -
   classified as still resident, adopted, restored to
   mother

	Resident		Adopted		With mother	
	No.	Mean	No.	Mean	No.	Mean
White-white	10	101.2	17	113.0	9	98.2
Black-white	7	109.3	7	119.9	5	102.2
Black-black	8	105.6	0	-	1	106.0

Ages: all children 4.5 years.
Institutional history in common: admitted to nursery
before 4 months, remained until at least 2 years of age.

data and the following is offered with that qualification
understood.   As for the natural mothers, the occupations
of all were known and they included significantly fewer
skilled workers and significantly more unskilled workers
than the norm for London and south-east England. (40)   As
for the fathers, Tizard tells us that there was no difference between the proportions of manual and non-manual
workers in the different racial groups. (41)   She suc-

ceeded in determining the occupations of 49 of the fathers
of the children in her second group (the 64 children aged
4½ years):   35 per cent of them were either semiskilled or
unskilled. (42)   The 1966 census for London and the Mid-
lands reveals the following: 50 per cent of West Indian
males were in such occupations and 26 per cent of males
born in England and Wales. (43)   It appears that a skill
gap of about 25 per cent between the races in England was
eliminated among the natural parents.   Given that the
semiskilled and unskilled working class in England is
about 4 points below the remainder of the population genotypically (about 6 points phenotypically), this should
have made a difference for the children tested of one or
two IQ points.

J.J.D. Greenwood has suggested a second source of bias
in Tizard's results, namely, selective migration: he
hypothesizes that black immigrants to Britain are of above
average socioeconomic status in their homelands. (44)
The major source of West Indian migrants to England is
Jamaica and we have considerable data on the occupations
male migrants claim to have pursued at home, albeit that
researchers suspect the existence of inflated claims. (45)
Comparing this data to the occupational distribution of
the male population of Jamaica, and focusing on data which
includes migrants from 1955 and after (the period of
greatest migration), we find that professional and non-
manual occupations are not overrepresented.   However, the
figure of 69 per cent for unskilled workers in Jamaica
reduces to from 33 per cent to 37 per cent among migrants,
largely due to the failure of unskilled farm workers to
migrate. (46)   It is doubtful that a developing country,
one in which unskilled farm labourers constitute a majority of the population, has the same correlation between

occupation and IQ as Western industrialized nations, but
let us make that assumption: with the rural labour force
largely unrepresented, we would expect migrants to be 2 or
3 points above the population mean genotypically (4 points
phenotypically). (47)   Those who emphasize selective migration rarely take into account how rigorous the selective mechanism must be in order to make large differences.
Recall Eyferth: when the US armed forces used actual
mental tests and eliminated something like the bottom 30
per cent of American blacks, they raised the mean IQ a
maximum of 4 points in genotypic terms (6.5 points phenotypically).   It would be extraordinary if the usual sort
of selective migration did not have a lesser effect.

Returning to Tizard, there was a familiar difference
between the mothers of the black-black children and the
black-white: the mothers of all of the latter were
white. (48)   If the black pre-natal environment is proven
to be disadvantageous in America, and if studies like
Tizard's show that this is not true in England, this would
count against the possibility that black genes dictate the
disadvantage in question.   It is always possible that
West Indian blacks and US blacks are separated by genetic
differences.   Fortunately America has a large West Indian
population of its own and it would be of interest to compare that population with US blacks in general.   Another
point, Tizard points out that the children she studied in
English residential nursery homes seem to have profited,
as far as intellectual development is concerned, from an
environment superior to that of many private homes. (49)
The nurseries she describes are of good quality but they
are not elite institutions.   The staff were not highly
paid professionals, armed with graduate degrees, prepping
children for IQ tests, but rather women whose backgrounds

were rather modest: all were daughters of skilled workers
or small shopkeepers, all had left school at 15 or 16 with
from zero to four 'O' levels, and all were studying for or
had received a diploma in nursing. (50)   In America,
social workers sometimes make frantic efforts to get young
children into temporary private homes (prior to adoption)
rather than leave them in institutions.   I have no doubt
they are correct, but this tells us something about the
level of social services in America, not about a universal
truth concerning the merits of institutional care.

This completes our survey of the direct evidence on race
and IQ.   I have limited myself to studies which deal with
black and white but, within that area, I have tried not to
omit studies generally thought to be significant.   The
blood-group studies (for what they are worth), Witty and
Jenkins, Eyferth and Tizard all point in the direction of
equality between the races.   Scarr and Weinberg points in
two directions at once, but on balance it must count on
the other side of the ledger.   All of these studies involve small numbers, indeed, taking black and white together, they give a grand total of 598 children tested (I
have not included the blood-group studies) of which 44 per
cent are from Eyferth.   All of them possess difficulties
in the research design, problems in determining ancestry,
lack of precise data on parents, confounding variables
such as the pre-natal environment, and so forth.   However, let us imagine that the above was the only evidence
that existed: if that were so, I think most reasonable
men would lean towards a hypothesis of relative equality
between the races, adding the proviso that they are not
dogmatically committed to a belief in absolute equality
and that they look forward to the accumulation of more

evidence.   And I want to stress that the above is the only direct evidence that exists.

Chapter 4

A PROBLEM FOR THE SOCIAL SCIENCES

The direct evidence on race and IQ stands as a source of
cautious optimism and contrasts sharply with the drift of
the indirect evidence as presented by Jensen.   In the
last chapter, I argued that direct evidence must prevail
on logical grounds, which means that if such evidence were
to continue to favour an environmental hypothesis after we
had accumulated an impressive number of studies, and if
those studies eliminated most of the problems we have encountered in terms of research design, then we would have
settled the debate on race and IQ no matter what the indirect evidence seemed to imply.   However, no scholar
whose intellectual interests extend beyond race and IQ,
and no man who claims to have any real regard for the
speculative intellect, could be satisfied with that.

Assume that direct evidence accumulates in favour of an
environmental hypothesis about the IQ gap between black
and white.   Now also assume that the methodology of heritability estimates improves, that estimates for both
black and white America accumulate of .80 or above, that
all attempts to locate environmental handicaps peculiar to
blacks fail with humiliating regularity, and that all environmental factors which separate black and white quanti-
tatively rather than qualitatively prove to have little

effect on IQ - which is to say assume that Jensen's two-
step argument becomes ever more powerful within its own
terms.   Then we would have to accept something as true
which had been shown to be virtually impossible without
finding any flaw in the evidence to that effect.   We
would have to accept a hypothesis which was in direct conflict with a mass of evidence drawn from practically every
important branch of social science.   We would have a situation in the social sciences in which two bodies of evidence, both apparently extensive and reliable, pointed to
opposite conclusions on an important and highly specific
problem of causal explanation.   Physicists today find it
difficult to accept a situation in which the conceptual
system which explains subatomic physics cannot be integrated into the conceptual system which explains phenomena in
field physics;   but at least there is no clash between the
two bodies of evidence on a specific problem of causality.
The situation we would face in the social sciences would
be far worse and would amount to nothing less than a
scandal of the speculative intellect.

Therefore, we must attempt to weaken at least the key
links in Jensen's steel chain of ideas.   This means we
must attempt to perform at least one of the following
tasks: find reason to lower his h^2 estimates for IQ dras-
tically, say from .80 to below .40;   find a way to make
the concept of a blindfold seem more plausible, that is,
find evidence in favour of an environmental factor or factors confined to the black population and uniform within
it.   Or we must take on what amounts to a combination of
these two tasks, that is, lower h^2 estimates to somewhere
between .40 and .60 and find evidence of environmental
factors which, while not perfect blindfolds, are likely to
be much more prevalent and uniform among blacks than

whites.   I believe that the third alternative offers the
best prospect and will explore it over most of the remainder of this book.   In this chapter, we will examine the
methodology and evidence concerning h^2 estimates for IQ;
in the next chapter, we will examine the prospects for
specific environmental hypotheses on race and IQ.

Jensen usually offers the following as his estimate of the
heritability of IQ, at least within the white population
of America: $h^2 = .80$; $E^2 = .12$; $e^2 = .08$. (1)   He
feels that this is his best estimate because it is based
on the widest range of kinship data.   However, at times,
when attempting to discredit an environmental hypothesis,
he uses another set of estimates drawn from the data on
monozygotic (identical) twins raised in separated environments: $h^2 = .85$; $E^2 = .05$; $e^2 = .05$; test error =
.05. (2)   The first set of estimates has been adjusted so
as to take test unreliability into account.   As for the
division of the environmental component, E^2 refers to
between-family environmental differences, factors which
distinguish one family from another such as socio-economic
status, nutrition, child-rearing practices, and cultural
advantages; while e^2 refers to within-family environmental differences, factors which differentiate the environment within almost every family for that family's children, such as birth order effects (which child is the
eldest and which the youngest) and maternal age at birth.
The second set of estimates as I have presented them
assume that Jensen would divide the environmental component into E^2 and e^2 on a basis of approximate equality.
    Eventually we will want to see if the sort of data on
which Jensen has based his estimates is subject to another
interpretation, an interpretation which would give lower

h^2 estimates and a greater role for environmental factors.
But first I want to analyse something else: a study by
Jensen himself which may not appear to have any relevance
to the subject of heritability estimates but which, by the
time we have done with it, may put the reader in a recep-
tive mood.

In 1977 Jensen published an analysis of sibling data
from the total state school enrolment (about 1,300 children) of a small rural town in south-eastern Georgia, an
area of low socio-economic status.   The children were
tested on the California Test of Mental Maturity (1963 Re-
vision) which is a standardized test of general intelligence comparable to other leading IQ tests.   By an ingen-
ious method, Jensen established that IQ differences in the
lower and upper parts of the scale were equivalent; which
is to say he defended himself against a possible objection
that the test in question was not valid in the lower range
of the IQ scale - a possible objection that it exaggerated
differences for low-IQ blacks as compared to the higher-IQ
whites.   The white sample of 653 had a mean IQ of 102 and
showed no decrement in IQ between younger and older siblings, that is, no tendency for IQ to decline between the
ages of 6 and 16.   The black sample of 826 had a mean IQ
of 71 and did exhibit a decrement: over the age range of
6 to 16, IQ decreased by 1.42 points per year yielding a
total decrement of about 15 points.   The most significant
aspect of this study is Jensen's contention that the most
reasonable interpretation of the decline is an environmental one.   A genetic interpretation is logically possible:
it could be argued that there are genetic differences between the races such that blacks reach a higher proportion
of their ultimate mental development at an earlier age,
and therefore the gap between black and white would widen

with age setting environmental factors aside.   However,
if there is a genetic effect correlated with race, it
should show up among black children everywhere (differences in locale and environment should not matter) and
Jensen found no such decrement among black children in
California.   He thinks it likely that the fact that
Georgia blacks are more disadvantaged in terms of environment than California blacks is responsible for the decrement. (3)

Here I wish to add my own contribution to the analysis
of Jensen's data.   A mean IQ of 71 for the black school
children taken collectively, plus a linear decrement
amounting to 15 points (from ages 6 to 16), give us a good
estimate of their mean IQ upon leaving school at 16,
namely, a mean of 63.5 (71.0 - 7.5 = 63.5).   This last
stands as a maximum estimate of the mean IQ of the entire
population of adults in the black community of this
Georgia town.   It may surprise the reader that such a
thing is possible, that there could be a community of significant size in America with a mean IQ as low as 63.5.
It may surprise him all the more to learn that the black
adult population has an appearance of normalcy in terms of
everyday life - they are not in the care of institutions
or benevolent white guardians but live their own lives.
This community and others like it stand as a caution to
those who would classify members of minority groups as
'retarded' on the basis of IQ scores alone, a point made
by scholars ranging from Jane Mercer to Jensen himself.
A mean IQ of 63.5 is of course 21.5 points below the average for black America in general (85.0 - 63.5 = 21.5) and
this brings me to another point.   In his California study
in which he failed to find a similar deficit for blacks
over the age range of 5 to 12, Jensen expresses doubt

about the existence of such before the age of 5:   'it
would seem unlikely, if environmental effects on intellectual development act cumulatively like compound interest,
that such cumulative effects would not continue beyond age
5.' (4)   Whatever the truth of this, the converse is almost certainly true: if there is a linear decline in mean
IQ at a steady 1.42 points per year from ages 6 to 16, it
would be most remarkable if it did not extend back before
age 6 to the date of birth as well.   And if that is true,
the total IQ decrement for blacks in this Georgia town
from birth to age 16 would be approximately 22.7 points
$(1.42 \times 16 = 22.7)$.

It may be asked why we do not posit the continuance of
the decrement after the age of 16 into adulthood.   In
answer, IQ tends to stabilize after 16 and, moreover, even
if there is a continued decline among black adults in our
Georgia town this may be matched by a similar decline
among the black population in general.   (Blacks suffer
from more unemployment and often get less intellectually
demanding jobs after they leave school, factors which may
encourage a further widening of the IQ gap between black
and white.)   Recall that the IQ gap between our adult
Georgia blacks and American blacks in general is 21.5
points.   The most reasonable hypothesis is that this IQ
gap is entirely environmental in origin.

This makes it worth taking a closer look at one of
Jensen's most potent arguments, namely his attempt to show
how high h^2 estimates could render an environmental hypothesis about the IQ gap between the races implausible - by
way of forcing us to posit a huge number of standard deviations between the average black environment and the
average white environment.   While conceding that all the
evidence is not yet in, Jensen asks us to make certain

assumptions so that he can demonstrate the compelling
logic of his analysis, an analysis which will prove valid
if h^2 estimates for both black and white remain high in
the light of future evidence.   The assumptions are that
the heritability of IQ is the same for both black and
white;   that the mean IQs are 85 and 100 respectively;
that IQ variance and the standard deviation are the same
for both (SD = 15);   and that environmental effects on IQ
are normally distributed in both populations. (5)

   As for the h^2 estimates assumed, Jensen has presented
his analysis on three occasions using a variety of values.
However, in his most detailed presentations and in his
graphs, he uses the values he derived from studies of
identical twins raised apart, namely: $h^2 = 85$; $E^2 = .05$;
$e^2 = .05$;   and test error = .05.   He singles out the
value for E^2, that is, the percentage of IQ variance explained by between-family environmental factors for
reasons which seem valid.   Recall that within-family factors are primarily things like birth order and maternal
age at birth.   As Jensen points out, social reformers do
not seriously propose to manipulate such factors, for example, hope for a society in which every family produces
one set of twins at the same maternal age.   They focus on
between-family factors such as SES and cultural ·advantages
and so forth.   The data Jensen uses from the studies of
identical twins raised apart is complex, but we can sim-
plify his analysis by noting that it is mathematically
equivalent to assuming a value for E^2 of .05. (6)

   Using the above values, Jensen calculates the standard
deviation of between-families environmental effects at
3. 35 IQ points.   He explains the meaning of this: if two
individuals are identical in terms of genotype for IQ, and
if they nonetheless differ in terms of their test scores

(true-score values) by 3.35 IQ points, then they differ by
one standard deviation in terms of between-families environmental effects.   He goes on to calculate what an environmental hypothesis about the 15-point IQ gap between
black and white entails, namely, that the means of the two
populations differ by 4.48 SDs in terms of between-families environmental effects (15.00 ÷ 3.35 = 4.48).   And
this means, according to Jensen, that the average black
environment is 'something below the 0.003 percentile of
systematic environmental effects on IQ in the white population.'   Which is to say that only 3 whites in 100,000
fall below the mean for blacks.   Actually Jensen has made
a mistake in reading his tables: rather than finding the
percentage left at 4.48 SDs below the mean, he has read
for approximately 4.00 SDs;   the correct reading would be
the 0.0004 percentile - which implies that only 4 whites
in a million fall below the mean for blacks.   And that is
hard to believe.   It is hard to believe that only about
800 whites in the whole of America fall below the average
environment of the black population!   Jensen leaves environmentalists with a way out of this absurdity but it is
an escape which is equally absurd, namely, we can always
posit a blindfold: we can posit an environmental factor
or factors which affect blacks but not whites and which
have a uniform effect within the black population.   All
in all, an environmental hypothesis would seem to make the
black population of America 'too incredibly different.' (7)

Details of calculations:

(1)   Formula: $\sqrt{E^2} \times SD = X$.   X represents the number
       of IQ points per standard deviation on the scale
       of between-family environmental effects.

(2) E^2 = .05 and SD = 15;   thus $\sqrt{.05} \times 15 = 3.35$.

(3)   IQ gap (between black and white) $\div$ X = X_1. X_1
      represents the number of SDs apart in terms of
      between-family environmental effects black and
      white would have to be if the IQ gap were entirely
      environmental.

(4)   IQ gap = 15 and X = 3.35;   thus 15 $\div$ 3.35 = 4.48.

(5)   From table: 0.0004 per cent of higher population
      would fall below the mean of the lower.

The above presentation of Jensen's analysis speaks as
if one could assume that actual people and actual environments are distributed on a normal curve that matches the
curve of between-family environmental effects.   However,
Jensen himself uses language to that effect.   For example, when speaking of a difference of 3.2 SDs between
two populations on an environmental scale, he says that
this means that 'only 0.07 per cent of the lower group
exceeds the median of the higher group.' (8)   Jensen may
well not wish to be taken too literally here, but any
damage done will be repaired in a moment when we get to
our discussion of a possible 'threshold hypothesis'.

We have reviewed Jensen's analysis of the IQ gap between black and white in America.   Let us now make a
similar analysis of the IQ gap between the adult black
community of our Georgia town and American blacks in general.   We will make a set of assumptions similar in kind
to those made by Jensen: that the heritability of IQ is
the same for both populations (h^2 = .85 and E^2 = .05);
that the mean IQs are 63.5 and 85.0 respectively;   that IQ
variance and the standard deviation are the same for both
(SD = 13 for blacks);   and that environmental effects on
IQ are normally distributed in both populations.   This
gives a value for the standard deviation of between-family
environmental effects of 2.91 IQ points.   As for what an

environmental hypothesis about the 21.5 point IQ gap between the two populations entails, the means must differ
by 7.39 SDs in terms of between-families environmental
effects (21.50 ÷ 2.91 = 7.39).   And this means that the
average environment of adult blacks in our Georgia town
is at the 0.0000000000074 percentile of systematic environmental effects on IQ within black America in general.
Which implies that only about one person in ten million
millions from the general black population would fall
below the average environment of the local population!

   Details of calculations:

(1)   Values: E^2 = .05;   SD = 13;   environmental decre-
      ment = 21.5 IQ points.

(2)   Calculations: $\sqrt{.05}$ × 13 = 2.91;   21.50 ÷ 2.91 =
      7.39.

(3)   From table: 0.0000000000074 per cent of higher
      population would fall below the mean of the lower.

   At the close of one of his attempts to demonstrate the
implausibility of an environmental hypothesis (about the
IQ gap between black and white), Jensen asserts that it
would be more sensible to use a value for E^2 derived from
a wide range of kinship data, rather than the very low
estimate he derived from the data on identical twins
raised apart.   He attempts to make amends by using a
value of .10 and in a brief passage in a recent article,
he finally uses his usual value of .12.   I think it unfortunate that Jensen did not use his usual value in his
principal analyses of the IQ gap between black and white.
Many readers are likely to retain the impression that
given Jensen's h^2 estimates, the environmentalist must
posit an environmental difference between the races of
monstrous size;   the three SDs that a value of .12 dictates are quite bad enough.   Even when Jensen uses .12,

he blurs the issue by speculating that the IQ gap between the races may be as much as 20 points, which allows him to posit an environmental gap of 'some three to four standard deviations' on behalf of the environmentalist. (9)

In order to be fair to Jensen, let us go back to his Georgia town study and alter two of our assumptions: we will assume .12 as his value for E^2; and assume that he would attribute only part of the 21.5-point gap between adult blacks in this Georgia town and American blacks in general to environment.   For example, he might argue that the yearly IQ decrement before the age of 6 was less than thereafter (I personally doubt the plausibility of such an assumption) and that some of the gap was due to selective migration.   This would suggest a division of the 21.5-point gap as follows: 18.5 environmental (15.5 after age 6 and 3.0 before); 3.0 genetic (say selective migration). However, even using these values we get a huge gap between the two populations, namely, they would have to differ by 4.21 SDs in terms of between-families environmental effects (18.50 ÷ 4.39 = 4.21).   And this gives almost precisely the result Jensen felt was so damning to his opponents, that is, only 1.3 persons in 100,000 from the general black population (about 260 blacks from all the rest of America) would fall below the average environment of adult blacks in this Georgia town.

Details of calculations:

(1)   Values: E^2 = .12; SD = 12.67 (adjusted for absence of test error variance); environmental decrement = 18.5 IQ points.

(2)   Calculations: $\sqrt{.12}$ × 12.67 = 4.39; 18.50 ÷ 4.39 = 4.21.

(3)   From table: 0.0013 per cent of higher population would fall below the mean of the lower.

A community in which systematic environmental effects on IQ reach these depths is clearly worth our attention. The identity of the town in question is confidential but we are told its location (south-eastern Georgia) and the size of its school population (about 1,300). From this, we can determine that its black population has a median family income which probably does not fall below $US 3,079; and that the figure cannot possibly fall below $US 2,705. (10)   A quick run through the census data (census of 1970) reveals over 170 counties in America in which the median family income of blacks is below the higher figure and 70 counties in which it is below the lower. (11)   In other words, the black population of our Georgia town is poor by American standards but it is by no means unique.   It is easily on the scale of naturally occurring environments for blacks in America.

In sum, Jensen's own data in this study raises some interesting problems.   We environmentalists no longer need feel so lonely: in order to avoid absurdity in our hypothesis that the IQ gap between black and white is environmental, we must attempt to lower h^2 estimates or render respectable the concept of a blindfold or attempt a combination of the two.   Now Jensen is in a similar position: in order to avoid absurdity in the hypothesis that the IQ gap between the adult black population of his Georgia town and the black population of America in general is environmental (or that about 85 per cent of the gap is such), he too must look for record low h^2 estimates or take refuge in a blindfold or try a bit of both.

Jensen might well acknowledge that he has to undertake a task similar to our own but he might add that he will have a much easier time accomplishing it.   I refer to his 'threshold hypothesis' concerning environmental effects.

The hypothesis states: that environmental differences at
one part of the environmental scale (the very bottom) have
a greater impact on IQ than differences at other parts of
the scale (more favoured environments); and that we
should therefore find lower h^2 estimates for populations
in depressed environments.   However, this raises the
question of how depressed an environment must be to fall
below the threshold and thus fall beyond the reach of the
h^2 estimates Jensen usually posits.   The fact that the
mean IQ of adult blacks in our Georgia town is 63.5 is not
in itself sufficient.   Speaking of those in the IQ range
of 50 to 70 (those who are clinically normal), Jensen says
that they seem 'a part of the normal distribution of intelligence in the population, a distribution which is
determined mainly by polygenic inheritance.' (12)   We
must then look for the factors which would mark the black
environment in our Georgia town as below the crucial
threshold.   Jensen gives several descriptions of such an
environment: first 'children ... whose initial social environment was deplorable to a greater extreme than can be
found among any children who are free to interact with
other persons or to run about out-of-doors'; second,
'When I speak of subthreshold environmental deprivation
... I refer to the extreme sensory and motor restrictions
in environments such as those described by Skeels and Dye
(1939) and Davis (1947), in which the subjects had little
sensory stimulation of any kind and little contact with
adults'; third, 'typically culturally disadvantaged children are not reared in anything like the degree of sensory
and motor deprivation that characterizes, say, the children of the Skeels' study'. (13)   Jensen also refers to
the effects of malnutrition on growth (14) which calls to
mind his concession that severe malnutrition, the sort ex-

istent in areas of Africa in which children suffer from
severe protein deficiency, can affect brain development
and therefore IQ.

We see that the threshold hypothesis does not relieve
Jensen of the task of identifying environmental variables
in that the identification of certain variables is necessary to argue that the hypothesis is applicable.   Presumably we would take a sample of, say, the ten counties
closest to our Georgia town in terms of median income for
black families and look for certain things: do the parents deprive the children of virtually all sensory and
motor stimulation and prevent them from running out-of-
doors?   I rather doubt it.   Do the children show the
usual signs of severe malnutrition, that is, stunted physical growth, abnormal brain waves, head circumferences
below the tenth percentile, retarded rates of ossification
of cartilage, impaired performance on infant tests of sensori-motor development, or impaired memory? (15)   Almost
certainly not.   Jensen emphasizes that when Carter et al.
studied the very poorest families of Nashville, Tennessee,
they found that both black and white were above the standards recommended by the National Nutrition Survey for
healthy development.   And he says: 'Physical evidence of
malnutrition found to be correlated with lower IQs in
studies conducted in Africa, Mexico, and Guatamala have
not been found even in the poorest and lowest IQ segments
of the American Negro population.' (16)

I suspect that when Jensen looks for the relevant environmental variables, he will have to look for more
subtle factors, factors largely uncorrelated with SES.
The mere fact that the blacks in question are low in SES
is not good neough;   for example, it appears that the
threshold hypothesis does not hold for 'Eskimos living in

the icy wastes far above the Arctic circle', a group which
on the face of it seems to be more depressed than blacks
in Georgia. (17)   And once again, the threshold hypothesis does not relieve Jensen of the task of establishing
very low h^2 estimates, quite the contrary.   Unless whatever environmental factors are at work operate like a
blindfold, they must vary within the black population and
will account for a large proportion of IQ variance, thus
bringing h^2 estimates well down.   It might be difficult
to secure sufficient twin data, but we could get some
rough estimates from siblings separated at an early age,
sibling data in general, and calculation of regression to
the mean from parent to child.

The Georgia town study alters the situation.   Pre-
viously Jensen enjoyed a great advantage: the weakness of
social science methodology in establishing causal hypotheses is considerable and this includes hypotheses about the
determinates of IQ: and Jensen merely had to show that
the evidence for environmental hypotheses was weak.   Now
he must actually join us and help us to overcome this
weakness by isolating environmental determinates of IQ of
great magnitude;   otherwise he must leave some of his own
data inexplicable in its implications.   It would be a
salutory outcome of the debate on race and IQ if Jensen
were to make a positive contribution to causal analysis
comparable to the largely negative contribution he has
made thus far.   At any rate, it is nice to have the shoe
on the other foot.

Leaving our Georgia town behind, I am intrigued by something else which may someday influence our views on h^2
estimates even though its relevance is not immediately
apparent.   I refer to the unsettled question of whether

the IQ gap between twins and singletons is largely pre-
natal or post-natal in origin.   That there is such a gap
has been long established: various studies put the mean
IQ of twins 4 to 7 points below that of singletons, with 5
points most often cited as a reasonable estimate.   As
Jensen has pointed out, this difference seems quite unrelated to socioeconomic status, that is, we find much the
same gap over a wide range of SES groups. (18)   This last
suggested to many that the causes must be pre-natal, and
during the 1960s two studies noted a correlation between
IQ and birth weight: among monozygotic twins, the heavier
twin at birth tended to develop a higher IQ than his
lighter and genetically identical co-twin. (19)   The
average birth weight of twins is of course less than that
of singletons and presumably the difference is a result of
factors operating during gestation.

   However, in 1970 Record et al. published research which
seemed to provide overwhelming evidence of the influence
of post-natal factors.   Record took all the singletons
and twins born in Birmingham, England, from 1 January 1950
to 1 September 1954 and collected a wide range of birth
data; about 50,000 of the children remained in the Birmingham area long enough to take the verbal reasoning test
included in the eleven plus examination.   In order to
expand his sample of twins, he added all such born from 1
September 1954 to 1 September 1957, making certain that
standards of marking had not altered over the additional
period.   By these means, Record achieved a huge sample of
twins, large enough so that he could attempt something
new: he selected out those twins whose co-twins were
stillborn, died at birth, or died within a month of birth.
He found that in such cases the gap between twins and
singletons largely disappeared.   Indeed, when he standar-

dized the scores for maternal age and birth order, he obtained the following mean IQs: 41,195 singletons - 99.5; 1,924 twins plus co-twin - 95.2;   148 twins minus co-twin - 98.8. (20)   Which is to say that 84 per cent of the gap between twins and singletons had disappeared when someone gestated as a twin had not been reared as a twin.

Record anticipated certain objections to his results. He established that the mean birth weight of twins minus co-twin was actually less than that of twins plus co-twin, that is, 2.28 kilograms as compared to 2.52 kilograms. (21)   He thus ruled out the possibility of 'differential selection':   the possibility that in cases in which only one member of a twin pair is born alive, it is a twin who has 'won' the struggle for survival thanks to an above-average genetic endowment or pre-natal environment.   Record collected no data on the socioeconomic status of the parents of his twins.   But if we look at correlates with SES, such as maternal age, birth rank, and infant mortality, it seems that if anything, twins minus co-twin suffered from lower SES than twins plus co-twin. Recall that Record standardized his two groups of twins for maternal age and birth order, which would tend to standardize them not only for SES but also for the sort of within-family environmental factors that are usually posited.   He made no attempt to identify the specific environmental factors at work but referred to the usual hypotheses, that children reared as twins get less individual attention from parents, that twins tend to associate with one another at the cost of less verbal interaction with others, and so forth. (22)   In sum, Record's research appeared to lend credibility to the following conclusions: that post-natal factors account for an environmental decrement for twins of at least 3.6 points (98.8 - 95.2);

that these factors reflect between-family differences;
and that they have an impact over and above the influence
of SES.

And yet, in 1972, when Myrianthopoulos et al. attempted
to replicate Record's findings, they found entirely negative results.   They too had a large population base,
drawing upon data from the massive Collaborative Study
with its twelve participating institutions scattered about
the United States.   From a population of 56,249 births
they obtained: Stanford-Binet IQs at age 4 from 26,115
singletons, 592 twins, and 44 twins raised as singletons;
and WISC IQ data at age 7 from 3,401 singletons, 396
twins, and 33 twins raised as singletons. (23)   As for
their results: twins minus co-twin were .7 points below
twins plus co-twin at age 4 and only .5 points above them
at age 7.   The SES of twins raised as singletons was
lower than that of twins raised together but not significantly so.   It is true that the sample sizes of twins
raised as singletons (44 and 33) suffer by comparison to
Record's large sample (148); but they were large enough
so that a trend in favour of such twins should have been
in evidence, if it existed. (24)

The conflict between the results of the above studies
is total and this is unfortunate because the point at
issue makes a difference.   Let us call the factors we
described under Record, post-natal, between-families factors influential over and above SES, Record's factors or
R^2.   If we follow Record, we have evidence that R^2 is a
potent influence on IQ.   If we follow Myrianthopoulos, R^2
may well be potent, but we cannot look to the twin-single-
ton gap for evidence.

This takes us back to Jensen for Jensen has much to say
about R^2 although he does not call it by that name.   In

what follows, I will use what Jensen considers to be his
best-founded heritability estimates, a value of .80 for h^2
and .20 for all environmental factors combined (E^2 = .12
and e^2 = .08).   Concerning the environmental contribution
to IQ variance, Jensen asserts the following: (1) that a
major proportion and perhaps a majority proportion of the
sources of environmental variance are pre-natal; (25)   (2)
that indices of SES account for a major proportion of environmental variance and that once covariance between SES
and other environmental factors is eliminated, the latter
do not make a very significant independent contribution; (26)   (3) that within-family environmental effects
on IQ are slightly larger than between-family effects (27)
- a statement which is in mild conflict with his actual
estimates which assign only 40 per cent of the environmental component to within-family effects - I will therefore
follow the estimates.   These assertions collectively dictate an estimate for the sort of factors we described
under Record as contributing no more than .04 of IQ variance;   and this is true no matter how we relate them to
one another.   For example: (1) eliminating pre-natal
factors cuts .20 to say .10, then subtracting all post-
natal factors correlated with SES reduces .10 to no more
than .04;   (2) eliminating all factors correlated with SES
cuts .20 to no more than .08, then subtracting pre-natal
factors not correlated with SES leaves .04 as a generous
estimate;   (3) eliminating within-family factors cuts .20
to .12, then subtracting between-family factors correlated
with SES again makes .04 a generous estimate.

Let us test an R^2 estimate of .04 against Record's results by making use of some familiar assumptions.   Given
our two populations of twins plus co-twin and twins minus
co-twin, we will assume: that R^2 = .04 for both;   that

the mean IQs are 95.2 and 98.8 respectively;   that IQ variance and the standard deviation are the same for both (SD
= 15);   and that R^2 effects on IQ are normally distributed
in both populations.   This would mean that the populations differ by 1.2 SDs in terms of R^2 environmental
effects, which is to say that only the top 11.5 per cent
of twins plus co-twin overlap with the top 50 per cent of
twins minus co-twin in terms of the relevant environmental
effects.   I cannot prove this is untrue.   It is logically possible that in terms of, say, attention from the
mother, only one twin in nine gets the environmental quality that a majority of single infants get.   But it just
does not seem reasonable to assume that twins are disadvantaged to that extent.   A hereditarian could of course
elect to take the usual escape route from such an impasse:
posit a semi-blindfold, an environmental factor X that is
relatively uniform within the population of twins and
therefore, does not have much effect on h^2 estimates.
But this would be grist to the environmentalist's mill,
for it offers encouragement to those who hope to find some
semi-blindfolds with the population of black Americans.

   Details of calculations:

(1)   Formula: $\sqrt{R^2} \times SD = X$.

(2) R^2 = .04 and SD 15;   thus $\sqrt{.04} \times 15 = 3.0$.

(3)   IQ gap $\div$ X = X_1.

(4)   IQ gap = 3.6 and X = 3.0;   thus 3.6 $\div$ 3.0 = 1.2.

(5)   From table: 11.5 per cent.

   At present, all one can say about Record et al. and
Myrianthopoulos et al. is this: two groups of scholars,
both possessing impeccable credentials, both using an appropriate methodology, both having access to extensive
data, have produced evidence for opposite conclusions.
It would be too much to hope for a solution to this puzzle

in the near future, but I hope the relevance of a solution to the subject of h^2 estimates is clear.   If the causes of the IQ gap between twins and singletons are mainly pre-natal, thanks to the fact that twins possess an atypical pre-natal environment, the implications for h^2 estimates would be few.   But if the causes are mainly post-natal, that fact in itself would encourage scepticism about estimates which allot a very low value to post-natal factors uncorrelated with SES.

We have examined some studies that pose problems for high h^2 estimates, but no attempt to challenge such estimates will be taken seriously unless it addresses itself to the actual data on which they are based.   I will not attempt to give a comprehensive summary of the literature on the heritability of IQ, an extensive literature which is grow-ing day by day.   But I will aim at the following objec-tives: giving the general reader some notion of the theory that lies behind our methods of arriving at h^2 estimates;   emphasizing the controversy that surrounds those methods;   and making a few methodological points which, in my opinion, suggest that scholars may someday agree on values well below the .80 level.

   We will begin with the twin-study literature and the theory that lies behind methods for extracting heritabil-ity estimates from twin data.   The foundation of most heritability estimates is the 'intraclass correlation co-efficient'.   Its purpose is to measure the extent to which a twin and his co-twin are more alike in IQ (com-pared to two individuals selected at random from the gene-ral population) because of something they have in common (as compared to two individuals selected at random).   Let us take a sample of identical or monozygotic twins raised

apart (MZA). Assume that the fact they have been raised
apart means that, on the average, each twin and his co-
twin have no more in common, in terms of environment, than
randomly selected individuals. If that were true, and we
shall have reason to ask if it is ever true, the only
thing they have more in common is genes; and the intraclass correlation coefficient would measure the extent to
which they are more alike for IQ because they are unusually alike in terms of shared genes. This must be matched
against how much they would be alike for IQ if genes
accounted for all IQ variance and environment counted for
nothing. Since monozygotic twins are identical for
genes, they would be identical in IQ if genes were all
that counted. We make the intraclass correlation coefficient the numerator and the 'ideal' correlation the
denominator which gives: ICC ÷ 1.00 = h^2 (the percentage
of IQ variance accounted for by genetic factors). For
example, if the value for the ICC were .70, then .70 ÷
1.00 = .70; and we would say that 70 per cent of IQ variance is genetic and 30 per cent the total environmental
component, representing between-family differences (E^2)
plus within-family differences (e^2) plus test error.

The general expression of the above formula for MZA is:

$$h^2 = \frac{r_p \ (MZA)}{r_g \ (MZ)}$$

r_p (MZA) represents the ICC for the phenotype of the
monozygotic twins in the sample.

r_g (MZ) represents the ICC for the genotype of monozygotic twins in general.

Monozygotic twins who have been separated at birth and
raised apart are naturally very rare. The traditional
body of data on which h^2 estimates have been based comes
mainly from another source, namely studies of monozygotic

twins raised together (MZT) and fraternal or dizygotic
twins raised together (DZT).   The latter are essentially
no more alike than ordinary siblings which means that they
have about .50 of their genes in common.   Now let us
assume that a twin and his identical co-twin have exactly
the same degree of environmental similarity as a twin and
his fraternal co-twin.   Again, this may not be true, for
example, parents may treat identical twins more alike than
they do fraternal twins.   However, if we make this assumption, then a pair of monozygotic twins raised together
have no more in common in terms of environmental factors
(which affect IQ) than do a pair of dizygotic twins raised
together.   Therefore, if the former are more alike in
terms of IQ than the latter, this must be due purely to
the genetic difference between the two kinds of twins:
the MZT having 1.00 of their genes in common, the DZT
having only .50 of their genes in common.   We therefore
take our sample and calculate the intraclass correlation
coefficient for IQ for the MZT and subtract from that the
intraclass correlation coefficient for the DZT.   And
again, we match the result against what the difference between the ICCs would be if genes accounted for all IQ variance.   The actual difference becomes our numerator and
the 'ideal' difference our denominator: $h^2 = (ICC_{MZT} -
ICC_{DZT}) \div (1.00 - .50)$.   For example, if the correlations
for MZT and DZT were .85 and .50, then .35 $\div$ .50 = .70;
and once again, we would say that 70 per cent of IQ variance is genetic.

The general expression of the above formula for MZT/DZT
is:

$$h^2 = \frac{r_p \ (MZT) \ - \ r_p \ (DZT)}{r_g \ (MZ) \ - \ r_g \ (DZ)}$$

r_p (MZT) and r_p (DZT) represent the ICCs for the pheno-

types of the MZ twins and DZ twins in the sample;
r_g (MZ) and r_g (DZ) represent the ICCs for the genotypes of MZ twins and DZ twins in general.

NOTE: usually the denominator of the above is altered
so as to take both assortive mating (for IQ) and dominance into account.   Taken together, these factors
boost the genotypic correlation for fraternal twins, so
the denominator becomes: 1.00 - .55.

Let us leave theory behind and proceed to the twin studies
themselves.   We will begin with studies of monozygotic
twins raised apart and immediately, two questions arise.
The first has to do with the quality of the sample: do
the environmental gaps between twin and co-twin match the
gaps we would obtain if we had dispersed them into various
homes at random;   which is to say, does the sample represent the full range of environmental effects existent in
the population at large?   The second has to do with the
size of the sample: do we have enough twin pairs to
reduce the standard error, the error that sampling a population entails even if random, to a size which lends pre-
cision to our results?   The size of the sample needed is
easily determined by the appropriate formula.   Actually
the formula is not appropriate unless we believe our
sample to be random, but nevertheless it is suggestive:
given a typical value for the intraclass correlation coefficient, we need a sample size of 40 twin pairs to
reduce our standard error to .08.   To illustrate what
such a standard error means, assume our study of MZA gave
an h^2 of .70.   Then: there would be two chances out of
three that the true value of h^2 lay within the range of
.62 and .78 (that is .70±.08);   and there would be 19
chances out of 20 that the true value lay between .54 and
.86 (that is .70±.16).

Formula for the approximate Standard Error of h^2 calculated from MZA:

$$SE \simeq \frac{1}{r_g} \sqrt{\frac{(1 - r_p^2)^2}{N}}$$

Source: Loehlin et al. (1975). (28)

At one time, the largest sample of MZA was thought to have been collected by the late Sir Cyril Burt and his associates.   In a series of papers published between 1943 and 1966, Burt claimed that a total of 53 twin pairs had been tested and advanced an intraclass correlation coefficient of .87, very high indeed.   It is now clear that Burt's data must be set aside, a conclusion endorsed by all serious scholars from Jensen to Leon Kamin (at the environmentalist end of the spectrum).   I will not enter into the sad debate over whether Burt faked his data or was merely careless, over whether one or some or all of his supposed research assistants were fictitious, over who deserves credit for first exposing him, and so forth.   If the reader has the stomach for it, he can follow it beginning with the January 1977 issue of the 'Bulletin of the British Psychological Society' or read the summing up by Oliver Gillie in late 1978. (29)

There remain only three studies of monozygotic twins raised apart.   The largest of these, and the only one with a sample size even approaching 40 twin pairs, is that of James Shields who reported IQ data on exactly 40 pairs, almost all from Britain, and based a correlation of .77 on 37 of these. (30)   Shields himself is clearly convinced that hereditary influences on IQ are more important than environmental factors. (31)   However, his own data indicates, as he acknowledges in the text, that factors like 'not being brought up in the same family network' encouraged larger IQ differences;   and concerning the degree of

separation of twin and co-twin he asserts that 'large differences of social class do not occur often ... in the
present material.' (32)   This raises the question of how
separated twins raised apart should be if they are to be
taken as the basis of an h^2 estimate.   In Shield's
sample, 26 of the 40 pairs (whose IQs were tested) were
raised in related branches of the parents' families;   8
pairs were reared by their mother and her own mother, 7
others by siblings, e.g. their mother and one of her sis-
ters.   As Leon Kamin has pointed out, (33) if we take the
10 pairs who had neither been raised by related families
nor attended the same school, we get an intraclass correlation coefficient of only .47.   (When reading Shields
and Kamin, it is sometimes not easy to follow just which
twin pairs are supposed to meet the criteria being
applied.   As for Kamin's analysis: (1) among the 40
pairs of MZA tested, I find 14 not raised by related families (unless one counts a distant cousin as a relative);
(2) among these 14 pairs, I find 2 who clearly went to the
same school (pairs Sm8 and Sf1) plus 2 others who were reunited at times so that they must have done so at least
briefly (pairs Sm4 and Sm10).   This does leave 10 pairs:
Sm3, Sm5, Sf3, Sf5, Sf9, Sf10, Sf16, Sf17, Sf19 and Sf22.
And the intraclass correlation coefficient for these is
approximately .47 - I get .46 but this may be the difference between my modest pocket calculator and a computer.)
    Kamin's selection of 10 pairs includes pair Sf3
(Valerie and Joyce) and Joyce's score on the non-verbal
test (the Dominoes) was suspect in that she may not have
understood the instructions. (34)   If we were to keep
this pair but count only their scores on the verbal test
(the Synonyms section of the Mill Hill Vocabulary scale),
suitably weighted, the ICC would rise from .47 to .57.

On the other hand, converting from Shields's scoring system to conventional IQ scores would reduce the latter to .53.   As for Shields himself, he reacted to Kamin's analysis by offering an alternative method of classifying the twin pairs represented in his sample.   He excluded 12 of the 40 tested on criteria ranging from suspicion that the results were unreliable (because of the subject's age, first language, or failure to understand fully the test instructions) to rejection of those suffering from neurological disorders (syphilis, epilepsy, sclerosis).   From the 'purified' sample that remained, he made his own selection of the 12 cases that had the greatest environmental separation, pairs in which twin and co-twin had been separated before 18 months and had not been reunited in childhood; and then calculated an ICC of .84. (35)   I will resist the temptation to make my own selection. When you get down to a 'sample' of 10 or 12, you get into absurd situations, for example, the result can fluctuate wildly depending on the inclusion or exclusion of one twin pair, say a pair that has a radical effect on either total variance or within-pair variance.

As for the general question of how separated twins should be when we do studies of monozygotic twins raised apart (MZA), this is easy to answer in theory: we all know that on the average twin and co-twin should have environments as different as children randomly assigned to homes throughout the population being measured.   But since we never actually do assign our twins at random, we must ask if the differences in our sample match those we would get if we did such a thing.   In practice, this would mean matching their environmental differences with 'typical' environmental differences within the population in question.   And attempting that would be to assume that

we can agree about which variables affect IQ, for without
this we have no measure of whether two environments differ
in terms of the relevant differences.   At present, of
course, hereditarians and environmentalists cannot even
agree on whether variables uncorrelated with SES (socio-
economic status) play an important role and environmentalists cannot agree among themselves as to the identity of
such variables.   Therefore, for the present, one can go
to Shields's data and extract a high h^2 estimate (thanks
to an ICC of .84) or a low h^2 estimate (thanks to an ICC
of .47) depending on one's predilections.

   This last assertion, which may seem unexceptional on
its face, would provoke an acrimonious debate.   It
assumes that we should take the intraclass correlation coefficient as our h^2 estimate, an assumption we have not
questioned up to now.   In fact, scholars compete in
giving reasons why the ICC should be raised or lowered
before it is allowed to go before the world as an h^2 estimate.   For example, Jensen argues in favour of correcting
the ICC for both test error and 'restriction of range'.
He has a reasonable case for raising the ICC to compensate
for test error in that chance factors in test-taking or
test marking are not true environmental influences; and
naturally, when they are deducted from the non-genetic
portion of variance, the percentage of variance due to
genetic factors rises slightly.   The question of adjusting the ICC for restriction of range is more complicated:
intraclass correlation coefficients are calculated in
terms of the total IQ variance present in one's sample;
when the coefficient is revised upward for restriction of
range, this is done because the standard deviation and
therefore the variance ($V = SD^2$) of one's sample is lower
than that of the general population whose h^2 is being

measured.   This adjustment is appropriate unless the reduced variance is a result of factors that bias the balance between the variables being measured.

For example, assume that genuinely to separate siblings
at birth in England is essentially a working-class trait
and that the separate siblings usually end up in working-
class homes; and that the English working class comes
closer to the full range of genetic variance for IQ (in
the general population) than it does to the full range of
environmental variance.   Then the very factors that
account for reduced variance in a sample of MZA would also
bias the result in favour of a high h^2; and for the environmentalist, to raise the h^2 estimate further for 'restriction of range' would be to add insult to injury.   It
is a pity we know so little about the causes of reduced
variance in the MZA studies because clearly something
potent is at work: the SDs for the three studies existent
range from 9.0 to 13.4 (with SD = 15 for the general population). (36)   If we take the ten twin pairs Kamin selected out of Shields's study, those in which twin and co-
twin had neither been reared by related families nor attended the same school, they do seem to have been mainly
working-class both in origin and placement; but their SD
was fairly high, that is, SD = 14.2.   We have information
on the natural parents of only four pairs, all of whom
were working class with the possible exception of one
police sergeant.   We have better information on the 20
homes in which they were reared: only 6 were clearly
middle class or professional and only one child was less
than 13 months old when placed in such a home. (37)   A
few of the natural parents were rather unusual.   The
father of Berta and Herta sold the former to pay his debts
and attempted to sell the latter.   He came to a bad end,

eventually attempting suicide by swallowing broken glass, razor blades and a bottle of furniture polish. (38)

Some scholars not only argue against raising the intra-class correlation coefficient, they also argue that the ICC is already too high to be accepted as a genuine heritability estimate.   Thus far, we have emphasized only one of their reasons: looking at the three MZA studies exis-tent taken together, for two-thirds of the twin pairs, twin and co-twin were raised by related families. (39) As for additional reasons, even when twins are genuinely separated, adoption agencies try to get them all decent homes, thus eliminating the contribution of sub-standard homes to IQ variance.   Monozygotic twins are borne by the same mother and therefore they entirely miss between-family differences in pre-natal environment, say the dif-ference between a mother who during pregnancy gets proper nutrition and medical advice and a mother who does not. They are also borne in their mother's womb at the same time and therefore miss some within-family differences; for example, with singletons, a mother may contract rubel-la when bearing one child and not do so when bearing ano-ther.   Against this is the fact that about two-thirds of monozygotic twins share the same blood supply, one twin receiving blood only after it has passed through his co-twin.   This may add something to within-family differen-ces although, as Breland (1974) has shown, the evidence that the above phenomenon causes IQ differences within twin pairs is very weak.

When I spoke above of some scholars wanting to lower the intraclass correlation coefficient if it is to qualify as a heritability estimate, this should not be taken too literally.   Many environmentalists are really arguing that, at least as far as MZA studies are concerned, the evidence in question is just not adequate for a reliable h^2 estimate.   For example, Leon Kamin does not suggest taking his selection of 10 twin pairs, claculating an ICC of .47, and then lowering this figure to obtain a heritability estimate.   Setting aside the peculiar bias of the sample, a sample of this size would have a standard error of approximately .27.   To be given an h^2 estimate of say .40, and then be told that there are two chances in three that the heritability of IQ lay between .13 and .67 would not be very helpful.

The remaining studies of monozygotic twins raised apart both had very small samples: Newman et al. (1937) asked MZAs to volunteer by way of newspaper and radio appeals, collected 19 twin pairs, lodged them in Chicago, and tested them with the 1916 Stanford-Binet; Juel-Nielsen (1965) tested 12 twin pairs in Denmark using an adaptation of the Wechsler (WAIS) which had never been standardized on a Danish population - his sample achieved an average performance well above (6 or 7 points) the standard mean, most unusual for a twin study.   Newman in particular may have accepted as MZAs twins who had not actually been raised apart.   Those who were reluctant to come to Chicago were told they would get a free, all-expenses-paid trip to the Century of Progress Exposition which was being held there at the time.   This was a strong inducement, particularly during the great depression, and some may have succumbed to the temptation to lie about their degree of separation, so as to qualify.   As Leon Kamin points out, there are some odd cases: Ed and Fred claimed complete separation until the age of 24 and yet both worked as repair men for the telephone company and each owned a fox terrier named Trixie; Kenneth and Jerry were supposedly separated from 3 weeks of age until 13 years and yet

Kenneth's foster father was a city fireman with a very
limited education and Jerry's foster father was a city
fireman with only a fourth-grade education. (40)   Newman
reports an intraclass correlation coefficient of .67;
Juel-Nielsen reports .62 for a first testing and .69 for
two testings combined.

Howard Taylor has analysed all three of the MZA studies
in terms of a variety of criteria, criteria having to do
with the degree of separation between the environments of
twin and co-twin.   If one accepts the samples as given
and takes the average (weighted average) of the intraclass
correlation coefficients as reported (combined scores for
Juel-Nielsen), the result is .73.   If one selects out of
each sample first those not reared by related families,
second those who did not enjoy a childhood reunion, and
third those separated at 6 months or earlier, the average
ICC falls to .61, .55 and .61 respectively. (41)   (Taylor's case for the influence of related families and
childhood reunion is much stronger than his case for late
separation.   Dividing those separated after 6 months of
age from those separated at 6 months or earlier, the ICC
(three studies together - weighted average) is lower for
the latter;   but this is due to reduced total variance.
The average difference between twin and co-twin in terms
of IQ points is actually greater for those separated late
than for those separated early.)   It is important to note
that these criteria have been applied one by one and not
collectively.   If we take them collectively and apply
them to Shields's study, the only study of significant
size, we find that only three twin pairs meet all three
criteria.   Taylor argues against accepting any of the
above correlations as heritability estimates, indeed, he
refers to such as 'bogus heritability'.   He advances the

usual set of reasons, plus some interesting ones of his
own, and speculates that the actual heritability of IQ may
be far below .60. (42)

Studies of monozygotic twins raised apart capture the
public imagination because of their spectacular character.
However, the oldest and most widely used method of estimating the heritability of IQ is based on studies of monozygotic twins raised together (MZT) as compared to fraternal or dizygotic twins raised together (DZT).   Here we
have a much larger body of data, and presumably these
twins are distributed much more randomly in homes throughout the general population: they are after all not separated from their natural parents but remain with them
just as singletons do.   Jensen calls this method the most
efficient and least ambiguous base for an overall estimate
of heritability and he uses it when he derives his estimate of .80, the value for h^2 he designates as most reliable.

Once again we must raise questions about the quality of
samples and about sample size and, in this kind of study,
these are sometimes closely related.   Thanks to the fact
that a comparison of two intraclass correlation coefficients is involved (comparing the ICC for MZT with the ICC
for DZT), we need an unusually large sample to reduce the
standard error to a size we can tolerate.   Assuming that
our sample is random, we can use an appropriate formula.
That formula suggests: given typical values for the two
ICCs, we need a sample size of 400 pairs of each kind of
twin in order to reduce our standard error to .08.   In
order to get a sample of that size, it may be necessary to
sacrifice quality, that is, sacrifice the representative
character of the sample in favour of a systematic bias.

Formula for the approximate Standard Error of h^2 calculated from MZT/DZT:

$$SE \simeq \frac{1}{r_g MZ - r_g DZ} \sqrt{\frac{(1 - r_p MZT^2)^2}{N\ MZT} + \frac{(1 - r_p DZT^2)^2}{N\ DZT}}$$

Notation: r_g refers to genotypic correlations; r_p to phenotypic correlations; N to number of twin pairs.

Source: Loehlin et al. (1975). (43)

Calculation - values assumed:

(1) $r_g MZ = 1.00$; $r_g DZ = .55$.

(2) $r_p MZT = .85$; $r_p DZT = .60$.

(3)   N MZT = 400;   N DZT = 400.

There have been only two MZT/DZT studies in history which were based on 400 pairs or more of each kind of twin and both of these used data from an unrepresentative section of the population.   I refer to Nichols (1965) and Loehlin and Nichols (1976) who analysed the performance of American high-school students who took the NMSQT (National Merit Scholarship Qualification Test);   these students are of course an elite in terms of academic achievement and come to a disproportionate degree from unusually favourable environments.   Moreover, the NMSQT is not an IQ test;   as Loehlin and Nichols point out, the nearest thing they could get to a general ability measure was the students' total score which would contain a considerable academic achievement component. (44)

Setting aside these two studies, we are left with a large number of MZT/DZT studies with samples ranging from a few pairs up to the 215 (MZT) pairs plus 416 (DZT) pairs studied by Husen in 1959.   In 1976, Loehlin and Nichols surveyed the literature using the following criteria: the study must itself include both kinds of twin;   it must have a sample size of at least 25 pairs for each kind.

They compiled a table of 17 such studies and noted that
the intraclass correlations for MZT and DZT were such as
to give medians of .85 and .59 respectively (see Table
4.1).   They also note that these values give a smaller
gap between MZT and DZT than those based on the survey of
the literature made by Erlenmeyer-Kimling and Jarvik
(1963).   The reader should recall that it was the latter
Jensen used to obtain his h^2 estimate of .80 and also that
the smaller the gap, the less the role of the genetic difference between monozygotic and dyzygotic and the lower
the h^2 estimate.   Loehlin and Nichols assume that the
differing values are due to differing cirteria, i.e. that
Erlenmeyer-Kimling and Jarvik included studies involving
only one kind of twin or having very small samples;   they
point out that this makes meaningful comparison of the MZT
and DZT samples difficult.   However, they allow for the
possibility of a discrepancy in the studies located in the
literature. (45)

Now let us take the list compiled by Loehlin and
Nichols, eliminate the Burt data (as surely we must) and
use the appropriate formula for estimating the heritability of IQ (given on p. 137).   We get the following results: using the median values of the 16 studies, h^2 =
.53; using values obtained by weighted averages, h^2 =
.51.   I do not wish to rest my case on the studies done
by Loehlin and Nichols themselves, thanks to the reasons
given above, but it may be of some interest that their
results match our composite data almost exactly, both for
the values of the intraclass correlation coefficients and
for h^2 (as computed by the author) - see Table 4.2.

The reader must be warned that these h^2 estimates have
not been adjusted for test error or differences between
sample variance and the larger population variance;   these

TABLE 4.1 Indentical- and fraternal-twin correlations on measures of general ability in various twin studies. Studies with less than 25 pairs in each group not included

Test	Correlations		Pairs		Source
	MZT	DZT	MZT	DZT	
National and Multi-Mental	.85	.26	45	57	Wingfield and Sandiford (1928)
Otis	.84	.47	65	96	Herrman and Hogben (1933)
Binet	.88	.90	34	28	Stocks (1933)
Binet and Otis	.92	.63	50	50	Newman, Freeman and Holzinger (1937)
I-Test	.87	.55	36	71	Husen (1947)
Simplex and C-Test	.88	.72	128	141	Wictorin (1952)
Intelligence factor	.76	.44	26	26	Blewett (1954)
JPQ-12	.62	.28	52	32	Cattell, Blewett and Beloff (1955)
I-Test	.90	.70	215	416	Husen (1959)
Otis	.83	.59	34	34	Gottesman (1963)
Various group tests	.94	.55	95	127	Burt (1966)
PMA IQ	.79	.45	33	30	Koch (1966)
Vocabulary composite	.83	.66	85	135	Huntley (1966)
PMA total score	.88	.67	123	75	Loehlin and Vandenberg (1968)
General-ability factor	.80	.48	337	156	Schoenfeldt (1968)
ITPA total	.90	.62	28	33	Mittler (1969)
Tanaka B	.81	.66	81	32	Kamitake (1971)
Median of above	.85	.59			

TABLE 4.2   Author's h^2 estimates based on Loehlin and
Nichols data, Burt omitted, h^2 unadjusted

| | Correlations | | Pairs | | | |
	MZT	DZT	MZT	DZT	Gap	h^2
16 Studies – medians	.845	.605	1372	1412	.24	.53
16 Studies – weighted ave.	.84	.61	1372	1412	.23	.51
NMSQT – 1962	.87	.63	687	482	.24	.53
NMSQT – 1965	.86	.62	1300	864	.24	.53

adjustments, particularly the latter, are more complex
for MZT/DZT than for MZA but the general tendency is to
boost the h^2 estimate.   For example, my estimate based on
the NMSQT – 1962 is .53 as compared to Jensen's estimate
(for the same study) of .56. (46)   And a rough calculation on my part indicates that he would move my .51/.53
based on composite data up by at least .05 to say .60.
(Recall that Jensen's .80 derives not from such adjustments but from selection of a different set of composite
data.) (47)   Once again, such adjustments signal another
round of the debate between various scholars as to whether
the rough estimates are already inflated and should, if
anything, be lowered.   Take the NMSQT – 1962: we can
argue that the fact that its sample is drawn disproportionately from students who enjoy favourable environments
means that it does not measure the full range of environmental effects; and that therefore, the nature of its
sample inflates the h^2 estimate.   On the other hand, we
could argue that the test in question measures not only IQ
but also academic achievement; and that since the latter
is more influenced by environment than IQ, it overesti-
mates the effect of environmental factors.

As for the general method of estimating h^2 by way of

MZT/DZT studies, it is sometimes argued that its key methodological assumption is incorrect.   The method assumes,
as we have seen, that twin and co-twin are no more similar
in environment (in ways relevant to IQ) for monozygotic
twins than for dizygotic twins.   If they are more similar, this of course would inflate the h^2 estimate.   The
heritability estimate is based on the notion that the gap
between the correlations for MZT and DZT derives purely
from the fact that the former have more genes in common
(all their genes as compared to approximately half).   If
MZT also have more in common in terms of environment, then
the gap between MZT and DZT is a measure of more shared
genes plus more shared environment; and the h^2 estimate
is attributing to genes their influence plus part of what
properly belongs to environment as well.   This problem of
'overlap' is called the problem of covariance in the methodology of h^2 studies.   It will be recalled that it also
plagued our MZA studies: we had reason to believe that
the 'separated' twins were not only more alike genetically
than random individuals but also more alike environmentally (thanks to being raised by relatives).   And many feel
that this problem of covariance runs through all of the
methods we use to estimate the heritability of IQ.

    Critics of MZT/DZT studies present a wide range of
sociological evidence to the effect that identical twins
have more similar environments than fraternal twins.   It
is generally agreed that: twin and co-twin are more
likely to feel closely attached to one another, study
together, have the same friends, spend time together, and
be separated less often; they are more likely to be in
the same classroom and the same school; and their parents
are more likely to report that they were dressed the same
and treated similarly.   The key question is whether these

greater similarities in environment operate as a causal
factor so as to promote greater similarity in IQ.   I
believe that there is one discrepancy in the data which
makes an affirmative answer likely.   If the reader turns
back to Tables 4.1 and 4.2, he will see that the data on
fraternal twins raised together suggests an intraclass
correlation coefficient of about .60.   Now the ICC for
full siblings raised together is considerably less than
that, for example, the Erlenmeyer-Kimling and Jarvik data
used by Jensen gives a median value of .49 for 35 studies.
David Fulker has argued that this value is too low, that
it reflects the fact that siblings have often been tested
at different ages and under different conditions, which
would of course make them seem less alike for IQ than they
really are.   We do not know what value better studies
will give but I suspect that it will not go above .54,
based on the fact that the more recent, careful study of
Higgins et al. (1962) raises the ICC only slightly, from
.49 to .52.   If my guess is correct, there is a real difference between the ICCs for fraternal twins and full siblings raised together of about .06 (.60 - .54 = .06). (48)

The significance of a higher correlation for dizygotic
twins raised together (DZT) than for full siblings raised
together (FST) is that the former are no more alike in
terms of shared genes than the latter.   Therefore, if
they are more alike in terms of IQ, this would seem to reflect the impact of a greater similarity of environment.
Recall that monozygotic twins raised together (MZT) have
an even greater similarity of environment.   The fact that
the enhanced similarity of DZT over FST has a causal
effect on IQ does not prove that the enhanced similarity
of MZT over DZT has an additional causal effect;   but it
certainly makes this a viable hypothesis.   If the result

of these two factors were to inflate the gap between MZT
and DZT by even half of .06, by even as little as .03, we
would have to reduce our h^2 estimates by .07 to compensate.   This would just about match the usual raising of
unadjusted estimates for test error and atypical sample
variance - leaving my own estimate for h^2 at about .50.

On the other side of the ledger stands Loehlin and
Nichols's analysis of performance on sub-tests in the
second NMSQT study.   They agree that MZT have a greater
environmental similarity in certain respects than DZT but
they are sceptical about the impact of these differences
on IQ.   They selected out six measures of having had different experiences and correlated them with performance on
five ability/academic achievement subtests: different experiences appeared to have only a slight effect in terms
of differential performance for DZTs;   and the scores of
MZTs were actually more alike for those who had had more
different experiences! (49)   They also explored the hypothesis that it is not so much greater similarity of experience (dressed alike, same teacher, same school), but
rather greater identification with one another by twin and
co-twin that might count.   The theory is that MZTs are
more likely to want to be like one another and have the
same aspirations and interests, while DZTs (like many siblings) develop a greater sense of difference or rivalry
and attempt to contrast themselves;   the term used for the
impact of a greater sense of identification is the 'assim-
ilation effect'.   Loehlin and Nichols did find an assimi-
lation effect among MZTs but a modest one;   it was strong-
est on the science and mathematics subtests. (50)

Note that the findings of Loehlin and Nichols relate
only to the impact of whatever environmental differences
exist within the class of twins, say whatever differences

separate MZT from DZT.   And they have no direct relevance
to the impact of whatever environmental differences exist
between twins in general and singletons, that is, between
twins in general and the larger population.   I make this
point because sheer uniformity of environment within a
class will raise h^2 estimates; we learned this when we
read Lewontin, that is, the more uniform the environment,
the less it can account for differences in IQ.   Let us
imagine that the greater similarity of environment for MZT
over DZT is trivial as a causal factor; but that the
greater similarity for both sorts of twins taken together
over singletons is significant.   This would mean that
twins in general were an atypical sub-population with a
greater uniformity of environment than the larger population they are supposed to represent and therefore, MZT-DZT
studies would give us inflated h^2 estimates.   The above
would also mean that corrections for lower total variance
in our samples than we find in the larger population might
be inappropriate: it might be due to the absence of part
of the environmental portion of variance.   The general
reader will have to take on faith that the formula for
MZT-DZT studies is sensitive (in terms of a greater gap
between the ICCs of MZT and DZT) to uniformity of environment for twins in general, even when there is no greater
relevant uniformity for monozygotic twins.   (Those who
wish to pursue the matter further can reflect on the fact
that the ICCs can be crudely represented as follows:

$$ICC\text{-}MZT = \frac{2H + E}{2H + E + e} \text{ and } ICC\text{-}DZT = \frac{H + E}{2H + E + e}$$

Now imagine either E or e or both eliminated from both
equations.   The gap between the ICCs will increase.)

   The best evidence for twins in general as a sub-population with unusual uniformity of environment has already
been identified, the gap between the ICCs of fraternal

twins and full siblings;   and therefore, the day when
these values will be 'settled' is awaited with interest.

Studies of MZT/DZT may provide the 'least ambiguous' basis
for heritability estimates, but what of the other data on
which such estimates are sometimes based, namely: comparisons across other kinship categories (e.g. comparing
siblings and unrelated children reared in the same home)
and adoption studies (e.g. simply comparing unrelated
children raised together on the theory that they are uncorrelated for genes).   As mentioned above, all of these
research designs pose the problem of co-variance, our inability to adequately separate genetic and environmental
factors.   In order to make a start in dealing with this
problem, Christopher Jencks used path analysis which is an
approach that assumes certain causal sequences among factors: it thereby allows for a variety of estimates for
the extent to which genes and environment 'overlap' in
their effects on IQ variance, which is to say we can
attempt to estimate gene-environment covariance.   Jencks
restricted himself to studies using the Stanford-Binet and
samples drawn from the US population (as the most reliable
data and the most relevant).   He found that a variety of
values would fit a variety of data but advanced as his
'best guess' the following: $h^2 = .45$, $e^2 = .35$ (e^2 here
includes both between- and within-family environment), and
covariance = .20;   the covariance component as Jencks de-
fines it is an entirely environmental component, merely
one which happens to be correlated with genotype.   He
estimates his standard error at .10 and concludes that
'the chances are two out of three that the heritability of
IQ scores ... is between .35 and .55', that is,
.45±.10. (51)

Jencks's use of path analysis has not stood unchallen-
ged.   Loehlin et al. (1975) altered one of his path dia-
grams, altered his data slightly, and derived an h^2 of
.60.   On the other hand, Loehlin and another group of co-
workers have analysed data from the Texas Adoption Project
and have advanced a tentative h^2 estimate of .45 to .53
(with between-families environment contributing from .24
to .29 of total variance).   They emphasize features of
this data which make it far more suitable for heritability
estimates than earlier adoption studies and note that it
suggests correlations similar to those found in four other
adoption studies all done since 1975. (52)   The Honolulu
group of Rao, Morton and Yee have also pioneered the use
of path analysis, and in 1976 they derived values of .67
for children and .21 for adults. (53)   It is difficult to
tell whether or not to take this difference seriously.
If we did, it would raise a host of questions such as:
what of those studies that have estimated h^2 from samples
with a wide range of ages, e.g. Shields tested subjects
ranging from 8 years of age to 59; and what values
(childhood or adulthood) are we to use in applying h^2
estimates to the IQ gap between black and white?   I refer
to Jensen's attempt to use them to indicate that if the IQ
gap were environmental, then the average black environment
would have to be an impossible number of standard deviations (4.48 SDs) below the average white environment.
Goldberger has composed a searching critique of the Honolulu group in which he alleges: errors which bias their
calculations and render their models inapplicable, using
sample sizes as low as 19 (MZA) to resolve fundamental
problems, combining samples of same-sex fraternal twins
and ordinary siblings, and selecting data so as to avoid
an anomaly in their general model. (54)

Path analysis has brought us no closer to consensus than traditional methods.   It has not made good on its promise to help us separate the effects of shared genes and shared environment when these two appear to accompany one another.   As one researcher has remarked, (55) the situation calls for an analogy: Voltaire describes a man who killed swine with a mixture of prayer and arsenic;   if prayer were always accompanied by arsenic, so that we could never separate the two, we would never be able to solve the problem of causality.   If anyone is interested in my own 'best guess' about the heritability of IQ, I suspect that we may someday agree on values between .45 and .55 for white Americans and between .40 and .50 for black Americans (based less on the few contradictory studies that have been done on blacks than on the hypothesis that they are exposed to a wider range of environmental effects than whites).   However, I assume it is clear that the drift of the last half of this chapter has not been to obtain values but to underline that this whole area of research is in flux and that its methodology is crude;   and that the possibility of a value between .40 and .60, the target for someone who wants to weaken Jensen's steel chain of ideas, is a very open possibility indeed.

Presumably it is also now clear why I posited a range of values for the calculations used in Chapter 3, the calculations relevant to an interpretation of Eyferth's data on occupation children in Germany.   These were, it will be recalled, h^2 estimates ranging from .45 to .80 and corresponding values for h^2 narrow ranging from .40 to .70.

Chapter 5

A PROBLEM FOR BLACKS

We can show that the IQ gap between black and white is environmental without isolating the specific environmental factors at work. However, in order to avoid a clash between direct evidence and the indirect evidence, we must search for semi-blindfolds: potent environmental factors at work in the black community, preferably uncorrelated with SES (socio-economic status), and with a greater degree of uniformity than factors like SES. Having said this, I want to tell the reader what to expect. I do intend to identify a number of variables and put them forward as likely candidates; but some of them are highly general and others clearly work through mediating variables. I will be much more concerned with identifying promising areas which should be explored, slowly and carefully, in our research over the next few decades. There is no reason to be apologetic: the social sciences have not yet brought many complex problems of causality to a successful conclusion and the causes of intellectual development are complex. Our opponents have a tendency to demand a degree of success unparalleled elsewhere, but clearly such a demand is unjust.

Another point: the fact that we will be looking for factors uncorrelated with SES does not mean they will be

uncorrelated with other sociological criteria such as
race, sex and cultural traditions.   In the social sciences, positing psychological factors detached from sociology is the last refuge of a scoundrel.

I will try to track down some important environmental
variables by following a trail of evidence which leads
from the influence of IQ as an environmental variable,
through the importance of verbal interaction between
parent and child, towards recent advances in special education.   The studies analysed will include E.W. and S.C.
Reed on mental retardation, Willerman et al. on parents of
interracial children, Harrell et al. on the use of dietary
supplements, Barbara Tizard on the quality of talk within
residential nurseries, and the most recent developments in
Rick Heber's Milwaukee Project.
    What of IQ itself as an environmental factor?   I refer
of course to the influence that parental IQ has on the
child's IQ.   Ever since Binet invented his tests a debate
has raged between environmentalists and hereditarians.
The herediatarians argue that IQ scores signal the quality
of the parents' genotypes for IQ; and that parental IQ
influences the child primarily through the flow of genes
from parent to child with the impact of parental IQ on the
quality of the child's environment a minor factor.   The
environmentalists rarely deny a genetic factor but they
argue that the environmental impact of parental IQ is very
great.   They argue that the carry-over of low IQ from
generation to generation sometimes reflects no more than a
causal sequence of below-standard home environment, academic failure, limited opportunities, a new below-standard
home environment, and so forth.   This debate has often
seemed hopelessly unresolvable: how can we possibly dis-

entangle parental IQ as an index of environmental quality
from parental IQ as a measure of genetic quality?   The
record of our attempts to measure the heritability of IQ
is unlikely to encourage optimism.

In 1965 Elizabeth and Sheldon Reed published a study of
mental retardation on behalf of the Minnesota Human Genetics League.   The Reeds concluded that genetic factors
were more important than environmental ones as a cause of
retardation and they are enthusiastic advocates of eugenics as a solution to the problem.   Indeed, they emphasize
that since sterilization will be effective in either case,
it is irrelevant whether the basis of the trait is genetic
or environmental.   They set their standard for mental retardation at an IQ of below 70, note that 90 per cent of
retarded persons are functioning outside of institutions,
and urge an educational programme to encourage voluntary
acceptance of sterilization. (1)   The fact that this
would mean the sterilization of one-eighth of the total
population of black America is not mentioned.   Given the
Reeds' views, it is to their credit that their study includes data which, as they say, can be seized upon as evidence of environmental influence on intellectual development.

The Reeds compared 153 children born of unions in which
the mother was normal and the father retarded with 107
children born of unions in which the mother was retarded
and the father normal: the former had a mean IQ 8 points
above the mean of the latter. (2)   Let us make two
assumptions, both of which will be questioned in a moment:
(1) that the genetic advantage of having a normal rather
than a retarded mother is equivalent to the genetic advantage of having a normal rather than a retarded father;
(2) that the mean IQs of the two parental combinations, as

represented in the Reeds' sample, were equivalent - that
is, that normal mother + retarded father equalled, say,
an average IQ of 80 and that the reverse combination also
equalled 80.   Working with those assumptions, the 8-point
difference between the mean IQs of the offspring stands as
a measure of an environmental difference;   it measures the
environmental advantage of having a mother with an IQ over
90 rather than a mother with an IQ below 70.   Indeed it
underestimates that advantage in that if the father's IQ
exercises any influence whatsoever on the child, the
normal mother's IQ had to overcome the disadvantageous
influence of a retarded father.   Which is to say that the
8 points would measure this: the environmental advantage
of 90+ mother over 70- mother minus the advantage of 90+
father over 70- father.

   Now for the above assumptions.   Against the first
assumption, it has been argued that when a female is retarded she is likely to have a stronger genetic predisposition to mental retardation than a male.   It seems
that females have a greater resistance than males to the
influence of a deleterious environment, as evidenced by a
higher incidence among males of a wide range of childhood
physical and emotional disorders.   When Lemkau and Imre
surveyed the entire adult population of a county in Maryland, they found that 1.69 per cent of white males scored
an IQ below 70 as compared to 1.02 per cent of white females.   If the greater resistance of females extends to
environmental factors which encourage mental retardation,
this suggests the following difference between the sexes:
women who are retarded, being more resistant to environmental influences, have a greater genetic proclivity;
while men who are retarded, being more susceptible to a
deleterious environment, have a lesser genetic proclivity.

In other words, a retarded mother may be someone whose
genes have dictated her own IQ to an unusual degree, a
degree beyond what occurs in the case of a retarded father
or in the case of a normal parent of either sex; and presumably her genes would have an unusual influence on the
IQ of her offspring.   And this last would mean something
unfortunate for our research design: the children of the
normal mother-retarded father combination would have both
a genetic and an environmental advantage over the children
of the retarded mother-normal father combination.   The 8-
point difference between the mean IQs of the offspring
could not be counted as measuring a purely environmental
advantage.

I know of no studies that would allow us to estimate
the size of the unusual genetic predisposition of female
retardates (towards mental retardation) on the basis of
data.   The best I can do, as before when faced with such
difficulties, is attempt to be generous enough to achieve
some credibility.   To say that a retarded mother's genes
have a greater influence over the IQ of her offspring is
to say that her own IQ is more genetically transmissible:
and that means we must posit a higher estimate for h^2
narrow for the retarded mother-normal father combination
than for the reverse combination.   Let us say that the
latter has an h^2 narrow of .55 and the former has .65, a
difference of .10; this is quite a large difference when
we take into account that the unusual 'genetic potency' of
the retarded mother is being diluted by her not unusual
mate.   In effect, it assumes that the unusual genetic
predisposition of female retardates (their predisposition
over and above that of male retardates) lowers their own
IQs by a full 7 points.   It is worth noting that we have
to subtract only 3 points from our criterion for mental

retardation to get equal percentages of men and women, that is, following Lemkau and Imre   the percentage of men under 67 equals the percentage of women under 70. (3)

In order to use values for h^2 narrow, we need data about the actual IQs of the parents and this brings us to our second assumption, that the mean IQs of the two parental combinations were equivalent.   Fortunately, the Reeds had parental IQ data for about half of their 260 children. Taking these 131 we find: 82 children for whom the mean maternal IQ was 92 and the paternal was 62;   and 49 children for whom the mean maternal IQ was 63 and the paternal 98.   Which is to say that the second group of children, those with retarded mothers and normal fathers, actually had an advantage in terms of the mean IQ of their parents, an advantage of 3.5 points (80.5 as compared to 77.0). This genetic advantage would almost exactly offset the hypothesized genetic disadvantage of having retarded mothers - using the usual formula, both groups of children would be expected to have a mean IQ of 87.   The calculation is no better than the h^2 narrow values it assumes and these, of course, were invented for the purpose.   Despite this, it serves to show that the hypothesized unusual genetic potency of retarded mothers would have to be very great, I would say implausibly great, to unbalance the research design.   As for the results, within the sample of 131 children, once again it was the children with the normal mothers who had the higher mean, the gap being the same 8 points. (4)   We are therefore left with our old estimate intact, our estimate that children with normal mothers enjoy an 8-point environmental advantage.   But now we can be more precise about what those points measure: the environmental advantage of a maternal IQ of 92 over one of 63 minus the advantage of a paternal IQ of 98 over one of 62.

As we said a few pages ago, the above must give an under-estimate of maternal IQ as an environmental factor, unless one assumes that the paternal IQ is literally a null factor.   For example, if the above paternal IQ gap is worth even 2 points, the maternal gap would be worth 10 points.   Moreover, SES is much more highly correlated with the IQ of the father than the mother and therefore, the children with normal mothers and retarded fathers almost certainly had an added environmental disadvantage to overcome.   No doubt some of the effects of socio-economic status have already been taken into account, for the father's influence on his child's IQ would be partially exercised through his influence on his family's SES. Still a paternal gap of 36 IQ points should signal a very large gap in terms of SES and it is unlikely that the latter makes no independent contribution.   The normal mother is after all attempting to raise her children both with a less intelligent spouse to help her and with fewer middle-class amenities available, as compared to the sub-normal mother.   Allowing even a point or two for SES as an additional factor would give an estimate of 11 to 12 points as the total environmental advantage a child enjoys from having a normal mother rather than one 30 points below normal.

In the fifteen years since the Reeds published their data no one has attempted to collect similar data.   At times there seems to be a malevolent invisible hand at work in this area which guarantees that really important research, even research relatively easy to do, will never be replicated.   As for the future, what we need are studies comparing groups of children whose mothers have an IQ of 100 and whose fathers have an IQ of 85 with children for whom the reverse situation holds.   Studies of this

sort would have even greater value in terms of both methodology and relevance: since they would deal with subjects
clearly in the normal range of IQ scores, the complication
of the presence of female retardates would rarely arise;
and at any rate, we cannot assume that the environmental
impact of a mother 15 points below the mean will bear a
linear relationship to that of a mother 30 points below.
However, we face a complication largely absent when the
Reeds did their study.   In recent years, the traditional
division of labour between men and women in terms of child
rearing has begun to erode, and therefore we would have to
differentiate couples in which the mother assumed primary
responsibility from those in which father and mother had
equal contact with their pre-school children.   Setting
aside such complications, if there were even a modest difference in favour of the mother 100-father 85 group, this
would be of great interest.   For example, assume a difference of 3.5 points plus data proving a large disadvantage in terms of SES.   Allowing, say, 1.5 points for the
combined impact of the paternal IQ-SES disadvantage would
lead to the following conclusion: that even within white
America, the environmental advantage of a maternal IQ of
100 rather than a maternal IQ of 85 would be approximately
5 points.

Even the accumulation of such data would leave important questions unanswered.   First, maternal IQ has no
direct impact on the quality of the child's environment
but works through mediating causal factors.   It is not
the activity of a mother taking an IQ test and scoring 100
which confers quality on the child's environment;   presumably, as compared to a mother with a lower IQ, she is
likely to surround the infant with a higher quality of
verbal interaction and to have enjoyed better diet and

medical care during pregnancy.   But as yet we have no
right to do more than speculate about the identity of the
mediating causal factors.   Second, as the last sentence
implies, we do not even know the balance between pre-natal
and post-natal factors.   And third, we do not know the
extent to which the relevant variables, whatever they may
be, differentiate white and black in America.

There has been one important attempt to establish
whether or not there is an environmental difference between the races without identifying the relevant mediating
variables, namely, the papers published by Willerman,
Naylor and Myrianthopoulos in 1970 and 1974.   The National Institute of Health has been co-ordinating a massive
study of the offspring of approximately 42,000 women who
registered during pregnancy at 12 hospitals scattered
across the United States.   The children are routinely
tested at various intervals up to the age of 8.   At 8
months they were tested with a research version of the
Bayley Scale of Mental Development, at age 4 they were
tested with the abbreviated version of the Stanford-Binet
(Form L-M).   In the data collected, Willerman et al.
found IQ scores for 129 interracial children, 101 of whom
had white mothers and black fathers, 28 black mothers and
white fathers.   The latter sample size is of course quite
small.   If the parents in each category were typical of
the larger populations they represent, we would get an
estimate of great interest: the environmental advantage
of having a white mother rather than a black mother minus
the advantage of having a white father rather than a black
father, assuming that the advantages run in the direction
described.   Willerman et al. found that at age 4, the
mother-white children had a mean IQ 8.67 points above that
of the mother-black children. (5)

The best way to establish whether each category of
parent is typical of its larger population would be to
calculate the mean IQs of the parents and make the relevant comparisons.   But we have no data on the parental
IQs and must make do with information about the number of
years of school completed.   Unfortunately Willerman et
al. do not give us the ages of the parents, but the fact
they are all of child-bearing age suggests a comparison
with 1970 census data for the age groups 25-34 or 25-44
(it makes no real difference which we choose). (6)   We
find that the black fathers are almost exactly typical of
black males of the relevant ages.   The black mothers and
white mothers also pose little problem: both groups are
one year plus below their respective population means but
the two deficits are comparable, being within .5 of a
school year of one another;   it is likely that their circumstances (almost half of them are unwed mothers) rather
than genes have limited their educational attainments.
The white fathers are another matter: they are a full two
years of schooling below the mean of the larger population
of white males.   Therefore, it can be argued that the
black mother-white father combination has a lower genetic
value for IQ than the white mother-black father combination.   And this would mean that some of our 8.67 point
gap is due to genes rather than to the environmental advantage afforded by a white mother.

As usual, rather than making no estimate at all, I
prefer to make a rough one rendered more credible by being
generous to the hereditarian.   A generous allowance for
the educational deficit of the white fathers would be an
IQ deficit of 7 points, giving them a mean IQ of 93.
This would lower the black mother-white father combination's average by 3.5 points;   using a Jensen-level value

for h^2 narrow (.70), we would anticipate that the effect on the offspring would be 2.45 points.   Thus taking 2.45 from 8.67, we get an estimate of 6 plus IQ points as the environmental advantage of having a white mother rather than a black mother.   In fact such an estimate must be a gross underestimate.   We have considered whether or not the mothers in question are typical of their larger populations in genetic terms, but not whether their environmental circumstances are typical.   Under normal conditions, white mothers are fully integrated into the fabric of white culture and enjoy to the full whatever advantages that situation confers over functioning within black culture.   In this case, the fact that both white and black mothers are functioning in an interracial situation has clearly acted as a leveller: for example, there is no significant difference between the two parental combinations in terms of SES.   Normally the white mother would have the advantage of raising her children in a socioeconomic setting from 1.0 to 1.3 standard deviations above that enjoyed by a black mother.

Another example: Willerman's sample gives us 39.3 per cent of the black mothers unwed and 50.5 per cent of the white mothers unwed.   This is typical for blacks (40 per cent of black children are being raised by women alone) but not at all typical of whites (for whom the figure is 12 per cent). (7)   If we weighted Willerman's data in terms of the percentages given above for the general populations, the gap between white-mother children and black-mother children would rise from 8.67 IQ points to a full 11 points.   It must be said that such a procedure is very crude;   as Meehl has pointed out, 'matching' as a procedure for dealing with 'nuisance variables' raises many methodological problems. (8)   Weighting the white-mother

group in favour of married couples might well raise the
educational level of the parents and therefore their genetic value.   On the other hand, not to weight the data is
to ignore the social realities of the fact that the children being studied are of mixed race.   In America, half-
black children are socially classified as black: thus the
unwed white mothers in Willerman's sample are in the unusual position of raising a child who is both illegitimate
and black.   The excess number of this unusual sort of
unwed white mother may entail a greater environmental
deficit than would be entailed by an equal excess of the
usual kind.   Remember the Scarr and Weinberg adoption
study, the pathetic fact that almost all of the half-black
children given up for adoption were given up by white
mothers.   These mothers must suffer from considerable
ambivalence and stress.

These are weaknesses in the Willerman study which can
be overcome only by replication.   First, there is the
lack of IQ data on the parents.   Second, the data on the
black-mother children contains an apparent anomaly: the
mean IQ for males is almost 19 points below the mean IQ
for females.   Later on I will argue that black males
suffer from a greater environmental disadvantage than
black females but I can offer no explanation for a difference as large as this.   The small number of black-mother
children in Willerman's sample (11 males and 17 females)
takes on added significance.   Finally, since all of these
studies measure the differential impact of mother and
father, we must have some information on the allocation of
child-rearing responsibilities between the parents, at
least where both parents are present.

The replication of Willerman et al. would tell us more
about environmental differences between the races.   How-

ever, as we have implied, such studies cannot solve our
other problems, namely, the identity of the mediating
variables which link mother and child and the balance between pre-natal and post-natal factors.   Willerman et al.
hypothesize that post-natal factors are operative on the
grounds that while the mother-black children had the lower
mean IQ at 4 years, they were actually superior on the
Bayley Scales of Infant Development at 8 months. (9)   The
latter fact is of interest but the question of the significance of mental tests given at so early an age is much
debated.

There are three important studies which attempt either to
identify mediating variables or to separate pre-natal and
post-natal influences.   Perhaps the reader will recall
the research published in 1956 by Harrell, Woodyard and
Gates (see Chapter 3).   They attempted to assess the
effects of maternal diet during pregnancy on the offspring's IQ and we will now examine their research in
greater detail.

Harrell et al. gave dietary supplements during pregnancy to 1,200 welfare mothers in Norfolk, Virginia of
whom 80 per cent were black.   At age 4, 370 children were
available for testing, the attrition being due mainly to
the failure to achieve a viable child at term, deaths and
departure from the Norfolk area (by far the largest
factor).   On the Revised Stanford-Binet (form L):   91
children whose mothers had received thiamine, riboflavin,
niacinamide and iron had a mean IQ 8.1 points above the
placebo group;   and 181 children whose mothers had received thiamine or ascorbic acid alone were 4.3 points
above.   They attempted the same experiment with 1,200
mothers from a very poor county (Leslie County) in

Kentucky, all of whom were white.   Here the population
was less transient and 811 children were tested at the age
of 3:   there were no significant differences between those
whose mothers had received dietary supplements and the
placebo group. (10)   Taking the results of these two experiments together we can interpret them in a number of
ways: (1) they contradict one another and therefore, both
are doubtful;   (2) they complement one another, showing
that even poor whites have an advantage over poor blacks
in terms of the adequacy of their usual or unsupplemented
diet;   (3) they suggest that there is a difference between
white and black in regard to nutritional needs which goes
beyond the environmental.

Harrell et al. provide some data which allows us to
explore the second interpretation.   There were some minor
differences between the Virginia and Kentucky groups:
travel problems caused by the poor roads in rural Kentucky
made it more difficult to ensure that the dietary supplements were always taken by the mothers involved;   the mean
duration of supplementation was less for the Kentucky
group, 114 days as compared to 134 days.   The authors
also emphasize some factors that undoubtedly limited the
effect of dietary improvement on both groups.   As indicated, the duration of supplementation was no more than $4\frac{1}{2}$
months, that is, about half of the term of pregnancy.   It
occurred at variable times during pregnancy, not necessarily during the period of rapid brain development.   And
there were no supplements given to the children themselves
during their first two years of life, a time when the central nervous system continus to develop.   However, the
major difference between the Virginia and Kentucky groups
was in the quality of their usual or unsupplemented diet,
a crucial factor in that only if the usual diet is defi-

cient, would we expect supplements to have much effect.
The researchers attempted to get dietary histories by way
of interview, but had to abandon this in the face of
demonstrated gross fabrication by the (mostly) blacks in
Virginia and the extraordinary reluctance of whites in
Kentucky to be questioned.   Their observations were as
follows: that the diet of the Virginia group was poor and
limited;   that the diet of the Kentucky group was plain
but not conspicuously inadequate.   The researchers noted
that in Kentucky there was a daily use of pork of fowl,
succulent vegetables and fruits, both fresh and home pre-
served, and they conclude that there was a significantly
higher intake of ascorbic acid, vitamin A and vitamins of
the B complex in Kentucky than in Virginia. (11)

Even if these observations are correct, we cannot use
them to generalize about dietary differences between poor
blacks and poor whites in America.   The poor whites above
were in a rural area and in urban areas, where pigs and
chickens are likely to be absent, the white poor and the
black poor may have a similar diet.   It is a pity that
the 80 per cent blacks and the 20 per cent whites in the
Norfolk, Virginia, sample were not compared to one another
either as to diet or as to the effects of dietary supplementation on the IQ of the offspring.   Moreover, we do
not know what proportion of black Americans in general
suffers from dietary deficiencies similar to those of
black mothers on welfare in Norfolk.   It is true that
one-third of all black children in America today are with
mothers who receive welfare under the aid to broken families programme, (12) but some of these may well be better
off nutritionally than their Norfolk counterparts.

This brings us back to the variety of interpretations
which can be placed on the results of Harrell et al.   The

difference between the reactions of mostly blacks in Virginia and whites in Kentucky to dietary supplements is so
striking that we must wonder whether environmental factors
are entirely responsible: assume that further research on
wider populations were to show the same striking difference between the races even when samples were matched for
adequacy of diet.   We would then have to entertain the
possibility of a genotype X environment interaction.
This term refers to a phenomenon observed in laboratory
animals, namely: in a certain shared environment, populations A and B each attain a certain level of performance;
then in a different shared environment, we get a much more
dramatic alteration in performance from population A than
we do from B.   For example, Cooper and Zubek selectively
bred two strains of rats for 'brightness' and 'dullness'
respectively in terms of finding their way through a maze.
Although the 'bright' strain easily outperformed the
'dull' when both were reared in a normal laboratory environment, the two did equally well when reared in a restricted environment and the 'bright' strain did only marginally better when both had enjoyed an enriched environment.
In Henderson's experiments with six inbred strains of
mice, strain A/J lagged behind strain C3H when both were
in a standard environment but forged far ahead in an enriched environment.   In sum, genotype X environment
interaction exists when different genotypes respond in
different ways to the same environmental factors.

The implication is obvious: we know that the races
differ in their reactions to certain foods.   Over 70 per
cent of American blacks develop an intolerance for the
lactose in milk as compared to 8-15 per cent among whites,
an intolerance which causes abdominal pain and diarrhoea
and which begins in blacks sometimes as early as the first

six months, often during the first four years, sometimes later. (13)   It may be that black and white differ in terms of their nutritional requirements or in terms of their optimum intake of vitamins; if so, dietary supplements which have a marked effect on black IQ and the development of the central nervous system might have little or no effect on whites. Even if the discovery of such an interaction only closed the overall IQ gap between black and white by a few points, it might have a very significant impact on the academic performance of, say, the lower third of the US black population. As this last sentence indicates, I am not inclined to rest my case for black equality on speculation about a radical genotype X environment interaction effect. As the reader knows from Chapter 3, I think it unnecessary to concede that blacks would have a mean IQ less than whites if both races were equally distributed over the range of environments which exist in America today. To concede that black performance would be worse under those conditions and speculate that the performance of the races would be reversed if only great unnamed environmental changes were to occur, such a line of argument smacks of desperation. However, my reservations about genotype X environment interaction do not extend to ignoring the possibility of the sort envisaged above, a verifiable interaction of a highly specific kind.

Let us return to the post-natal environment, our task of identifying mediating variables therein, and the research of Barbara Tizard and her associates, particularly their study of the intellectual development of 85 children in long-stay residential nurseries in England (1972). Tizard et al. studied 13 nursery groups from 11 nurseries. They found all of these nurseries very different from the

grim foundling houses of an earlier era.   They were characterized by a high standard of physical care for the
children and children were divided into small groups, each
with its own suite of bedroom, bathroom and living room,
each with its own nurse and assistant nurse.   The rooms
were furnished in homelike style and plentifully supplied
with toys and books; outside there was usually a large
garden and play equipment.   In all of the nurseries,
children over 3 attended a play group, where sand, paint,
water and so forth were available, and the children were
always read to at least once a day.   All of the nurseries
were generously staffed by most standards and the major
difference between the best and the worst was whether one
or two nurses were in continuous contact with each group
of children.   All nurseries had long waiting lists of
applicants for staff posts and staff turnover was relatively low.   The backgrounds of staff from nursery to
nursery were similar: all were studying for, or had
achieved, their nurse's diploma, all were the daughters of
skilled workers or small shopkeepers, and all had left
school at 15 or 16 with from zero to four 'O' levels.
Tizard et al. were clearly impressed by the standards that
prevailed and speculate that the environment provided is
in fact superior to many private homes. (14)

Despite these similarities, Tizard et al. suspected
that subtle differences between the nurseries in terms of
social organization might well affect the children's development.   They choose four criteria all of which they
suspected would affect the quality of interaction between
staff and children.   First, they gave each nursery group
a score based on the number of day-to-day decisions the
staff and children made for themselves.   The nurseries
differed in terms of whether the nurse attending the

children could decide to take them for a walk or turn on
the TV or whether the day's activities were timetabled
with departures requiring the permission of a matron.
The theory was that the greater the group's autonomy the
more stimulating the interaction between nurses and children, the more likely that there would be mutual interest
in one another, discussion, and active co-operation.
Second, each group was given a staff stability score based
on the number of trained nurses who had worked with the
group for at least a week in the past two years.   Third,
the mean age of the children in each group was calculated,
the theory being that young children were likely to benefit from the presence of older children.   And fourth, a
measure of the staff-child ratio was obtained for each
group by dividing the number of staff hours worked per
week by the number of children present.   They then gave
each nursery group a 'composite score' and ranked them
from one to thirteen.   They also divided the groups into
three categories: those more than one standard deviation
above the mean in terms of their composite score, those
within an SD of the mean, and those one SD or more below
the mean. (15)   The fact that some nursery groups were
one standard deviation below the mean does not contradict
the above assertion that differences between the groups
were not great.   The standard deviation is merely a
measure of whatever differences exist within a population
and if differences are small, it will be small.   The fact
that 3 of the 13 nursery groups were put in the lowest
category means little more than that they were ranked in
places 11, 12 and 13 in terms of composite scores.

   In order to measure the significance of the above environmental differences, Tizard et al. arranged for mental
tests to be given to 85 children divided among the 13 nur-

sery groups.   The children were aged from 24 to 59
months;   70 per cent had entered a residential nursery
before the age of 12 months, 86 per cent before 24 months,
and all had been resident for at least 6 months.   All 85
children were tested on the Reynell Verbal Comprehension
Scale and the Reynell Expressive Language Scale and 54
children aged 3 years and older took the Minnesota Non-
Verbal.   The testing was done by a clinical psychologist
who was not a part of the research team and who knew
nothing of their hypotheses.   As for whether the children
in various nursery groups differed not only environmentally but also for genotypes for IQ, Tizard et al. had not of
course randomly assigned them to groups, and therefore
could not ensure that genotypes were the same.   However,
they found no evidence of genetic bias: the occupations
of about two-thirds of the fathers were known and there
was no significant difference between the proportions of
manual and non-manual workers in the various groups;   the
occupations of all of the mothers were known and there was
no significant difference between the social class distributions for the best and the worst nurseries.   Essentially the children had been placed in whatever nursery had a
vacancy at the time. (16)

Tizard et al. compared the mean score (on each of the
three mental tests) of the children in each nursery group
with the 'composite score' they had assigned each nursery
group.   They emphasize that the correlation is high for
the Reynell Comprehension and low for the Minnesota Non-
Verbal, with the Reynell Expression in between. (17)
However, they also report the mean scores for children in
their three categories of nursery groups, those above-
average, average, and below-average in the composite score
rankings. (18)   If we merge the above-average and average

nursery groups so as to get adequate numbers (36 to 52
children on the various tests) and compare them to the
below-average nursery groups (15 to 27 children), we find
a noticeable difference on all three tests.   Children in
the better groups have a mean score advantage over those
in the below-average groups as follows: .71 standard deviation units on the Reynell Comprehension;   .65 SD units
on the Reynell Expression;   and .49 SD units on the Minnesota Non-Verbal.   If we converted the children's scores
into conventional IQ scores, this would amount to an advantage ranging from approximately 7 to 11 IQ points.
The mediating variables which appear to make this difference are of course quite common sense;   the reader will
not be surprised to find that children benefit from ini-
tiative, attention and continuity on the part of those who
care for them.   However, common sense does not help us to
quantify such variables or measure their impact.   Recall
that the standard of child care was good in all the nurseries compared: if such variables make a difference of 7
to 11 points within such a context, similar variables may
make a very great difference between black and white.   In
America, fully 25 per cent of black children are being
born out of wedlock to teenage mothers, as compared to 4
per cent for whites.   The gap in quality of child care
between black and white in America is likely to be much
greater than that existent in even the best and the worst
of Tizard's 13 nursery groups.

     Tizard et al. also made a more ambitious attempt to
measure mediating variables.   They hoped to show a correlation between the composite score of nursery groups and
the quality of staff talk to children, and then a correlation between the latter and the children's test scores.
Using systematic time-sampling observations, they deter-

mined such things as: how frequently the staff spoke to
the children and how frequently the child replied; the
proportion of informative talk ('That's not a sweet, it's
a piece of a puzzle') versus mere ritual talk ('That's
nice,' 'Aren't you clever,' 'Lucky boy'); the proportion
of commands with explanations versus commands without;
and the length and complexity of the sentences staff used.
They found significant correlations between the nursery
group's composite score and most of the above measures of
quality of staff talk.   On the other hand, correlations
between the latter and the children's test scores were
more ambiguous, there being a high correlation for the
Reynell Comprehension only. (19)   Tizard et al. note that
the differences between the nursery groups were small on a
number of indices: for example, the mean sentence length
was 4.75 words with a range from worst nursery group to
best of 3.72 to 5.50 words; and the range for percentage
of time spent in talking to children was from 36.8 per
cent to 61.5 per cent. (20)   They believe that the overall range of verbal quality was relatively narrow: it
will be recalled that the staff of all the nurseries were
remarkably similar in their social and educational backgrounds.

Despite the ambiguity of Tizard et al.'s attempt to
measure the quality of talk between adult and child, I see
no alternative but to apply similar techniques so as to
compare various classes and racial groups in America: if
the range of quality of adult-child talk is greater than
in Tizard's studies, then correlations between her indices
and IQ may emerge more clearly.   In saying this, I do not
mean to imply that verbal quality should be the only candidate for the role of mediating variable examined.
Martin Deutsch (1960) found that even lower-class white

children virtually all came from homes that offered books, organized meals, and activities and trips with parents. The lower-class black children were different: 50 per cent reported that they did not have a pencil or pen at home, over 50 per cent reported no books at home, only 30 per cent reported being kissed good-night (ages 9-12). (21)   And I do not mean to imply that we should ignore remote variables other than parental IQ: the absence of the father from the home cannot be a direct influence, clearly its influence is mediated by its effects on the child's environment, but nonetheless, there is evidence which suggests that it is of considerable significance. (22)   However, I do wish to say that whatever evidence we accumulate will not be conceded to be relevant if, as has been generally true up to now, we do not control for genetic factors.   Even assuming we find significant correlations between variables in the home environment such as verbal quality, books, etc., and the child's IQ, the hereditarian will say in reply: parents with superior IQs both speak with greater complexity and give their child better genes for IQ and the latter is by far the more important factor.   In this regard Barbara Tizard had an advantage thanks to studying children in an institutional setting, that is, although children were not placed in nursery groups at random, at least they were not being raised in private homes by those responsible for both their environmental and their genetic endowment.

The sort of research design needed is easier to describe than to realize in practice, but ideally we would: (1) pair families with one another where the mean IQ of the parents are the same but where, thanks to a 'mismatch' between maternal and paternal IQs, one mother has a higher IQ than the other; (2) see if we find a positive correla-

lation between maternal IQ and variables such as verbal
quality;   (3) see if we find a positive correlation between the latter and the child's IQ.   The point of number
(1) is of course to control for genetic factors.   If we
get the correlations described, we would have taken a
first step towards identifying variables which act media-
tors between parental IQ (as an environmental influence)
and the child's IQ.   We would of course have to do such
studies for both black and white America;   and also compare black and white homes to see what differences there
are between the races in terms of the variables identified.

Thus far we have spoken of identifying variables but
what of attempts to manipulate the factors which influence
IQ?   Most attempts in the area of 'compensatory education', such as the majority of projects undertaken under
the rubric of Project Head Start, have been so modest that
their effects could not help but be minimal;   typically
they did not begin until the child was 4 years old and
left the home environment untouched.   (Hunt and Kirk have
provided an excellent analysis of why Project Head Start
did not have more dramatic results.   This is not to say
that it did no good or that it should be terminated.
Bernard Brown has accumulated evidence in favour of long-
term benefits to the children involved, such as a reduced
percentage of children being placed in special education
classes or being retained in grade. (23))   In 1967, Professor Rick Heber and his associates at the University of
Wisconsin began a far more ambitious programme, namely the
Milwaukee Project.   Heber was primarily concerned about
those who are classified as mentally retarded but who exhibit no identifiable gross pathology of the central nervous system;   about 80 per cent of those with IQs below 75

exhibit no such pathology. He was convinced that compensatory education in such cases could be successful only if
it began at an early age, focused on language and cogni-
tion, and attempted to rehabilitate the whole family.
Therefore he took the following steps: children entered
his programme at from 3 to 6 months; they spent from 8.45
a.m. to 4.00 p.m. five days a week at learning centres in
which they enjoyed a comprehensive programme designed to
promote cognitive-language, social-emotional and percep-
tual-motor development; the staff were carefully selected
paraprofessionals whose cwn education ranged from 10th
grade to one year of university; the children were provided with food and medical and dental care; and the
mothers of the children received vocational training and
training in home-making and child-care skills. (24)

   Heber selected 40 mothers from a residential area in
Milwaukee characterized by the lowest family income, the
most dialpidated housing, and the greatest population den-
sity per living unit: although it contains only 2.5 per
cent of the city's population, it yields about one-third
of the children classified as mentally retarded by the
city's state schools.   All of the mothers selected were
black and all had an IQ on the Wechsler of less than 75.
As the babies were born, they were assigned to two groups,
the first lot of 4 to the Experimental Group, the next lot
to the Control Group, until each group had 20 children.
The experimental children were those who entered Heber's
comprehensive programme.   The control children were left
in their natural environment save for the fact that they
were subjected to the same mental tests as the Experimental Group and to a medical evaluation.   Heber also tested
all of the siblings of both the experimental and control

children and selected out those (all but five) who had not been exposed to his programme.   Finally, he had earlier conducted a study of a group of over 200 children from the same residential area all of whom had low IQ mothers (mean maternal IQ = 68).   All in all he had three groups (called the Control, the Sibling and the Contrast groups) he could use for purposes of comparison;   three groups against which he could measure the advantage the experimental children might derive from his programme. (25)

Table 5.1 presents the fluctuation of the IQ scores of the experimental children over time and matches them for age with those in the three comparison groups. (26)   I have used scores from the Wechsler only (the siblings may be an exception) in order to achieve uniformity.   From the comparison groups, it is clear that the experimental children would have ended up (at age 14) with a mean IQ of 70 ± 5 points if Heber had not intervened.   As for the progress of the experimental children over time, this is best analysed in four stages.

First, in the pre-school years from ages 4 to 6, the children were reasonably stable around a mean IQ of 111.5. Which is to say that they had made all the progress they were to make in their infancy and that from the age of 4 on Heber's programme merely held the ground gained. Second, after the age of 6 there was an immediate drop of 8 points (from 111 to 103).   At six, the programme was terminated and the experimental children entered state schools.   Heber clearly believes they suffered from considerable stress at that point: some children report going to school hungry or inappropriately dressed;   the verbal facility of the children proved a mixed blessing and led to adverse comment from teachers;   some parents responded with beatings and threats;   parents sometimes

TABLE 5.1 IQ data from the Milwaukee Project. All groups tested on the appropriate form of the Wechsler save for the Sibling Group (test unspecified)

Age in years	4/4+	5/5-	5/5+	6/6-	7/7+	8/8	9/9	10/10	13/13	14/14
Experimental	114	111	110*	111	103	104	106	105	–	–
Control	85	81	88	81	80*	82*	85	85	–	–
Sibling	82	82	82	86	83	87	85	82	76	–
Contrast	81	77	77	78	78	78	74	75	70	66

Note: The author has altered the presentation of Heber's data as follows: (1) some of the values used above are based on a reading of Heber's graphs; (2) the values marked with an asterisk appear to vary by about one point from graph to graph; (3) the match between the ages of the Sibling and Contrast groups on the one hand and the Experimental and Control groups on the other is not always exact – above the age of the former groups precedes the age of the latter.

could not read the teachers' notes and did not respond;
despite the fact that Milwaukee offers speciality schools
as an alternative to the usual school experience, only one
child entered such, partially due to parental fear of
things like signing official forms.   One little girl of
high intellectual ability refused to speak during her
first two months of school. (27)   During the third stage,
from ages 7 to 10, the children have not continued to decline but rather have stabilized around a mean of 104.5.
However, as they enter the fourth stage from ages 11 to
14, they are at risk.   Both the Sibling and the Contrast
Groups were relatively stable up to the age of 10 and then
suffered a loss of 6 to 9 points thereafter.

In sum, the most likely outcome of the Milwaukee Project is that the experimental children will have an eventual mean IQ of 100 ± 5 points, depending on whether or not
their gains are eroded as they enter adolescence.   The
effects of intervention will almost certainly be more than
20 IQ points, perhaps 30 or more.   Heber laments that the
attempt to rehabilitate the total family environment had
only limited success.   The programme did succeed in plac-
ing the mothers in jobs but could not hope to control
other factors: between 1967 and 1976, the percentage of
children living in solo-parent homes went up from 20 per
cent to 50 per cent;   by 1976, more families were without
telephones, a sign of economic distress.   Moreover, despite some success in engendering self-confidence in the
mothers, many of them did not become capable of dealing
with the problems inevitable in their circumstances, problems such as disciplining children, conflicts with family
and friends, and conflicts with police and other community
agencies. (28)

As Jensen points out, the Milwaukee Project cannot pos-

sibly settle the debate about race and IQ.   Even if the
eventual IQ of these black children matches the white mean
of 100, we will never be able to compare their environment
with that of the average white American: it was undoubtedly worse from conception to the age of 3 to 6 months;
it was undoubtedly far more enriched from infancy to the
age of 6;   it was almost undoubtedly worse thereafter.
Moreover, if IQ is heritable at all, the experimental
children must be well below the average black American in
terms of genotype for IQ: depending on where we put the
parental mean IQ and what h^2 narrow estimate we use, we
could get a genotypic deficit of anything from 4 to 10
points.   And, as some of Heber's critics have pointed
out, (29) his programme does not help us to identify the
specific environmental variables at work: he manipulated
so many factors that we cannot assess the impact of any
one factor.   However, on another level, Heber's experiment was an absolutely crucial experiment.   If he had
failed, it would have shown that contemporary social science was ignorant of even the general nature of what
affects intellectual development, so ignorant that future
progress was most unlikely.   The fact that Heber succeeded to the degree that he did is further evidence that
parental IQ and the verbal, psychological and social factors which seem correlated with parental IQ are of great
importance, no matter how inept we are at present at identifying specific variables.   And finally, Heber has shown
something of great human significance: it appears that
there are alternatives to mass sterilization in dealing
with the problem of mental retardation among America's
black population.

There are a number of peculiarities in the data on race

and IQ which may open up new areas of research.   Under
this heading, we will look at both the top and bottom of
the IQ scale and at factors such as sex, self-image and
cultural traditions.

During the last ten years, a debate has begun about
sexual differences within the black population, particularly at high IQ levels, which raises many questions of
general interest.   The points at issue include at least
the following: (1) is there a striking surplus of black
girls at high IQ levels; (2) if so, is this an independent phenomenon or merely a result of differences between
the mean IQs of black males and females in general; (3)
what relevance do sexual differences have to the race and
IQ debate; (4) what relevance do sexual differences have
to the significance of IQ scores for blacks?

In 1972 Thomas Sowell cited evidence that black girls
outnumber black boys at high IQ levels (120 and above) by
ratios of at least 2 to 1.   Sowell argues that since
black males and females have the same ancestors, the
causes of this phenomenon must be environmental rather
than genetic.   He hypothesizes that the environmental
factors which lower black IQ as compared to white have a
differential impact on the sexes, males suffering more
than females, and this is what we see when black girls
out perform black boys on IQ tests. (30)   Jensen appears
to concede the existence of the phenomenon in question,
but he has very different views on its significance.
Jensen argues that the surplus of black girls is merely
the result of a small difference between the sexes in
terms of their mean IQs.   He appeals to the mathematics
of a normal curve: a small difference at the mean can engender large differences at the extremes; he has evidence
of a 1.5- to 4.5-point gap at the mean in favour of black

girls; and this difference is sufficient to explain
ratios of 2 to 1 in favour of black girls at high IQ
levels.   However, this argument leaves Jensen with a
problem: his evidence on the white population also shows
the mean for girls above the mean for boys; and yet, at
high IQ levels, there are fewer white girls than boys.
For example, at 140 or above, boys lead by a ratio of 1.2
to 1.   He explains this last by pointing to the fact that
boys have a greater variance than girls.   The greater
variance 'spreads' the boys out enough to outweigh their
small disadvantage at the mean. (31)

I will first examine the evidence for what Sowell and
Jensen have in common, a belief in the existence of a surplus of black girls at high IQ levels; and then I shall
discuss the validity of Jensen's attempt to explain that
phenomenon in terms of the mathematics of a normal curve.

In 1935 Martin D. Jenkins submitted one of the most important and rigorous doctoral dissertations ever written
in the field of educational psychology.   Using a method
similar to that of Terman, he screened 8,145 black children in grades 3 to 8 (ages approximately 7 to 14) of seven
state schools in Chicago in an effort to select out those
with high IQs.   He succeeded in securing a group of 103
children all of whom scored at 120 or above on the Stanford-Binet.   He also found something quite unexpected:
the ratio of girls to boys among these superior children
was 2.3 to 1; among a smaller group of gifted children at
140 or above, the ratio of girls to boys was 3.1 to
1. (32)   Jenkins was clearly surprised by these results
and noted that two earlier studies of superior black children, both done in Washington, DC, had produced mixed results: Proctor had found a ratio of 1.3 to 1 in favour of
girls in a study of 30 children with IQs of 129 or above;

but Long had found a ratio of 1.1 to 1 in favour of boys
in his study of 34 children at 120 or above.   Despite the
latter, Jenkins noted the preponderance of girls held at 6
of the 7 schools he canvassed and hypothesized that more
girls than boys would be found in the general black elementary school population. (33)   Years later, E.G.
Rodgers needed a sample of high-IQ blacks to do another
doctoral dissertation.   He went back to the records from
September 1933 of the state schools of Baltimore: among a
group of 35 children with IQs of 130 or above on the Illi-
nois General Intelligence Scale, he found a ratio of almost 5 to 1 in favour of girls.   Rodgers's results encourage suspicion about the sampling procedure, but in
fact his method left no margin for error: the score of
every child in the fourth grade (usual age 9 years) in
every black school in Baltimore was examined, a total of
2,652 children; at 130 or above there were 29 girls and 6
boys. (34)   It is of interest that Proctor and Long, neither of whom found a clear surplus in favour of girls, did
not attempt to screen the local black school population
with any rigour. (35)

   I have summarized the findings of these four studies in
Table 5.2 and there is no doubt that the main drift is in
favour of a surplus of black girls at high IQ levels. (36)
However, I also wish to present one piece of evidence on
the other side.   In 1940 the US Office of Education collected test data on 4,032 students entering black col-
leges: there was a superior group whose median score on
the American Council on Education Psychological Examination (the ACE) was at the 68th percentile for college
freshmen; the group numbered 159 and boys outnumbered
girls by a ratio of 2 to 1.   Their performance would correspond to a median IQ score of approximately 116 with

TABLE 5.2   High-IQ black school children - ratios between the sexes

IQ	Proctor G - B	Long G - B	Jenkins G - B	Rodgers G - B	Totals G - B	Ratios G ÷ B
120 and above	——	16-18	72-31	——	88-49	1.8-1.0
130 and above	16-13	——	40-18	29-6	85-37	2.3-1.0
140 and above	7-6	——	22-7	——	29-13	2.2-1.0

only half the group above that score of course.   A smaller group of 24 had an IQ equivalent of 128 or above, but we have no breakdown of the sexes at that level. (37) The data is difficult to evaluate.   The ACE was a poor IQ test: it gave a gap between black and white college freshmen of 1.75 standard deviations which seems far too high; (38) it was discontinued in 1954 because of low validity and problems of interpretation. (39)   However, it was an IQ test of some sort and it is hard to imagine boys not having some advantage at high-IQ levels on the basis of these results.   When comparing data from the college level with data from the elementary-school level, we must remember that the former is less reliable in regard to the sexes due to a differential drop-out rate beginning in secondary school.

I feel considerable frustration at all of this. Martin Jenkins put forward his hypothesis about black girls in print in 1936.   All over America, there is massive data, classified by sex and race, stored in innumerable state schools which would settle the question; yet at present, all of our direct evidence dates from the period of 1925 to 1940.   Both Sowell and Jensen are forced to cite indirect evidence when they want current data, namely, the Moynihan Report of 1965.   This report does supply ratios in favour of black females over males on a number of variables which have a positive correlation with IQ: honour rolls in high school, 7.5 - 1 to 9.0 - 1; high-school graduates, 1.3 - 1; white-collar jobs, 4.0 - 1; government employment (Department of Labour), 2.3 - 1. (40)   In sum, on the available evidence, I suspect that there is a surplus of black girls at high IQ levels but at present we cannot take this for granted.

Let us assume, for the sake of argument, that the phenomenon in question exists and proceed to examine Jensen's explanation.   Jensen appeals to the mathematics of a normal curve but when we look at the data he has collected, we find that his mathematics simply does not work.

Jensen analysed eight studies on race × sex comparisons, the only studies in which tests were administered to both whites and blacks at the same time under the same conditions, and these together covered 34,041 children. In Table 5.3, I have translated his summary results which

TABLE 5.3   Race × sex comparisons - based on 8 studies collected by Jensen

	Number	Mean	Variance	SD
White	18,803	100.0	225.0	15.0
Black	15,238	83.5	206.4	14.4
W. male	11,827	99.5	235.0	15.3
W. female	6,976	100.5	208.0	14.4
B. male	7,817	82.5	227.2	15.1
B. female	7,412	84.5	184.7	13.6

Note: The above values are approximations based on the following assumptions: white mean = 100;   white SD = 15; all distributions are normal distributions

are expressed in standard deviation units and ratios (41) into values expressed in IQ points: the gap between black girls and boys at the mean is only slightly larger than for whites, 2 points as compared to 1 point;   but the advantage of black boys over girls in terms of greater variance is considerably larger than for whites, a ratio of 1.23 to 1 as compared to 1.13 to 1.

At this point, one thing must be clearly stated: you cannot calculate a normal distribution or compare two distributions without values for both means and variances. In Table 5.4, projected ratios of boys to girls are calcu-

TABLE 5.4 High-IQ whites and blacks - projections of
ratios between the sexes compared to actual ratios

IQ	White B/G Projected	White B/G Actual	Black B/G Projected	Black B/G Actual
120 and above	1.0 - 1.0	————	1.5 - 1.0	1.0 - 1.8
130 and above	1.2 - 1.0	————	2.0 - 1.0	1.0 - 2.3
140 and above	1.3 - 1.0	1.2 - 1.0	2.3 - 1.0	1.0 - 2.2

lated on the basis of Jensen's data.   The projected ratio
for whites matches the actual ratio for the sexes above an
IQ of 140 with almost Pythagorean elegance (1.3 - 1.0 $\simeq$
1.2 - 1.0).   The projected ratios for blacks at high IQ
levels gives a sexual balance that is almost precisely the
reverse of the ratios which both Sowell and Jensen assume
to be the case: rather than the actual ratios favouring
girls by more than 2 to 1, we get projections favouring
boys by about 2 to 1.

In other words, in the case of whites, where actual
values (for means and variances) explain the relatively
equal number of boys and girls at high IQ levels, Jensen
uses actual values.   In the case of blacks, where actual
values make the surplus of girls even more surprising than
it appears at first glance, he uses fictitious values.
He can 'explain' the sexual imbalance only by assuming
equal variances for black boys and black girls, an assumption he knows to be incorrect.   To be fair, Jensen half
admits he is on shaky ground: he says that it is 'not
known' (42) why greater variance does not increase the
percentage of black boys at high IQ levels.   But this is
not good enough.   The causes of the dearth of black boys
is indeed unknown, but one thing that is known is this:

Jensen's own data, and it is extensive data, rules out the mathematics of a normal curve as an explanation.   The most obvious interpretation of the data is that real causal factors of considerable potency are at work at high IQ levels within American's black population, factors which cripple boys as compared to girls.

In Table 5.5, I have attempted to drive this last point home by going back to Martin Jenkins. (43)   His study of high-IQ blacks is the only one which gives us sufficient data to calculate the pattern of girl to boy ratios at a variety of high-IQ levels, namely, 150 and above, 140 and above, 130 and above, 120 and above.   There is a simple test of whether a 2- or 4-point difference at the means accounts for a ratio at an extreme: if it does, then by subtracting say 3 points from all of the girls' scores, we should reduce their number at any given level to that of the boys.   As Table 5.5 makes clear, we would have to

TABLE 5.5   High-IQ black school children - ratios between the sexes - data from Martin Jenkins

IQ	Girls	Boys	Ratios G/B
150 and above	7	4	1.8 - 1
140 and above	22	7	3.1 - 1
130 and above	40	18	2.2 - 1
120 and above	72	31	2.3 - 1

deduct at least 10 points: when we locate the girls at a particular level (say 150 and above), we must go down to at least the next level (say 140 and above) to locate an equal number of boys.   If causal factors are at work whose differential impact begins to take effect at high IQ levels, they are quite potent;   at least on the basis of this very limited data.

Both Sowell and Jensen, while differing on the potency of the factors at work, agree that the most parsimonious explanation of black sex differences is environmental rather than genetic. (44)   However, a strong hereditarian might argue as follows: 'Using height as an example, we might well find one race in which men and women are equally tall and another in which men tend to be taller.   It is quite plausible that the latter difference is primarily genetic in origin.   Therefore, given that we know of strong genetic influences on IQ, there is no reason to assume that sex differences among blacks are due to environmental factors.'

In answer, this view is logically possible but very improbable.   Aside from forms of mental retardation known to be due to a single gene, genetic influences on IQ appear to be polygenic, that is, many genes make a contribution.   Therefore, the genetic influences on IQ should tend to distribute scores in the pattern of a normal curve.   If sex differences among blacks distort a normal distribution at its upper levels, it is likely that this is the result of environmental factors.   A hereditarian would have to argue that while ordinary blacks have a sex-related genetic tendency which favours girls by only a small amount, bright blacks have one which favours girls by a great amount.   However, what with the paucity of the data on ratios at high IQ levels, I prefer not to rest my case against a genetic hypothesis on the above argument alone.   Focusing on the advantage black girls have at the mean, there is some evidence that this develops over time, that is, between the ages of 7 and 14.   Jensen finds such a trend in the data of Baughman and Dahlstrom (1968) and also in one of his own studies covering approximately the ages of 5 to 12 (for verbal IQ only). (45)   These trends suggest the hypothesis of an environmental decrement although they are not of course sufficient to confirm that hypothesis.

I have emphasized the paucity of evidence about sexual differences within the black population and we must keep an open mind concerning three possibilities: that black girls and boys do equally well on IQ tests; that the ratio of the sexes at high IQ levels can be explained by an advantage of girls at the mean of 2 or 3 points (this would imply that our present data on ratios or variances or both was inaccurate); that there is a surplus of girls at high IQ levels which cannot be so explained.   However, the environmentalist can explore the debate about sexual differences with profit no matter which possibility is correct, thanks to something which is not debatable: black girls outperform black boys in terms of academic achievement.   Take the first possibility.   If black girls and boys have the same mean IQ, then IQ does not have its normal significance within the black population, or at least its normal significance is diminished.   In Chapter 2, when we developed the thesis that IQ measured something important, we set up a syllogism.   It ran: academic achievement is of significant personal and social value; IQ is correlated with academic achievement; therefore, IQ is significant.   The assumption of course was that the correlation is not a mere correlation but that IQ tests measure an intellectual skill, a skill which plays a causal role in enhancing academic performance. If IQ differences between the sexes do not run in the same direction as academic achievement differences within the black population, then something peculiar is going on well worth investigation.   It is possible that whatever diminishes the causal role IQ normally plays is also playing a causal role that affects IQ itself.

The second and third possibilities appear more likely than the first.   Following up Sowell's suggestion, we would hope that identifying the environmental variables which account for a gap between male and female would afford clues as to the gap between black and white.   If we had an ideal run of luck, we would find that these factors, whatever they may be, had a variety of effects.

1   A differential effect on the sexes.   The crucial task which is a prerequisite to all others is to identify the variables that favour girls over boys.   Since black girls and boys are automatically matched for SES within any sizable population, we would focus on psychological variables which look as if they might be a result of social forces other than SES, e.g. sexism (in this case boys having a worse environment within the black family than girls) and racism.   If the IQ gap between the sexes is as small as it seems (2 or 3 points at the mean), it may be very difficult to measure correlates.   Here a much larger differential effect at high IQ levels (say 10 points) would be most convenient in that differential variables would presumably be much more visible.   We could compare boys at 120 with girls at 130, on the assumption they were equivalent for genotype for IQ, and so on up the IQ scale looking for a larger difference in terms of variables than we find among average boys and girls.

2   A differential effect on the races.   Assume we find variables which exhibit small differences between black boys and girls in general, enhanced differences at high IQ levels, and even larger differences between black and white.   We would then have reason to believe that they played an important role in the IQ gap between the races.

3 A common effect on the sexes.   It is often said
that factors which separate the sexes by only 2 or 3 IQ
points cannot be very important.   After all, raising the
mean IQ of black males by that amount would raise the mean
IQ of all blacks by only 1.0 to 1.5 points; and raising
the IQ of the top 1 per cent of blacks by even 10 points
would not have much overall effect.   The fallacy of this
is the assumption that the differential effect on the
sexes of the factors at work is equivalent to their total
effect.   Actually when we measure their differential
effect we are measuring their adverse effect on black boys
minus their adverse effect on black girls.   This difference may well be small compared to what boys and girls
suffer in common.   Black males and females have not only
ancestry but also virtually all of their childhood environment in common and it is surprising that there is a
sexual differential at all.

4 A common effect on blacks as such.   When we identify the above factors (and in fact the following is true of
all factors we identify), they should be tested for
'blindfold quality', that is, for their degree of uniformity throughout the black population.   The fact that
these factors have limited differential effect on the
sexes throughout most of the black population does not
mean that they have a limited differential effect on individuals.   Still the kind of factors which have been suggested as explaining the unusual problems of black boys,
it remains to be seen whether they actually do, have been
ones connected with racism and the peculiarities of black
culture.   If any factors are relatively uniform among
blacks, presumably these would be the ones.

The research done up to now on sexual differences among
blacks has focused on boys and girls in general rather

than at high IQ levels.   The emphasis is on the matriarchal family among blacks plus the fact that the gap between occupational aspirations and achievement is much
less for girls than for boys.   In American society, males
are supposed to achieve more than females in terms of
steady employment and occupational status; within black
America the women, as we have seen, outperform the men and
the man often bears the burden of being 'unreliable' and
'a failure', thus presenting an unsatisfactory model for
black boys.   In the 40 per cent of homes in which the
father is absent, black boys presumably have an even
greater problem. (46)   All of this is highly theoretical,
but fortunately Martin Deutsch has made a start at quanti-
fying the variables involved.   Deutsch studied two
samples of elementary-school children, approximately 400
in all, half from a lower-class ghetto school which was
over 99 per cent black, half from a similar school which
was 94 per cent white.   He achieved parity in terms of
the 'crowding ratio', almost 60 per cent of both groups
had more than 1.4 persons to a room which meant that both
suffered from extremely crowded living conditions (over
1.0 per room is considered crowded).   He did not achieve
complete parity in SES: the whites had slightly higher
incomes, greater job stability, and far fewer broken
homes.   The variables which most interest us, negative
family atmosphere and negative self-image, were measured
by an index compiled on the basis of a sentence completion
test.   For example, if a child completed the sentence
'When I look in the mirror I ...' with 'see myself', he
got a low (or good) score; while if he wrote 'I cry' or
'am sad' or 'look ugly' (as did 20 per cent of black
boys), he got a high (or bad) score. (47)
    I have collected the relevant results of Deutsch's

study in Table 5.6 with a view to comparing boy-girl differences within the black sample with black-white differences. (48)   As we would assume, black boys and girls are
virtually the same on the crowding ratio index of socio-
economic status.   Their difference in academic achievement, which is greater than the difference between black
and white, is all out of proportion to any possible difference in mean IQ;   clearly these black boys are not
'trying' as hard at school as the girls.   Note how the
gap between the sexes narrows as we go down the list of
tests to the Digit Span Backward which has the highest
correlation with IQ: the gap on this test would be equivalent to no more than 3.4 IQ points (.264 × 13).   The
gap between black boys and girls in terms of negative
family atmosphere is also greater than the gap between the
races, that is, it appears that black boys do see the
matriarchal family as a less friendly environment.   However, of greatest interest is the remaining variable of

TABLE 5.6   Deutsch's study of 200 black and 200 white
school children selected for similarity of SES: all
differences expressed in standard deviation units;   a
positive score indicates that the first group is better
off than the second, e.g. black girls are not as over-
crowded as black boys

Variables	Black G/B gap	Both races W/B gap
Crowding: no. per room	+.051	-.051
Stanford Achievement Test	+.773	+.717
Digit Span Forward	+.566	+.076
Digit Span Backward	+.264	+.354
Negative family atmosphere	+.404	+.307
Negative self-image	+.127	+.717

negative self-image: the difference between black boys
and girls is negligible while the gap between black and
white is very large.   Moreover, Deutsch asserts (without
detail) that negative self-image varied little between individuals within the black group, there being little difference between high and low achievers (which makes it
hard to argue that poor self-image was a mere effect of an
awareness of one's own intellectual inferiority). (49)
Clearly we must try to discover whether or not a significant difference in self-image between black boys and girls
emerges at very high IQ levels.

Deutsch's results cannot be generalized for two
reasons: since the black and white samples are similar
for SES, and normally whites are much higher in terms of
SES, the self-image gap between the races is probably an
underestimate;   since the black sample is composed mainly
of lower-class blacks, without much of the middle class,
the uniformity of negative self-image therein may be an
overestimate.   Another line of research which has attempted to measure racial differences in self-image is the
'doll experiments' pioneered by Clark and Clark (1940).
Clark and Clark took 253 black children aged from 3 to 7
years and showed them dolls identical in every way save
for skin and hair colour: 67 per cent preferred the white
doll to play with and an almost equal percentage said that
the coloured doll looked bad and was not a nice colour;
when asked to give someone the doll that 'looks like you',
over 30 per cent of the black children chose the white
doll, although the percentage of those who identified with
the white doll dropped to 20-25 per cent for those children with darker skin colours. (50)   The experiment has
been replicated many times with additional data pointing
towards a low self-image based on colour.   In 1965 Coles

found that black drawings of black children, as compared to white drawings of white, were often smaller in size with missing or mutilated body parts. (51)   Morland (1958) asked children directly whether they were white or coloured.   All white children identified themselves as such while 32 per cent of black children claimed they were white and 16 per cent maintained they did not know or refused to answer. (52)   Pettigrew reports many cases of tension when such questions were asked and cites the example of a small black boy who hung his head and murmured, 'I guess I'se kind of coloured.' (53)

In the 1970s several scholars, notably Hraba and Grant, have argued that the black movement may have altered black children in the direction of preference for and identity with their own colour. (54)   There is some evidence that earlier studies were too simplistic on the point of self-identification, for example, Greenwald and Oppenheim (1968) introduced a mulatto doll and got largely accurate identification of children with dolls for both black and white.   They also assert that children did not appear disturbed by questions about their colour. (55)   However, setting *identification* aside and focusing on the *preferences* of children, the evidence right up to the present is heavily on the side of Clark and Clark: in 12 studies using photographs and pictures, published from 1934 to 1972 and involving a total of some 2,000 children, the consistent trend has been for blacks to prefer white far more frequently than whites prefer black.   As for dolls, only 2 studies out of 11 have failed to produce a majority of blacks who prefer white dolls. (56)   This is true even of Greenwald and Oppenheim, although it must be said that the mulatto doll was rather unsatisfactory: it had to be specially coloured and this produced a 'light gray' skin

colour; its lack of popularity may indicate merely that
neither race contains many necrophiliacs. (57)   To this,
I wish to add a piece of evidence which has impressed me
deeply, namely, the testimony of physicians such as Dr
Harrison-Ross as to the problems black mothers have in
accepting the colour of their new-born child.   While the
first question of white parents is usually about the
baby's sex or whether it is normal and healthy, the first
concern of black parents is its degree of blackness; only
after a depressed 'he's going to be black' or a jubilant
'she looks almost white' does attention turn to counting
fingers and toes. (58)

A few words about the lower end of the IQ scale: schools
tend to use IQ tests to diagnose mental retardation, the
usual criterion being an IQ below 70.   However, as Jensen
himself has observed, white middle-class children who
score below 70 just seem much more retarded than black
lower-class children below that level.   In her study of
Riverside, California, Jane Mercer developed a test of
adaptive behaviour to see whether or not there were important differences between social groups classified as mentally retarded.   She used an age-graded set of indica-
tors, for example, can set the table at 3, lace his own
shoes at 5, run errands with money at 6, and as an adult,
can keep score at baseball, work with little or no super-
vision, read books and newspapers, and so forth.   A pass
(at this level) meant that one could perform approximately
two-thirds of the tasks appropriate to one's age group.
On the basis of a tested subsample, Mercer asserts that
none of the whites with IQs of less than 70 passed, while
20 of 22 blacks passed. (59)
     Jensen has his own analysis of such results.   He could

argue: that the competence of such black children in
everyday life reflects associative learning ability
(skills which involve things like memory and rote learning); that the races may be relatively equal for such
skills; but that this does not mean that the races are
equal for cognitive ability (skills which emphasize problem-solving and abstract thinking).   Indeed, Jensen has
constructed a whole theory of intelligence which divides
skills into Level I, associative ability as tested by say
digit span memory tests, and Level II, cognitive ability
as measured by Raven's Progressive Matrices.   The former
is supposed to be a prerequisite but not a sufficient condition for the latter. (60)   Now the key question here is
the extent to which those with high Level I ability but
low Level II are genetically incapable of the latter, as
opposed to possessing a capacity for the latter which
their environment has discouraged.

Heber has shown that massive intervention into the environment can develop cognitive or Level II ability in
those who, on the basis of their mother's IQ, were unlikely to develop such.   Guinagh has experimented with a much
more limited intervention, namely, a short course designed
to train children in abstract problem-solving.   From a
population of 105 black children of low SES, he selected
20 who scored high on Level I (digit span) and low on
Level II (Ravens) and compared them to another group of 20
who were low on both.   Each group was divided randomly
into 10 who received seven half-hour sessions on the con-
cepts behind Ravens (not on the test items themselves) and
10 who served as controls.   The children who had a high
Level I score improved significantly on Ravens while most
of those with a low Level I score did not.   In addition,
Guinagh studied two groups of white low-SES children, and

here both the high and low Level I children made significant gains. (61)   This last can be interpreted in two
ways: as signaling a racial difference favouring white
over black; or as evidence against Jensen's hypothesis
that Level I ability is a prerequisite to developing Level
II ability.   However, the important thing about the gains
children of both races made is whether or not they have
any larger significance.   We know that Heber's programme
had effects that went beyond improved performance on a
particular IQ test; his children have done well on both
the Wechsler and the Stanford-Binet and have done far
better than controls at school on achievement tests. (62)
The gains Guinagh achieved are impressive: comparing all
experimental children with all controls, the former gained
more than one standard deviation, the equivalent of 16.5
IQ points.   But it remains to be seen whether Guinagh's
sort of course can improve performance on anything save
the Ravens test itself.

The work of Mercer, Heber and Guinagh, taken together,
opens up the possibility that the majority of black children classified as mentally retarded suffer from no genetic
barrier to abstract thought.   Rather they may suffer from
an environmental handicap, that is, the ghetto environment
places strong emphasis on immediate gratification, present
experience, and dealing with concrete problems, with
little emphasis on abstractions, non-verbal symbols, and
problem-solving for its own sake.   We should certainly
continue with attempts to manipulate the environment but
we should also do comparative studies: select children
with high Level I only, then children with both high Level
I and Level II, and compare them for environmental differences.

In his book 'Black Education' (1972), Thomas Sowell

notes the features of the ghetto environment which place
the concrete ahead of the abstract.   But he also emphasizes the absence of intellectual interests and values
within black culture.   Naturally black parents want their
children to 'do well' at school but too often they simply
have no realistic appreciation of what education in the
sense of intellectual development entails, they do not
comprehend it as something beyond school attendance requiring the acquisition of certain habits and skills.   A
study of black children in Prince Edward County, Virginia,
where the schools were closed for several years found that
those who had never attended school could not even hold a
pencil, let alone follow detailed instructions or take a
test. (63)   As for Sowell's own experiences, the contrast
between his upbringing and that of Seymour Sarason, who
describes life in a Jewish immigrant neighbourhood, illus-
trates the point.   Sarason's neighbourhood was also low
SES but he tells us that to say there was respect for intellectual achievement is to use too weak a word: the
value placed on it was compelling, unrelenting and omni-
present.   When one of his cousins chose to play football,
this provoked disbelief and rage - what if he were injured
and could not go to college? (64)   When Sowell won a
place in a selective high school (Stuyvesant), his black
parents were pleased but they could not believe he had to
spend that much time at the library.   They feared he was
off getting into trouble and pleaded with him to tell them
what was 'really going on' and promised to try to understand. (65)   Sowell's environment just did not possess a
viable social role for someone who wanted to achieve academic or cognitive skills.

It may be said that today a majority of blacks have
attained a reasonable socio-economic status.   There has

been progress but its significance depends on what statistics you select for emphasis.   I remain impressed by
those to which I have referred throughout this chapter:
as of 1976, 40 per cent of all black children were living
in homes in which the father was absent (12 per cent for
whites), 25 per cent were being born out of wedlock to
teenage mothers (4 per cent for whites), and one-third
were receiving welfare benefits under the aid to broken
families programme. (66)   It is not easy to see these
teenage mothers attempting to cope without the support of
a spouse providing an antidote to Sowell's experience.
All of these statistics signal a swift deterioration over
the past decade vis-à-vis the white community.   And if
the black child does not get an impetus towards intellectual achievement at home, he is most unlikely to get it at
a ghetto school.   The Coleman Report (1966) focused
debate on the size and importance of the difference between black and white schools in terms of expenditure,
facilities, libraries and staff.   This is a great pity in
that for anyone who has ever observed a ghetto school, it
becomes clear that none of these things matter compared to
the atmosphere of these schools.

First, there is the desperate struggle to maintain discipline.   In Deutsch's study, he found that 50 to 80 per
cent of all classroom time was spent on discipline and
other non-academic tasks in the black low-SES school;
such activities occupied 30 per cent of classroom time, at
a maximum, in the white school selected as a control.   He
reports an extraordinary level of antagonism between black
boys and girls with a core of boys who were continually
literally pushing, kicking and playing tricks on the
girls.   The volume of noise was at times so great that no
one including the teacher could be heard. (67)   Then

there is the uncontrolled activity of the children.   A
young Harvard-trained teacher in a black ghetto school has
left a poignant account: 'What impressed me most was the
fact that my children (9-10 years old) are already ...
hostile, rebellious, and bitter.... They are hyperactive
and are constantly in motion.   In many ways they can be
compared to wild horses that are suddenly fenced in.' (68)
Even those children who remain in their seats are often
moving to the rhythms of unheard popular music or, at the
intermediate school level, high on drugs.   These schools
have to be seen to be believed and the most significant
finding of the Coleman Report was that 'very few future
teachers of either race wished to teach in predominantly
minority schools.' (69)

   A word of warning: I believe that anyone who wishes to
do research on the academic achievement of blacks in
ghetto schools must arrange for the administration of
standardized tests himself.   In some cities at least, the
testing that goes on in the schools is simply corrupt:
children are given answers in advance to memorize, 'slow
learners' are siphoned off into 'special assemblies' on
the day of the test, and staff fill in unanswered questions while marking.   The motive is to demonstrate progress in, say, reading whether any progress has occurred
or not.   We have a precedent for this in Stalinist Russia
in which production targets were met on paper whether the
goods actually existed or not. (70)

This chapter has been the most tentative and least sat-
isfactory of any in this book.   However, fully half of
the 10 major studies analysed are the product of the last
decade, and thus we may hope for better things in the
future.   I assume that its message is clear: there are

some plausible candidates for the role of blindfold; variables such as parental IQ, poor nutrition (particularly during pregnancy), lack of stimulation in early childhood, lack of complex verbal interaction between parent and child, family dislocation, low self-image, the chaos of the ghetto school, lack of an intellectual tradition and so forth may well handicap the intellectual development of blacks as measured by IQ tests.   I consider the preliminary evidence in favour of the impact of these variables more impressive than does Jensen.   Some of them clearly have a very significant effect that persists even when we are comparing samples that are equivalent for socioeconomic status.

The above poses a problem for blacks which may well make Jensen's message look more attractive than my own. Jensen never denies that blacks suffer from injustice within the context of American society: his proclivities are too generous and humane for that.   And he certainly believes that reforms in education could improve black academic performance, perhaps by way of a stronger emphasis on associative learning techniques.   Still, as far as intellectual development goes, his message is that in terms of their capacity for abstract thinking, the American environment has not done blacks much harm vis-à-vis whites.   On the other hand I have argued that the black experience in America does blacks grave harm in terms of intellectual development, that thanks to child-rearing patterns, relations between the sexes, the values and traditions of black culture, blacks really do end up damaged.   There seem to me two alternatives here: the environment really does cripple blacks and the IQ gap is environmental; or that it does not and the gap is primarily genetic.   I know that logically there is a third

alternative, namely, that the problem is with the tests
themselves.   I doubt that anyone can still believe that
black examiners and tests translated into ghetto English
will make much difference.   But it can be argued that
better tests will disclose a high level of abstract thinking going on among blacks, thinking which has as yet gone
undetected and which is just as valuable in its potential
for scientific and technological progress as 'white' abstract thinking.   In the absence of one shred of evidence
for this, I remain a sceptic.

From the outraged reaction to the Moynihan Report, I
know how unpopular my message is likely to be.   When a
group suffers from an unjust environment which does them
grave harm, it is only human to focus on the injustice and
pretend that the harm affects primarily one's external
circumstances rather than one's personal development.   We
see this in the women's liberation movement, that is, a
reluctance to acknowledge that the roles assigned women in
our culture have done harm to their characterological development, save perhaps for a willingness to admit to
lowered self-confidence.   Some intellectuals today take a
similar position about blacks: that black children are
not linguistically deprived or cognitively underdeveloped;
that while their language patterns are different, it is
racist to assert that white language patterns are better
than black. (71)   I take the naive view that an unjust
and deleterious environment damages one's capacities as
well as one's opportunities, and believe that the above
sort of extreme cultural relativism usually lacks the
courage to face up to unpleasant facts, such as a probable
causal relationship between certain patterns of communication and thinking on the one hand and a high level of progress in science and technology on the other.

If you measure a culture against itself at a particular
time, the relationship is one of identity and nothing is
wrong by definition.   If you measure the achievements of
a particular culture against the norms of another, they
are very likely to fall short and much will be wrong by
definition.   But there are alternatives to extreme relativism and sheer ethnocentrism.   I will ignore my own
favourite (which derives from Aristotle) for a less con-
troversial alternative: measuring a culture against how
well it allows its population to fulfill their aspirations, preferably their realistic aspirations.   Many
blacks aspire to academic success in American and want to
see blacks match whites in areas where the ability to
handle abstractions is important.   I think this is a realistic aspiration in terms of the genetic potential of
blacks.   For blacks with such aspirations, certain aspects of black culture act as a barrier and I doubt that
they will be loath to see those aspects of black culture
go.   Historically these cultural patterns derive from
racism but they exist for all that.   There are many other
aspects of black culture (e.g. a disproportionate contribution to the arts) in which blacks can take great pride.
That is fortunate.   Every responsible person engages in a
lonely and difficult struggle to improve his own talents
and to encourage his children to be better human beings
than their parents.   A very large number of blacks find
themselves surrounded by an environment of crushing force.
Group identity, a sense of racial pride, an atmosphere of
comradeship and mutual aid, these things can do much to
render their struggle less solitary.

Chapter 6

CONCLUSION AND SUMMARY

Today a great drama is being played out: the social sciences are attempting to clarify an issue of real philosophical and political importance, namely, whether the races differ in terms of certain intellectual skills because of genetic differences. Those who have pleaded with social science for relevance may well have got more than they bargained for. In the past, attempts by social science to clarify important problems have been almost universally embarrassing, the major exceptions being in certain areas of economics. It is as yet unclear whether social science will clarify the race and IQ issue or whether the issue will act as a mirror revealing contradictions and flaws within social science. As for my reasons for entering the debate, having read Jensen I suspected that the evidence on race and IQ was subject to another interpretation; and I wanted to make my own contribution, for what it is worth, to the intellectual respectability of the environmentalist position. Also Jensen threatens to dominate the debate by the range of his learning, his skill as a controversialist, and the sheer volume of his contribution. In much the same way, Saint Augustine the Bishop of Hippo overwhelmed his opponents concerning whether Christianity had played an important role in the

213

fall of Rome and I have never been sure that Saint Augustine was correct.

After having reviewed the evidence in detail, I am
quite convinced that an environmental interpretation is
viable.   However, there is not one piece of evidence on
either side so firm that it is proof against exacting
critique.   I have criticized twin studies, the evidence
for high h^2 estimates, the claim that environmentalists can
do no better than posit a mysterious 'factor X'.   But my
own evidence is subject to critique: the blood-group
studies are suspect on grounds of genetic theory; Witty
and Jenkins should have selected a contrast group from the
local population they studied; most of Barbara Tizard's
children were of an age (under 5) at which IQ tests have
only quasi-respectability; Sandra Scarr's results are
ambiguous; even Eyferth is subject to interpretation by
way of a variety of scenarios.   The sample sizes are
small and the possibility of sampling error great.   However, I am impressed by this: the environmentalist finds
himself explaining away primarily the indirect evidence;
the hereditarian must explain away the main drift of the
direct evidence.   Therefore, there is reason to say that
the hypothesis that black and white are roughly equivalent
for genotype for IQ is the more probable.   Those who are
dissatisfied with this conclusion and want something
stronger want more than the evidence will bear.   If they
want 'far more probable' or 'almost certain', let them
improve on the research presently at hand.

Having said this, I will content myself with a brief
summary of this book designed to render explicit its logical structure.   From the beginning, we must follow truth
but one truth is this: the contention that two-thirds of
the present IQ gap, say 10 points, between black and white

is genetic adds epistemological respectability to the
arguments of racist ideologues; albeit it does so only in
selected areas, such as immigration policy and support for
white rule in Africa.   There are of course other (non-
racist) arguments for a conservative opinion on such
issues but these are not the concern of this book.   The
most efficient (but not the only) way to attack the racist
ideologue is to dispute his factual premises.   This means
a critique of the conceptual system that Jensen, ironi-
cally a fierce opponent of racism, has constructed and the
evidence he has accumulated.   Jensen has formulated a
two-step case of great force: he uses high h^2 estimates
to suggest that only factors far more uniform within the
black population than seems conceivable (they would have
to be omni-present blindfolds) could provide an environmental explanation; and then he carefully destorys the
credibility of every candidate for such a role, indeed, he
attempts to falsify virtually every hypothesis in favour
of factors of large effect on IQ (within the range of
naturally occurring environments in a nation like
America).

We can of course evade Jensen's argument by raising our
standards of evidence so high that no evidence in any area
of social science could hope to meet them until the Second
Coming.   We can demand an experimental design equal to
that we have in plant breeding before we take any h^2 estimate seriously.   We can emphasize the possibility of a
radical genotype X environment interaction such that we
could not even say those afflicted with Mongolism have a
worse genotype for IQ: perhaps they have an unknown genetic resistance to radiation and after the almost inevitable nuclear 'accident' our future promises us, they will
be the only ones who are safe from severe brain damage.

I have found throughout my career as a social scientist
that standards for evidence escalate dramatically when
some come along we rather dislike: they remain surpris-
ingly relaxed on other issues and no effort is usually
made to achieve consistency.   In my opinion, all of this
is a sign of panic within the ranks of environmentalists
and panic I believe to be premature.   The best answer to
Jensen is to accumulate direct evidence: evidence concerning the effects on IQ when, usually due to historical
accident (war) or an accident of personal history (going
to a residential nursery), black and white actually exchange or merge environments.   And I believe that what
direct evidence exists favours an environmental hypothesis
concerning race and IQ.

However, even if the accumulation of such evidence continues to point towards relative equality between black
and white, to stop at that is just too absurd: it would
leave us with a scandal of the intellect in which what
begins to seem almost certainly true also seems impossible - impossible in the light of a mass of evidence not
directly relevant but still suggestive.   Therefore, we
must make a case for environmentalism that goes beyond the
narrow issue of race and IQ and it too must have two
steps: (1) evidence for h^2 estimatss in the range of .40
to .60 and eventually a between-families component of
variance on the order of .25 to .35.   This last would
imply an environmental gap of from 1.7 to 2.0 standard
deviations between white and black in America, even assuming environmental effects have a normal distribution and
that the factors which account for differences between the
races are the same as those which explain variance within
the races;   (2) but we should also attempt to challenge
those assumptions.   We must try to identify environmental

factors which are both potent and affect blacks adversely
(perhaps lower parental IQ or dietary deficiencies or lack
of verbal stimulation in early childhood); factors whose
effects deviate from a normal distribution (perhaps whatever affects high-IQ black boys); and factors which seem
relatively uniform within the black population (those connected with racism and the distinctive characteristics of
black culture).   In sum, we must search for semi-blindfolds as distinct from the implausible omnipresent blindfolds Jensen describes.   Once again, our success or failure in these two tasks is of secondary importance to the
race and IQ issue which will be settled on the basis of
direct evidence.   But success would relieve considerable
intellectual tension and save social science from the fate
of having several of its most important methodologies each
casting doubt upon the other.

Before we close: Bertrand Russell once analysed the
problem of egoism vs altruism with his usual intelligence.
When making a decision that affects both ourselves and
others, he advises that: we should carefully balance our
own interests against those of our fellow man and arrive
at a sober conclusion; and then throw a weight or two in
the altruistic side of the scales to cancel out our par-
tiality to self.   Perhaps when we assess the capabilities
of our own race against those of others, we should do
something similar.   All racial comparisons are not ethnocentrism but ethnocentrism is an ever-present temptation.
The genius of Aristotle did not save him from believing
that barbarians were natural slaves.   I find it beneficial to reflect on something J.B.S. Haldane recommends to
our attention.   At the time of the Moorish occupation of
Spain, a Moorish writer commented on the Northern Europeans who became our own (my own) ancestors: 'They are of

cold temperament and never reach maturity.   They are of
great stature and of a white colour.   But they lack all
sharpness of wit and penetration of intellect.'

BLACK SOLDIERS AND
WHITE SOLDIERS

In Chapter 3, I argue for the logical priority of direct
evidence over indirect.   Eyferth's study includes over 40
per cent of the total number of children tested in studies
which count as direct evidence.   In order to interpret
Eyferth's study, I offer a variety of key estimates, for
example: an estimate of the mean IQ of white troops who
served in the US occupation of Germany;   two estimates for
black troops, a maximum one and what I call a more realistic one;   and an estimate which asserts that at least 80
per cent of the usual IQ gap between black and white was
present among the above troops (from a genetic point of
view).   In Chapter 3, I claim that there is data to back
up those estimates and now it is time to make good on that
claim.

The reason for the fact that the mean IQs of both white
and black troops in Germany were above the means for their
respective larger populations was, of course, armed forces
selection, primarily the use of procedures and standards
that eliminated low-IQ blacks as ineligible to serve.
For much of the twelve-year period that concerns us, both
draftees and enlistees had to have a score of at least 70
on a mental test called the AGCT (Army General Classification Test), which score must not be equated with an IQ of

70.   I must immediately qualify this by saying that
during the Second World War, a period of recruitment that
contributed the fathers of at least half of Eyferth's
children, standards were much more relaxed.   In the later
war years, it would be roughly accurate to think of a
score of 50 as the usual criterion of eligibility and in
the earlier years, emphasis on schooling or literacy
rather than mental test scores allowed a large number of
blacks to qualify with scores well below 50.   The AGCT
was designed to have a mean of 100 and an SD of 20, although as we shall see the latter target was not achieved
in practice.   A modified version of the AGCT, called the
Armed Forces Qualification Test or AFQT, was substituted
in 1950, but the latter was correlated with the former in
terms of levels of performance and cutting lines, so this
need not concern us. (1)

The task of arriving at estimates of the effect of
armed forces selection poses two methodological problems:
first, given the armed forces data, how do we estimate the
extent to which black and white troops were above their
respective population norms on the AGCT;   second, given
those estimates, how do we translate them into estimates
relevant to Eyferth's study?   I am going to begin with
the second because it will provide a better introduction
to the overall problem of methodology - the first may be
logically prior but it is unlikely to arouse much controversy.

In my opinion, we need the following: an estimate of the
extent to which white troops were an elite group on the
AGCT, that is, how many standard deviation units (SDUs)
was their mean on the AGCT above that of US whites in
general;   a similar estimate for black troops;   and an

estimate of the correlation coefficient between the AGCT
and the Wechsler - I refer of course to 'r', that is, the
Pearson Product-Moment Correlation Coefficient.   The need
for the latter probably requires some explanation.

Eyferth tested his children on the Wechsler and we want
to know how much the fact that the potential fathers were
an elite group may have affected his results.   This means
that we must estimate how much the potential fathers were
an elite group as measured by the Wechsler and that an
estimate purely in terms of AGCT scores will not do.   The
technical reason for this is that heritability estimates
assume that measurement error has been reduced to a minimum, but an illustration may serve to get the point across
more clearly.   What the armed forces essentially did was
this: ranked the male population of America on a normal
curve in terms of their AGCT scores and by way of selection standards and procedures, eliminated most of those at
the bottom of the curve.   Now imagine that the armed
forces had ranked Americans on a normal curve in terms of
scores based on pure chance.   Eliminating those with 'low
scores' on such a curve would not give us an elite that
was an elite in any relevant sense: those eliminated
would not be the same as those who lie at the bottom of a
Wechsler IQ curve, indeed, those with high IQs would stand
as good a chance of being eliminated as those with a low
IQ.   The AGCT test results naturally have a better correlation with the Wechsler than the zero correlation of
random chance, but the match is not perfect.   I will
eventually argue that at least as far as blacks were concerned, the correlation could lie anywhere between .30 and
.77 and therefore, once again, the men the armed forces
eliminated would include not only those near the bottom of
the Wechsler curve but also men whose Wechsler IQs would

be quite respectable.   Particularly if I am correct about
my suspicion of a very low correlation for blacks, no
method of analysing AGCT results that fails to take the
degree of correlation into account is appropriate.

To anticipate, I believe that a maximum estimate of the
effect of armed forces selection on blacks would be as
follows: that it raised the in-service mean .650 SDU
above the general population mean as measured by AGCT
scores.   A maximum estimate of the correlation between
the Wechsler and AGCT, when the latter was administered
under the actual conditions of armed forces testing, would
be .77.   Fortunately, when a rise in the mean is achieved
by eliminating the bottom end of a normal curve, there is
a beautifully simple relationship between the rise as
measured by one test and that measured by another: you
multiply the rise on the first test by the correlation coefficient and you get the rise on the second.   Thus, .650
SDU on the AGCT times .77 gives a rise cf .501 SDU on the
Wechsler.   As for the rest of the relevant calculations,
following Jensen and using 13 as the black SD, we get a
rise of 6.5 IQ points taking a population mean of 85.0 to
an in-service mean of 91.5.   Using an h^2 narrow estimate
of .55, not the author's choice but one that will command
general respect, we get a rise of 3.6 points (6.5 × .55)
in terms of heritable IQ which gives a genotypic IQ of
88.6.   This figure rounded off to 89 was the maximum
estimate for blacks used in the author's interpretation of
Eyferth's results.   A similar calculation for whites, although here there is no difference between maximum and
other estimates, would run: values, .108 SDU rise on the
AGCT, SD = 15, h^2 narrow = .55;   thus, .108 × .77 = .083
SDU, .083 × 15 = 1.2 IQ points for a phenotypic IQ of
101.2, and 1.2 × .55 = .7 for a genotypic IQ of 100.7.

This last was rounded off to 101 for the purposes of Chapter 3. (This calculation (+SDU-1 × r = +SDU-2) assumes a bivariate normal distribution. It would underestimate the rise on the second test only if the correlation is higher (after correction for restriction of range) at the lower levels of the curves. In fact, as we shall see, the correlation tends to be lower at lower levels. All values for h^2 narrow (.40, .55, .70) are adjusted values, that is, they assume that measurement error has been partialed out and thereby eliminated. For example, my high estimate assumes: h^2 narrow = .70, dominance = .10, E^2 = .12, e^2 = .08, and measurement error = .00.)

Before I defend my general method against alternatives, I had better defend my estimate of the correlation between the AGCT and the Wechsler. Researchers have conducted three studies of sufficient relevance to be suggestive: Rabin (1941) put the correlation at .74 between the Army Alpha (the parent of the AGCT and correlated with it at the .90 level) and the Wechsler-Bellevue I (parent of the present Wechsler); Tamminen (1951) found .83 for the AGCT and the Wechsler-Bellevue I; and Watson and Klett (1968) found .74 for the AGCT and the present adult Wechsler. (2) It is of interest that almost all studies of the correlation between the present adult Wechsler (WAIS) and the children's Wechsler (WISC), when the tests are taken at the age at which the two overlap, put the correlation at .84 to .96 which is almost as high as most test-retest correlations. (3) At any rate, the average of the above three studies gives a correlation of .77. My reasons for accepting this as a valid figure for whites but suspect for blacks will be given later; for now, I will accept it for the purpose of giving a maximum estimate.

As for alternative methods of translating the AGCT

results, two methods are definitely not viable: first,
taking the gains of black and white troops on the AGCT
above their respective population means at face value;
second, taking the gap remaining between black and white
troops after military selection had done its work at face
value.   Both of these methods lead to nonsense conclusions thanks to the fact that the AGCT puts the general
population of white America almost 1.5 SDUs above the
general population of black America, unlike IQ tests which
separate them by only 1.0 SDU.   To illustrate: imagine
that armed forces selection had raised the white mean not
at all and the black mean by a full standard deviation;
if we equated the black gain with an IQ gain, we would
have to say that the AGCT had eliminated the black-white
IQ gap (1.0 - 1.0 = 0) among the troops, even though the
AGCT itself showed them still to be .5 SDU apart!   Or
imagine that selection had raised the black mean by only
half of a standard deviation;   if we looked at the gap remaining between black and white troops, we would find it
was 1.0 SDU (1.5 - .5 = 1.0).   And if we equated that
with an IQ difference, we would have to say that military
selection had left the gap at one standard deviation and
had had no effect whatsoever on closing the gap between
the races!

A colleague has suggested a third alternative to my own
method which evades these difficulties and which runs as
follows: (1) assume that the 1.47 SDU gap between black
and white Americans on the AGCT is equivalent to the 15
point IQ gap between the races;   (2) estimate the gain of
black troops as compared to black Americans in general,
i.e. + .650 SDU;   (3) divide the latter by the former -
which gives the percentage of the black-white gap on the
AGCT that was eliminated by the black gain, i.e.

.650 ÷ 1.470 = 44.22 per cent;   (4) multiply that percentage times the 15 point black-white IQ gap, i.e. 44.22 per
cent × 15.0 = 6.6 points;   (5) thus our estimate of the
phenotypic IQ of black troops in Germany becomes 91.6,
i.e. 85 + 6.6 = 91.6.   Naturally, we would do the same
for whites: .108 ÷ 1.470 = 7.35 per cent; 7.35 per cent
× 15.0 = 1.1 points; 100 + 1.1 = 101.1 as our estimate of
the phenotypic IQ of the white troops. These estimates
of 91.6 and 101.1 match my own with a discrepancy of only
one-tenth of an IQ point but despite this happy outcome, I
prefer my own method. The above alternative leads to no
absurdity but it is too inflexible: it allows us no way
of adjusting our estimates given the possibility of a low
correlation between the AGCT and the Wechsler.

The above method does raise one question of considerable interest. If we assumed that the AGCT was a better
measure of intelligence than the usual tests, the 1.47 SDU
gap between black and white Americans would translate into
an IQ gap of 22 points (1.47 × 15 = 22.1), much larger
than the 15-point gap the usual tests give. The estimate
of a 15-point gap is based on massive evidence drawn
mainly from IQ tests taken by school children and it is
unlikely to be abandoned. However, some explanation of
the extra gap produced by the AGCT seems in order.

From an environmentalist point of view, there would be
nothing surprising if the gap between the races tested as
adults (at say 18 to 40) were greater than the gap when
the races are tested as school children (most often at 10
or 11). After they leave school, blacks are more likely
than whites to be unemployed or get jobs that fail to exercise the skills tested by IQ tests and this may well
have some effect. However, I believe the principal explanation in this instance lies elsewhere and will discuss

two factors: the nature of the AGCT and a problem of
motivation.   As for motivation, when the armed forces
used tests, they brought into play an incentive system not
usually present in psychological testing, namely, if you
passed, you had to serve in the armed forces.   At the
time of the Second World War blacks faced an army which
was segregated, virtually without black officers, disproportionately commanded by white Southerners, in a word
racist.   Many blacks were alienated from American society
and therefore from its wars.   I suspect that far more
blacks than whites purposely failed so as to evade military service, thus lowering black performance.   I can
present no evidence for this at the time of the Second
World War but I can for the Korean War (when we get to
Table XI) and by Korea conditions for blacks in the armed
forces had much improved.   (During the Second World War,
on the pre-induction level, you passed or failed not the
AGCT but other tests.   However, I have counted failures
here as low scores on the AGCT (below 60);   and therefore,
in so far as these failures were intentional, they make
their contribution to the gap between the races.)

   As for the content of the AGCT, (4) it was a group test
and group tests always pose a problem for those with a low
level of education or literacy.   Johnson and Bond found:
that the directions of the AGCT required a reading level
slightly below the 6th grade;   that the arithmetic section
ranged from grade 6 to grade 7;   and that the vocabulary
ranged from grade 6 to near grade 10. (5)   In 1940, black
males in the relevant age group had completed barely over
6 years of schooling (6) and given the quality of that
schooling, the effective level of their education was undoubtedly lower than that.   Despite his general endorse-
ment of the AGCT, Tamminen notes that it cannot be substi-

tuted for the Wechsler at lower levels of education. (7)
It is likely that a large number of blacks simply gave up
on the AGCT or filled in answers at random; and it is
also likely that they would have done better on an indivi-
dually administered test such as the Wechsler.

Altus published an interesting study in 1948, a study
which would have had the fortunate result of separating
test content as a factor from low black incentive. His
sample consisted of men who had been originally classified
as illiterate, trained at a Special Training Centre, and
graduated into the Army on the basis of passing a test in
reading and arithmetic. The army then gave them the AGCT
which meant that doing poorly on it would not help them
evade service but merely give them less opportunity to
rise within the armed forces. Altus gave them four subtests of the Wechsler Form B (information, arithmetic,
comprehension and similarities). A sample of 225 whites
and 256 blacks had virtually identical scores on the
Wechsler, but on the AGCT the whites opened up a gap of
2.40 points. And on the MAT, an aptitude test with an
overlap of 60 to 80 per cent with the AGCT, the whites
opened up a gap of 4.85 points. (8) These gaps would be
equivalent to 2 or 3 IQ points: we cannot assume that
since blacks equal to whites on the Wechsler fall 2 or 3
points behind on the AGCT, blacks 15 points behind on the
Wechsler would fall 22 points behind on the AGCT; but the
tendency is in the direction of an expanded gap. Moreover, note that the army had trained all these men up to a
standard of literacy which would allow them to cope with
the AGCT. Therefore, the disadvantage of blacks on the
AGCT as compared to the Wechsler had been minimized.

I can contribute a piece of indirect evidence that unusual environmental factors were operating when blacks

took the AGCT, that is, the black distribution indicates
an unusually high variance.   My estimates of standard
deviations and variances will be defended in the discussion of Table III and for the moment, I will assume their
validity.   On IQ tests, Jensen puts the black standard
deviation at 13 and white at 15; but on the AGCT, my
calculations indicate that the black SD was 24.3 and
white 23.1.   If we convert the black SD to an IQ equivalent, it would be 15.8 points and therefore, variance
would rise from 169 (13^2) to 250 (15.8^2), a very great ex-
pansion.   This expanded variance may hold for only the
top 70 per cent of the black population but that in itself
would be sufficient to evidence the impact of unusual factors.   And indeed, the fact that the bottom 30 per cent
is probably an exception is also a sign of unusual factors; something has pushed the median black performance
too low (too close to zero) for a normal distribution of
the low scores to be possible.

In sum, we cannot be certain what caused the 1.47 SDU
gap between the races on the AGCT, but there are plenty of
environmental hypotheses available.   And that expanded
gap, whatever its causes, dictates in my opinion my own
method of translating AGCT results into estimates relevant
to Eyferth's study.   I now pass on to the methodological
problem we postponed, namely, how do we estimate the extent to which black and white troops rose above their respective population norms (on the AGCT) thanks to armed
forces selection.   Unfortunately, this means that the
next section must consist of a lengthy series of tables.
The reader may want to look them over quickly and refer
back to them as he reads the commentary that follows.

TABLE I   Second World War mobilization population –
estimate

	I	II	III	IV	V
White	6.36	29.82	30.87	26.44	6.51
Black	.24	2.68	9.56	39.90	47.62

Gap W/B mob. population: 1.470 SD Units.
Results of selection: white mean + .070; black mean
+ .401.
Gap W/B armed forces: 1.139 SD Units.

TABLE II   March 1941-May 1946, armed forces, enlisted men
plus 72 per cent of officers corps (9)

	I	II	III	IV	V
White	6.4	28.7	32.7	26.6	5.6
Black	.3	3.4	12.9	47.7	35.7

Results + 72 per cent officers: white mean + .018;
black mean + .359.
Results + 100 per cent officers: white mean + .049;
black mean + .364.
Gap W/B armed forces: 1.155 SD Units.

TABLE III   Second World War – Fulk and Harrell: comparison between author's estimates for Fulk and Harrell
sample and actual means reported; comparison between
author's estimate for troops Table IV and means based on
Fulk and Harrell plus education levels (10)

	W mean	B mean	Gap W/B
Fulk and Harrell estimates	94.5	70.1	24.4
Fulk and Harrell actual	95.1	68.5	26.6
Table IV estimates	100.0	71.9	28.1
Table IV - Fulk and Harrell	101.8	71.8	30.0

Note: all means expressed in terms of AGCT scores; all
means refer to EMO (EMO = enlisted men only).

TABLE IV   Spring 1945, armed forces, European Theatre, all blacks, white infantry (EMO)(11)

	I and II	III	IV	V
White	37	34	24	5
Black	4	13	49	34

Results (EMO): white mean + .089; black mean + .400.
Results (+ officers): white mean + .166; black mean + .411.

TABLE V   January-August 1946, armed forces, European Theatre (EMO) (12)

	I	II	III	IV	V
White	6.1	29.3	32.5	29.5	5.5
Black	.3	3.6	13.3	47.6	35.2

Results (EMO): white mean - .003; black mean + .381.
Results (+ officers): white mean + .096; black mean + .414.

TABLE VI   September 1946, armed forces, European Theatre (EMO) (13)

	I	II	III	IV	V
White	4.3	24.7	31.5	35.4	4.1
Black	.3	4.9	14.4	56.5	24.1

Results (EMO): white mean - .085; black mean + .547.
Results (+ officers): white mean + .029; black mean + .558.

TABLE VII   January 1948, army, within USA - 10,661 men (EMO) (14)

	I	II	III	IV	V
Black	.35	8.04	23.93	55.75	11.93

Results (EMO): black mean + .857.
Results (+ officers): black mean + .885.

TABLE VIII   March 1949, army (EMO) (15)

	I	II	III	IV	V
White	4.28	27.27	35.99	29.74	2.72
Black	.13	7.50	30.45	57.72	4.20

Results (EMO): white + .018; black mean + 1.034.
Results (+ officers): white mean + .122; black mean + 1.059.

TABLE IX   January 1950, regular army (EMO) (16)

	I	II	III	IV	V
White	4	27	40	28	1
Black	1	8	31	54	6

Results (EMO): white mean + .055; black mean + 1.095.
Results (+ officers): white mean + .161; black mean + 1.129.

TABLE X   January 1949-June 1950, air force, enlistees (17)

	I	II	III	IV	V
White	6.24	39.02	54.48	.26	nil
Black	.66	15.20	83.66	.47	.01

Results (enlistees): white mean + .428; black mean + 1.457.
Results (+ officers): white mean + .500; black mean + 1.465.

TABLE XI   May-August 1951, army, accessions (18)

	I	II	III	IV	V
White	8.85	19.31	27.70	33.06	11.08
Black	.34	2.06	9.77	38.99	48.84

Results (accessions): white mean - .159; black mean - .002.
Results (+ officers): white mean - .072; black mean + .042.

TABLE XII   1953, army, accessions (19)

	I	II	III	IV	V
White	8.7	27.0	34.2	27.0	3.1
Black	.6	3.9	17.5	54.8	23.2

Results (accessions): white mean + .101; black mean + .634.
Results (+ officers): white mean + .161; black mean + .658.

TABLE XIII   1953, air force, accessions (20)

	I	II	III	IV	V
White	10.3	29.4	37.5	22.8	nil
Black	.7	5.1	25.2	69.0	nil

Results (accessions): white mean + .301; black mean + .937.
Results (+ officers): white mean + .376; black mean + .954.

TABLE XIV   Estimates of mean phenotypic IQ of white and black US armed forces personnel in Germany

	White	Black
Maximum estimate	101.2	91.5
Alternative estimate I	——	88.5
Alternative estimate II	——	88.1
Maximum estimate (EMO)	100.1	91.3
Alternative estimate I (EMO)	——	88.3
Alternative estimate II (EMO)	——	88.0

EMO = estimate refers to enlisted men only.

TABLE XV Estimates of mean genotypic IQ of white and
black US armed forces in Germany - and of the genotypic
gap between the races which remained after armed forces
selection

	White	Black	Gap W/B	%
Max. est. + h^2 = .70	100.8	89.6	11.2	75
Max. est. + h^2 = .55	100.7*	88.6*	12.1	81
Max. est. + h^2 = .40	100.5	87.6	12.9	86
Alt. I + h^2 = .70	——	87.5	13.3	89
Alt. II + h^2 = .70	——	87.2	13.6	91
Alt. I + h^2 = .55	——	86.9	13.8	92
Alt. II + h^2 = .55	——	86.7*	14.0	93
Alt. I + h^2 = .40	——	86.4	14.1	94
Alt. II + h^2 = .40	——	86.2	14.3	95

Note: (1) % refers to the genotypic gap remaining as a
percentage of the 15-point phenotypic gap between black
and white; (2) * designates estimates used by the author
in Chapter 3.

From the above tables, the reader can see that I have
attempted to secure data on the AGCT distribution of black
and white troops for the entire period during which Eyferth's children were being conceived. The armed forces
have an unpleasant tendency to destroy records, particularly statistical records, and much of our data had to be
got from reading correspondence and reports at the National Archives. Concerning the nature of the data, armed
forces compilations on the performance of their personnel
on the AGCT rarely give actual scores, rather they give
the percentage of men who scored in certain categories of
significance to the armed forces; for example, you had to
score in classes I or II to qualify for officer training,
and at times you had to score in class IV (or even III)

to be acceptable for military service.   In 1947 in the
European Theatre (essentially the occupation army in Germany), you had to have a certain score even to try out for
the band. (21)

Recall our purpose in assembling this data: we want to
determine how much armed forces selection, primarily re-
jecting men considered illiterate or mentally unsuitable
but also failing to attract or deferring men in the upper
levels of ability, raised black and white troops above the
norms for their respective larger populations, at least as
measured by AGCT scores.   In order to do this, we must be
able to compare the AGCT performance of whites who did
enter the armed forces with the performance of all white
males in the relevant age group; and the same for blacks.
The general population of all males in the relevant age
group is called 'the mobilization population'.   As for
our comparison, we have our data on the performance of
armed forces personnel on the AGCT; but we need an estimate of how well the mobilization population would do -
and this is given in Table I.   The estimate is based on
Davenport's data which includes the performance of every
man who passed through an induction centre during the
Second World War, that is, from June 1941 through September 1945. (22)

I modified Davenport's data as follows.   First, there
was a change in the cutting line between class IV and V in
August 1942 and I have altered the percentages of men in
these classes before that date to correspond to the proportions of the period immediately after. (23)   Second,
Davenport's data includes all enlisted men but only those
officers who came up through the ranks - officers who were
commissioned directly from civilian life, ROTC, the military academies, etc., did not go through induction centres

to be tested.   I have added the missing officers making
the following assumptions: that 11 per cent of white
armed forces personnel and .87 per cent of black were
officers; (24)   that 68 per cent of them came up through
the ranks, leaving 32 per cent missing; (25) and that the
missing officers would have distributed themselves in
classes I and II in the same proportions as the men already there.   The third and last modification was to
allow for the portion of the mobilization population who
are missing because they were rejected on mental grounds,
that is, because of intelligence or literacy or both.   I
made the assumption that these men would have scored in
class V;   and used failure rates of 2.5 per cent for white
and 14 per cent for black in the period up to June 1943,
rates of 3.4 per cent for white and 30 per cent for black
for the period thereafter. (26)

As Karpinos, the statistician who served the Surgeon
General so well for so long, has pointed out, this should
give us a good estimate. (27)   The men still missing in
our estimate were, during the Second World War as distinct
from other times, not very significant.   Volunteers were
at a minimum after the executive order banning them in
December of 1942 and student deferments for high-IQ occupational groups (e.g. medical and professional) were very
low, particularly in the younger age groups from which
most of the troops were drawn. (28)   Despite all this, I
have encountered the view that a profile such as mine
underestimates the performance of the general population
because of occupational deferments.   In answer to this, I
present the following facts: the 1940 census shows that
15 per cent of American males in the relevant age group
had some college education - no doubt the percentage would
have risen slightly over the next few years;   my profile

of the mobilization population included 15.8 per cent with
some college education. (29)

Table I not only presents our estimate of how black and
white males in general would perform on the AGCT, it
allows for an analysis of their differential performance.
The distribution of the white population approximates a
normal curve and while there are some problems with the
lower end of the black distribution, I will deal with
these a few pages hence. Assuming a normal distribution
for both populations, the percentage of men in each class
allows us to compute the distance in standard deviation
units (sometimes called standard score units) of the cutting line of each class from the appropriate population
mean. By comparing the standard deviation units at each
of the four class boundaries for black and white respectively, we get four estimates of the gap between the black
and white means - and the average of these four is our
overall estimate of the gap between black and white performance on the AGCT, which is a gap of 1.470 standard
deviations.

The addenda to Table I offer an estimate for the Second
World War period of the extent to which selection raised
the means (in SD units) of black and white armed forces
personnel, raised them above the respective population
means. The method used was to imagine that a percentage
of the area at the bottom of a normal curve had been eliminated equal to the percentage of the mobilization population rejected on mental grounds; and then calculate how
much (in SD units) the mean of the remaining area would
exceed the mean of the original curve. Table II represents an attempt to check the validity of Table I by
calling on data from a different source, official armed
forces data, and covering a slightly different period than

Davenport, and seeing if the results tallied.   As the
reader can see, they tallied very well, particularly when
allowance was made for the fact that only 72 per cent of
officers were included. (30)

The method used for calculating the rise in means for
Table II merits discussion for the same method was used in
all subsequent tables, that is, Tables IV through XIII, the
data which sheds light on Eyferth's study.   Each of these
tables gives the black and white distributions on the AGCT
(or AFQT) for armed forces personnel at a particular time.
Sometimes my task was easy: where the distribution was
symmetrical, signalling an approximation of a normal distribution, I merely compared the armed forces population
with the mobilization population at each of the four class
boundaries; as above, the average of these four comparisons affords an estimate of the distance in SD units that
the mean of the armed forces population is above (or
below) the mean of the mobilization population.   This
method was appropriate for the data on whites in Tables
IV, V and VI and for the data on both races in Table XI.
However, usually the armed forces data was not symmetrical, rather it suggested a curve which had once been
normal but which had had the bottom chopped off - had had
men chopped off at about the point corresponding to the
armed forces minimum standard for accessions at that time.

Such data called for a more complex method in four
steps: (1) I took a certain percentage from the bottom of
the appropriate mobilization population - sometimes this
constituted part of class V but at other times it constituted the whole of V and part of class IV as well; (2) I
added this on to the bottom of the armed forces data, adjusting the data so that the total would still be 100 per
cent; (3) now we have 'normalized' the distribution of

our armed forces data by creating an artificial population inclusive of the 'men rejected' - and if calculations show that this artificial population is equivalent to our mobilization population at the cutting lines, we have added on the correct percentage of rejects; (4) we then calculate how much deleting that percentage from the bottom of a normal curve would raise the population mean. Just to spell the method out by way of a hypothetical example: (1) assume we take 50 per cent from the bottom of the black mobilization population, which would be all 47.62 per cent in class V and 2.38 per cent from class IV; (2) we then add these to a table of armed forces data on blacks - taking each percentage given times .5, adding 2.38 per cent to the product we get for class IV, and adding 47.62 per cent to the product we get for class V; (3) once again, if the population we have created is equivalent to our mobilization population at the cutting lines in terms of SD units, we have used the correct percentage; (4) therefore, we calculate how much deleting 50 per cent from the bottom of a normal distribution would raise the mean - in this case the mean would rise by .798 SD units.

I must emphasize that this method is merely a useful calculating device. I do not mean to imply that the pattern of military selection was ever so simple as to just screen out a certain percentage at the bottom of the general population curves. However, I applied this method because I wanted a maximum estimate for blacks: it has little effect on the estimate for whites because the percentages involved are so low; but by assuming that all missing blacks were eliminated from the very bottom of a normal curve, it raises the black in-service mean above the black population mean by the largest possible amount.

The above four-step method gives us an estimate which
applies to the military personnel represented in a particular table.   Normally the table refers to men actually on
duty at a particular time and includes enlisted men only,
which means that the entire officers corps is missing.
Table II is an exception in that it refers to accessions
(men at the time of their induction rather than on duty)
and covers a period of over five years - which means that
many of those inducted as enlisted men were serving as
officers by the end of the period; but even here 28 per
cent of the officer corps is missing.   In order to allow
for the presence of officers absent from our tables, two
things are necessary: an estimate of how much the performance of white officers on the AGCT was above the white
population mean plus a similar estimate for blacks;   and
the percentage of white and black armed forces personnel
who were officers.   The latter is of course a matter of
record.   As to the former, Table I tells us that the top
36.18 per cent of whites were eligible to be officers,
that is, those in classes I and II combined;   taking this
percentage as a proportion of the area at the top of a
normal curve, we find that this group had a mean 1.035 SD
units above that of the white mobilization population.
The top 2.92 per cent of blacks were eligible to be officers and their mean was 2.278 SD units above the black
population mean.   These estimates were checked against
data on the educational level of officers and the IQ
typical of various educational levels at that time. (31)

Table III makes use of the data collected by Fulk and
Harrell and provides the best possible check on the accuracy of our estimates.   From personnel rosters of men
serving during the Second World War, Harrell selected a
sample of 2,174 whites and 2,010 blacks and recorded the

AGCT score attained by each man.   As we have seen, most
of our data does not give us actual AGCT scores but only a
distribution of performance divided into AGCT categories,
that is, the percentage of men in classes I through V.
Fulk and Harrell compiled a table from their sample which
gives us the following: (1) a breakdown of both races in
terms of years of schooling, i.e. the number of whites
with zero years of formal education all the way through
13+ years and the same for blacks;   (2) the mean AGCT
score for each of their cells, e.g. the mean score for
whites with zero years of schooling, plus the SD for each;
(3) the overall mean AGCT score for black and white plus
the overall SD for each. (32)   All in all, they give us
an opportunity to compare our estimates with actual
values.

I arrived at the first set of estimates in Table III by
using the Fulk and Harrell data to classify their men into
the usual AGCT categories of I through V, that is, I used
their data to construct a replica of one of my tables,
which tells us no more than the percentage of men in each
AGCT class.   I then applied my usual method of analysis
and 'predicted' that the overall means for white and black
would be 94.5 and 70.1 respectively (Fulk and Harrell
estimates);   the actual values reported are 95.1 and 68.5
(Fulk and Harrell actual).   I then turned to Table IV, my
first table of data on armed forces personnel serving in
Germany.   Fortunately the source for this table classi-
fies the men not only by AGCT category but also by educational level. (33)   My usual method of analysis applied
to Table IV 'predicted' means for white and black of 100.0
and 71.9 (Table IV estimates);   using Fulk and Harrell
means for various educational levels allowed me to calculate another estimate based on the educational levels of

the men represented in my table - giving values of 101.8
and 71.8 (Table IV - Fulk and Harrell).   Now the largest
discrepancy disclosed by these attempts to check my estimates is 1.8 AGCT points and this would mean an error of
only .5 IQ points - when translated into the estimates I
use to interpret Eyferth's study.

Values: white SD on the AGCT = 23.1; correlation AGCT
and Wechsler = .77; white SD for IQ = 15.0; h^2 narrow
= .55.

Calculations

(1)   1.8 ÷ 23.1 = .078 SDU - discrepancy on AGCT.

(2)   .078 × .77 = .060 SDU - discrepancy on Wechsler.

(3)   .060 × 15.0 = .9 IQ points (phenotypic).

(4)   .9 × .55 = .5 IQ points (genotypic).

However, to focus on the size of one discrepancy is to
miss something more significant, namely, the overall
effect of the discrepancies collectively: the effect of
the discrepancies is to underestimate the gap remaining
between black and white troops after military selection
had done its work.   As Table III shows, my estimates consistently put that gap at about 2 AGCT points less than
the values used to check them.   Given that an environmental interpretation of Eyferth's results is rendered more
plausible the greater the gap that remained, the overall
effect of the discrepancies is entirely against the
author's 'interests'.

It is good to have my estimates so closely confirmed by
more detailed data.   But while on the subject of the
accuracy of his estimates, the author wishes to detail
some minor inaccuracies that he suspects are existent.
Thanks to my attempt to provide a maximum estimate for
blacks, I have probably given an overestimate of the rise
of the black in-service mean over that of the general

black population.   First, I tried to err on the side of
caution when constructing my profile of the performance of
black America in general on the AGCT.   For example, I
assumed that everyone rejected on grounds of literacy
would have scored in class V.   The effect of this was
undoubtedly to artificially lower general black performance on the AGCT - and the effect of that would be to
inflate the gap between the in-service and general population means.   Second, when analysing the black in-service
data, I assumed that all 'missing men' were located at the
very bottom of the black population curve.   This was
equivalent to assuming that military selection was so
efficient that all blacks were rejected who were below the
minimum AGCT standard at the time.   We of course know
this was false: particularly during the early Second
World War period when simply having four years of schooling got you in, many with low scores slipped through, as
attested to by scattered references to black soldiers with
scores in the 20s and 30s and by Fulk and Harrell
data. (34)

The above factors probably had only a modest effect:
rough calculations (available on request) show they were
worth only about .065 SDU - which would lower my estimate
of the black rise on the AGCT from .650 SDU to .585 SDU.
The factor of low black incentive may have had a greater
effect.   Whenever a black failed with intent during the
Second World War the gap between the in-service mean and
the general population mean became partially an incentive
difference and not an IQ difference.   But I could see no
way of making even a rough allowance for this.   None of
the above factors require an alteration in my estimate for
whites: almost no whites were rejected as illiterate;
when analysing white in-service data, I generally assumed

that the distribution of scores approximated a normal
curve.

A few words about the calculations used to prepare
Table III.   The reader may wonder how I can calculate a
mean for in-service personnel in terms of a specific AGCT
score on the basis of my tables, when all my tables give
me only distributions in terms of AGCT categories.   The
key is that we know the scores that constitute the cutting lines between the AGCT categories.   Using these, we
can calculate a best fit for the distributions of our
black and white mobilization populations (Table I), a
best fit in terms of means and standard deviations expressed as AGCT scores.   The result for the two mobilization
populations is as follows: white - mean 97.9, SD 23.1;
black 62.2, SD 24.3.   Once we have these, we can calculate the means of the in-service personnel, because we
know how many standard deviation units they are above
their respective population means.   The estimate for
standard deviations may arouse scepticism in that the AGCT
was supposed to yield an SD of 20.   However, whatever the
intent, when the test was actually used, it was the in-
service population whose SDs were approximately 20.   Fulk
and Harrell show this clearly: they found SDs of 21.2 for
white and 20.7 for black in a sample that included enlisted men only.   This implies that the general population
would have SDs well above 20:   for blacks, the general
population included those who failed to qualify for service (say the bottom 10 per cent plus about .5 of the 11th
to 30th percentiles), all low scores who would add substantially to variance;   for whites, it included those who
failed and the potential officers corps (say the bottom 3
per cent plus about .3 of the 64th to 99th percentiles),
both of which would also add to variance.   Indeed if we

assume in-service SDs of 21 for white and 20 for black, we get rough estimates of the general population SDs of 23.5 and 25.0 respectively.   Therefore, my own estimates are certainly not too high to be plausible.

The estimate of a black SD of 24.3 for the general population raises a problem mentioned earlier, the fact that the black curve clearly does not have a normal distribution at its lower end.   A curve should be able to accommodate 3 SDs below its mean and the black curve reaches a score of zero at 2.56 SDs.   This implies that those blacks who failed to qualify for the armed forces must be assigned scores somewhat higher than a normal distribution would dictate.   And this in turn implies that my estimate of 62.2 as the general black population mean on the AGCT is too low.   But fortunately that estimate is a mere calculating device of no practical consequence and the estimates that are important are not rendered suspect by the above.   First, take the estimate of the black in-service mean of 71.9 (for Table IV - enlisted men only). If the distribution of in-service scores look like a normal curve with its bottom 20 to 30 per cent missing (and they do), then the estimate of the black in-service mean will be correct whatever the distribution of the 'non-existent' scores.   Second, there is our main concern, our estimates of the effect of military selection in terms of raising the mean IQ (of the armed forces above the population mean) for recall, we are interested in AGCT scores only because of their correlation with IQ. Since black IQ scores are normally distributed at the bottom end, it does no harm to give black AGCT scores a pseudo-normal distribution at the bottom end, just so long as the AGCT has a reasonable rank-order correlation with IQ.   And if the AGCT does not have a reasonable correla-

tion with IQ, then armed forces selection did not much
raise the mean IQ of blacks and I am being over generous
to the hereditarian (in evaluating Eyferth's study) in
assuming that it did.   In other words, on this point I
cannot lose: either the correlation is there and the calculations are well founded;   or the correlation is not
there and the calculations need not have been done.

Having described and defended my methodology, I now proceed to the tables that actually refer to the potential
fathers of Eyferth's children.   Therefore, I will discuss
them in the context of his chronology.   Eyferth divided
his children into five groups according to age.   The
oldest children were conceived in February 1945, each of
the five groups spans 19 months, which means that the
groups collectively take us from February 1945 up through
the end of 1952. (35)   He gives us the number of children
in each group and this allows us to state what percentage
cf the total number were conceived in each of the five
periods.

   February 1945-August 1946:   45.78 per cent of white
children conceived, 43.09 per cent of black;   Table IV and
Table V.   Since this period witnessed the conception of
over 40 per cent of Eyferth's children of both races, it
is fortunate we have such excellent data, data from the
European Theatre itself which is essentially Germany in
that Austria seems to have been considered part of the
Mediterranean Theatre of Operations.   The data in Table
IV was collected as part of a study of the use of screened
volunteers as black combat infantry on the Western Front
in 1945, most black troops having been used in service and
supply roles.   Consequently the black infantry was an
elite group, but fortunately figures are given for all

blacks in the European Theatre.   The white data is for
infantry only but white combat troops were not an elite,
indeed, the distribution of these troops in terms of educational levels is an almost perfect match for the distribution of the army as a whole (enlisted men only) at that
time. (36)   This data is the best indication of the AGCT
quality of the 3,000,000 US army and air force personnel
who poured into Germany beginning in February 1945.

During this period, the occupation forces were reduced
from 3,000,000 to just under 300,000 (37) and the data in
Table V, which is from early 1946, signals the situation
towards the end of the period.   There is clearly a minor
error in the figures for whites in that they total slightly more than 100 per cent; I have treated the excess as
if it were in class III, so as to neutralize its effect on
cutting lines above and below the mean.   The data shows
exactly what events at the time would lead us to expect,
the quality of white troops had fallen off with the rush
to return to civilian life, while the quality of black
troops who rather preferred Germany to America did not.
At this time, the air force was still part of the army and
the data covers all US occupation forces.

The calculation for officers was made by the usual
method, the relevant figures being: Table IV - 8.13 per
cent of whites were officers and .56 per cent of blacks;
Table V - 9.54 per cent of whites and 1.73 per cent of
blacks. (38)   Unless otherwise stated, all officer data
refers to Germany itself.   To get an overall estimate for
this period, the results of selection in Tables IV and V
were averaged.   At one time, I experimented with weighting the data within each period so as to allow for fluctuations in the size of the occupation force, but this
turned out to make so little difference to the overall

result (less than one-tenth of an IQ point) that I abandoned it.

September 1946-March 1948: 19.28 per cent of white
children conceived, 24.31 per cent of black; Table VI and
Table VII.   During this period the occupation forces were
reduced from 290,000 to approximately 115,000, counting as
always only male personnel in that females were unlikely
to have fathered any occupation children. (39)   Table VI
reveals the continued decline in the quality of white personnel.   This disturbed the theatre command but they were
even more disturbed, beginning as far back as late 1945,
by the difficulties they were having with black troops.
The latter had very high rates of misconduct in terms of
desertion, crime and repeated contraction of venereal disease. (40)   In an effort to upgrade the quality of personnel, the minimum standard for enlistment and re-enlist-
ment (with minor exceptions) was raised to an AGCT score
of 70 as of March 1946, a score well up into class IV
(which runs from 60-89). (41)   The impact was far greater
on blacks than whites and Table VI shows a noticeable improvement in the scores of black troops.

Table VI refers to Germany and to all the occupation
forces stationed there.   But beginning with Table VII, we
encounter two problems: first, most of the data refers to
the army only and does not include the AGCT scores of air
force personnel; second, it refers to army personnel in
general rather than those serving in Germany.

As to our second problem, every piece of evidence indicates that the forces in Germany were typical of the armed
forces in general.   Look back to Tables IV and V which
are specific to the European Theatre, then compare them to
Table II which refers to all armed forces at that time.
The match for both black and white is almost uncanny.

Moreover, scattered references in the archives reveal the same kind of correspondence.   For example: in the summer of 1946, we are told that 49 per cent of blacks in the European Theatre had AGCT scores of less than 70; (42) and then, on 4 December 1946, a War Department source states that 50 per cent of blacks throughout the army were under 70. (43)   I very much suspect that data specific to Germany exists in the reports issued by Lieutenant Colonel Marcus Ray, Negro troop advisor from August 1947 to August 1950; (44)   frantic efforts by myself and several archivists proved unsuccessful in locating these.

As to the fact that beginning in 1948 we lack continuous air force data, there is enough data to show that the problem is negligible.   During the period 1948-52, the army comprised 84.4 per cent of the occupation troops in Germany and the air force only 15.6 per cent. (45)   In addition, we can compare the two services at two times. First, look at Tables IX and X which indicate that in 1950, the gap between black and white was actually greater in the air force than in the army.   Then note Tables XII and XIII which allow us to compare accessions for the Korean War period.   Here the higher minimum standard of the air force (which began to bite in 1948) has made for a lesser gap between the races.   The difference between the services is small, however;   and more important, even if we projected this difference over the entire period of 1948-52, it would not reduce the gap between black and white for the occupation forces in toto.

This last assertion must seem odd so let me explain. Precisely because of the air force's higher standards, the percentage of blacks therein was considerably lower than was the case in the army.   For example, in Germany during 1948-52, there was one white in the air force for every

five in the army; the ratio for blacks between the services was one to ten. (46)   Therefore, the high-quality
whites in the air force were actually pulling up the mean
for the white armed forces in toto to a greater, not a
lesser, extent than the high-quality blacks in the air
force were pulling up the black mean.   In sum, the
missing air force data would undoubtedly increase our
estimate of the gap between the races in Germany rather
than diminish it.   A last point, the most important of
all the estimates we are calculating is the mean genotypic IQ of the black troops in Germany.   The above
tables, plus the ten to one ratio for blacks, plus the
fact that we have air force data prior to 1948 (by then
55 per cent of blacks fathers were already accounted for)
mean this: the missing data could not possibly raise our
estimate by more than one-tenth of one IQ point.

To return to the period September 1946 to March 1948,
the overall estimate of the results of selection for
whites is based on Table VI only - Table VII gives no
data for whites.   The overall estimate for blacks is
based on an average of both tables.   The relevant officer
percentages are: Table VI - 10.18 per cent of whites were
officers and .66 per cent of blacks; Table VII - 1.97 per
cent of blacks. (47)

April 1948-October 1949: 18.07 per cent of white children conceived, 18.78 per cent of black; Table VIII.   We
now enter an era in which the number of occupation forces
remains fairly stable, fluctuating between 105,000 and
130,000 men. (48)   Table VIII, dated 31 March 1949, shows
that by raising their minimum standard (it was now up to
an AGCT score of 80), (49) the army had finally begun to
raise the quality of its white personnel, although the
extent to which it could achieve a mean above that of the

mobilization population always remained limited.   Once
again, the rise in the black mean was much more dramatic,
reflecting the higher proportion of blacks in the mobilization population who could not meet a standard of 70 to
80.   Such standards did not of course eliminate all army
personnel below them, thanks to the carry-over of men from
previous eras.

The estimates of the results of selection in Table VIII
stand as the overall estimates for black and white during
this period.   The estimate for whites was calculated in
the usual way;   for blacks I took the unusual step of ignoring the first cutting line (between classes I and II)
and beginning with the second.   It would have been to my
advantage to have taken the figure for blacks in class I,
only .13 per cent, at face value because this would have
reduced the rise in the black mean.   And in this case, we
actually have the rough data of the officer who compiled
the figures and these do indicate that only 90 blacks in
the entire army were in class I - which would dictate a
figure of .13 per cent. (50)   However, I just could not
accept this as accurate on the basis of all our other
data.   Fortunately, the percentages for the other classes
are what one would expect.   The relevant officer percentages: Table VII - 10.2 per cent of whites were officers
and 2.00 per cent of blacks. (51)

November 1949-May 1951:   14.46 per cent of white children conceived, 7.73 per cent of black;   Table IX and Table
XI.   There was a decline in occupation forces from
105,000 to 93,500 by June 1950, the outbreak of the Korean
War, and then the number rose to 185,000. (52)   It took
some months to train the Korean War accessions and they
began to arrive in the overseas commands at the beginning
of 1951.   This breaks the period into two parts: the

fourteen months from November 1949 to December 1950 - here
the regular army of the inter-war years is dominant as
represented by Table IX: the five months from January to
May 1951 - here the AGCT quality was a blend of the regular army and the arriving accessions, a blend of Table IX
and Table XI.   In calculating my overall estimate for
this period, I weighted the data accordingly, that is,
Table IX was given a weight of 14 and the average between
Tables IX and XI was given a weight of 5.

I ignored the first cutting line for blacks in Table
IX, not because I thought that the 1.0 per cent for class
I was a mistake, but because it is clearly something like
.6 or .7 per cent rounded off.   There were never as many
as a full 1 per cent of blacks in class I in any service
at any time between 1945 and 1952.   Table XI (as well as
Tables X, XII and XIII) poses a problem we have not encountered since our Second World War data.   It does not
refer to men actually posted and serving as enlisted men
with a separate officer corps serving alongside them.
Rather it refers to 'accessions':   this term designates
men entering the army, both draftees and volunteers, and
all of them did indeed enter the army as enlisted men;
however, a few of them would have been selected out,
trained as officers, and posted as such.   I made allowance for this possible 'overlap' between enlisted men and
officers by way of a deduction, by subtracting from the
number of officers the percentage of them who came up
through the ranks at the relevant time.   This was also
done for the other tables whose data was similar in character.   The relevant officer percentages were: Table IX
- 10.80 per cent of whites were officers and 2.84 per cent
of blacks;   Table XI (after deductions) - 7.32 per cent of
whites, 1.94 per cent of blacks. (53)

Table XI is worth some extra attention.   On the face
of it, the quality of accessions during the first year or
so of the Korean War was worse than the quality of the
larger mobilization population, worse for blacks as well
as whites.   It looks as if the mental test had gone
astray, as if it was flunking not those at the bottom of
the curve but rather a sample from all levels of ability -
with a slight bias against intelligence.   The explanation
lies in the archives: in point of fact the accessions in
class V had flunked the exam; they were admitted 'on the
assumption that the individuals involved failed the AFQT
deliberately'. (54)   Class V represents only 11 per cent
of white accessions but fully 48 per cent of black, which
would imply that something like 25 per cent of all blacks
who took the test attempted to fail!   Surely this cannot
have been true, but it does shed light on a problem discussed earlier: recall that during the Second World War
the AGCT test showed a larger gap between black and white
than do IQ tests of school children; it appears that my
reluctance to take the larger gap as valid has some foundation.   I should add that as the Korean War wore on, the
number of blacks admitted in class V was reduced from 48
per cent to 23 per cent - see Table XII.

June 1951-December 1952: 2.41 per cent of white children conceived, 6.08 per cent of black; Table XI and Table
XII.   The Korean War buildup continues and the occupation
forces in Germany go from 185,000 to almost 300,000. (55)
I use Table XI once again because it tells us the scores
of accessions at the beginning of this period, while Table
XII will have to do as indicative of the distribution
during 1952.   Actually, it refers to 1953 but no data
from the previous year seems to have survived - and there
is no reason to suspect that the two years would differ by

much.   The overall estimate for this period was obtained
by averaging the results of selection in Tables XI and
XII.   The relevant officer percentages: Table XI (after
deductions for overlap) - 7.32 per cent of whites and 1.94
per cent of blacks; Table XII (after deductions) - 6.43
per cent of whites, 1.46 per cent of blacks. (56)

Having reviewed the data, we come to the summary tables
which were the point of the whole exercise.   Table XIV
presents my estimates of the mean phenotypic IQ of US
armed forces personnel serving in Germany from February
1945 to December 1952.   This should not be taken literally in that the estimates have been weighted to have the
greatest possible relevance to Eyferth's study.   To elab-
orate, as we have gone along, I have indicated how I calculated the black and white rises on the AGCT for each of
our five periods, the rises being expressed in standard
deviation units (SDUs).   To get an appropriate overall
estimate, I took these and weighted them in terms of the
percentage of Eyferth's children conceived in each of the
five periods.   For example, the overall estimate for
whites was obtained as follows: the SDU rise for our
first period was multiplied by 45.78 per cent, the second
by 19.28 per cent, the third by 18.07 per cent, the fourth
by 14.46 per cent, and the fifth by 2.41 per cent; the
products were added and divided by 100 per cent.   The
overall estimate for blacks was obtained in the same way
using the appropriate percentages.   The results: an
overall rise of .108 SDU for whites - .010 SDU for enlisted men only; an overall rise of .650 for blacks - .626
SDU for enlisted men only.   As these results show, the
presence of officers was not as important as one might
have thought and Table XIV spells this out in its estimates

Concerning the maximum estimates presented in Table
XIV, thanks to our earlier discussion (see pp. 222-3), the
reader is familiar both with them and with the method by
which they were calculated; white, .108 × .77 (correlation coefficient) × 15 (SD) = 1.2 and plus 100 = 101.2;
black, .650 × .77 (correlation coefficient) × 13 (SD) =
6.5 and plus 85 = 91.5.   However, the correlation of .77
assumed between the AGCT and Wechsler plays an important
role and I want to say this: I accept it as valid for
whites and therefore, Table XIV presents no alternative
estimates for the phenotypic IQ of white troops; but I
think it suspect for blacks, and therefore have presented
two alternatives to my maximum estimate for black troops.

Before I discuss the problem of the correlation coefficient, let me dispose of my tables.   In Table XIV, alternative estimate I for blacks assumes a correlation coefficient between the AGCT and the Wechsler of .41 which
gives: .650 × .41 (correlation coefficient) × 13 (SD) =
3.5 and plus 85 = 88.5.   Alternative estimate II for
blacks allows not only for the possibility of a low correlation but also for the fact (see p. 242) that the black
rise on the AGCT was probably nearer to .585 SDU than to
our maximum estimate.   These values give: .585 × .41
(correlation coefficient) × 13 (SD) = 3.1 and plus 85 =
88.1.   In my opinion, this is a realistic estimate, as
distinct from a maximum estimate, of the phenotypic IQ of
our black troops.

In Table XV, all of our estimates for phenotypic IQ are
converted into genotypic IQ by the use of a variety of
values for h^2 narrow: recall that we are interested in
these troops as potential fathers, and therefore we are
interested in the portion of their elite intelligence that
could be inherited by their offspring.   In Table XV I

also wanted to show how little difference it makes just
what value we accept for h^2 narrow, whether a Jensen-type
value of .70 (corresponding to an h^2 of .80), or a moderate one of .55 (corresponding to .63), or my own guess of
.40 (corresponding to .45).   As the reader can see from
the table, the value used for whites makes no difference
at all: whatever the value for h^2 narrow, all the result-
ing genotypic estimates round off to 101.   For blacks, as
far as the maximum estimate goes, the difference is plus
or minus one point.   I have chosen to use .55 so as to
carry most scholars with me and it gives a maximum estimate for black genotypic IQ of 88.6 and rounding this off
to 89 gives the hereditarian fully his due.   For blacks,
concerning the realistic estimates, the whole range of
these is only 1.3 points and I have selected using .585
SDU and .55 h^2 narrow for my 'most realistic' estimate,
namely, 86.7.   In Chapter 3, I mainly use the maximum
estimates but I could not resist using the most realistic
one, rounded off to 87, at one point.

At last, the reader has the evidence for my assertion
that at least 80 per cent of the usual black-white IQ gap
was present (from a genetic point of view) among US
troops in Germany: a gap of at least 12 points, based on
a genotypic IQ of 101 for whites and 89 for blacks, with
87 being more probable for the latter.   The difference
between the maximum and the most realistic estimates for
blacks is, of course, determined primarily by what correlation between the AGCT and Wechsler one assumes to be
valid for blacks.

Let us therefore, take a closer look at the correlation
of .77 we have assumed between the AGCT and Wechsler.   If
we were interested only in white Americans, we could make
a case for either raising the correlation slightly (for

restriction of range) or lowering it slightly (the administration of the AGCT was more carefully controlled than
under the actual conditions of armed forces testing).
But such minor changes would make absolutely no difference
to our final estimates for white troops and moreover, the
main point is this: the three studies on which the figure
of .77 is based are clearly relevant.   They are relevant
because the level of performance of the subjects tested is
reasonably close to the norms for the AGCT, which is to
say it is reasonably close to the level of performance
typical of white America.   When we turn to blacks, we
must question the whole relevance of the above studies and
ask whether the figure of .77 is not overgenerous even as
a maximum estimate.   As Anastasi points out, correlation
coefficients that are high for normal groups often drop to
a very low level for low scoring groups, if only because
their scores are unduly influenced by guessing. (57)   Now
certainly the AGCT reduced blacks to a low scoring group,
one with a mean almost 1.5 standard deviations below the
usual norm.   I referred earlier to a study by Altus
(1948) comparing black performance on the AGCT and on four
subtests of the Wechsler (information, arithmetic, comprehension and similarities).   For his sample of 256 blacks,
men originally classified as illiterate and then trained
by the army up to a reasonable competence in reading and
arithmetic, Altus calculated a correlation between the
AGCT and Wechsler of .285, a very low value indeed. (58)
The mean AGCT score of his black sample was 65.75 and this
level of performance is an almost perfect match for black
Americans in general with their mean of 62 plus.

Unfortunately, Altus gives us less information than he
should.   His sample is clearly standardized to some
degree for educational level;   and we know from Fulk and

Harrell that the standard deviation of such a sample could
be anywhere from 50 per cent to 80 per cent of that of the
larger population of American blacks.   If the variance of
his sample were clearly low (SD^2 = variance), this would
tend to lower the correlation coefficient and we would
have to revise it upward for 'restriction of range'.
Since Altus gives us no value for SD, the best we can do
is get an approximation from Fulk and Harrell.   They
divide their sample of 2,010 black troops into sizable
subsamples which are standardized for years of schooling:
the mean SD of their 14 subsamples is 16.5 but it is
better to take the mean for the two subsamples closest in
performance level to Altus's subjects – which gives SD =
16.0. (59)   Corrections for restriction of range are inev-
itably crude, but using that SD plus the American black
population SD of 24.3 means raising Altus's value of .285
up to a correlation of .41.   We cannot have any real confidence about the exact value of the correlation but we
can, in my opinion, be confident that .41 is much closer
to reality than the usual value of .77.   I suspect that I
have not put the case for Altus's result strongly enough:
actually he studied four low-scoring groups who had been
through army special training, groups of disadvantaged
whites, blacks, Mexican-Americans and American Indians.
The highest correlation between the AGCT and Wechsler he
found was .375 (for Indians) – the mean AGCT scores ranged
from 62 to 68, all near the mean score of black Americans
– and the sample sizes were 225, 256, 225 and 121 respectively. (60)   Compare this to the three studies usually
cited, conducted on inappropriate subjects and with sample
sizes of 100 or less. (61)

   Before we close, there is a problem about my use of
correlation coefficients, one which I consider minimal in

terms of likely practical effect but one which must be
stated none the less.   The only evidence we have that the
troops of the German occupation were an elite group is
that they were an elite as measured by the AGCT;   and from
1946 on accessions were actually screened by the AGCT.
However, recall that during the Second World War the
actual screening was done at induction centres and a
variety of criteria were used: from 1941 to mid-1943,
simply whether a man had four years of schooling and if he
did not, whether he could pass a literacy test or was
judged intelligent enough to absorb military training;
from mid-1943 to 1945, a mix of literacy and mental
tests. (62)   Now in my use of correlation coefficients, I
have assumed that the Second World War screening, taken
collectively, was not more efficient than the AGCT itself.
This was certainly the armed forces view.   It was their
dissatisfaction with black troops admitted during the
Second World War period which led them to use the AGCT
itself as a screening device from 1946 on.   The archives
are full of references to men who cannot count or keep
records and official reports continually refer to what was
called 'the problem of illiterate and untrained Negro
troops'. (63)   I think that anyone who looks at the evidence will accept the armed forces view: whatever the
merits of the screening from mid-1943 to 1945, the earlier
criteria were quite ineffective.   As we have seen, particularly when four years of schooling for blacks was
taken at face value, they let through blacks with AGCT
scores as low as the 20s (roughly equivalent to an IQ of
60);   and this at a time when the army wanted none with a
score below 50 (roughly equivalent to an IQ of 75).

     In other words, there is a problem for my use of corre-
lation coefficients only if the screening criteria of the

Second World War had a higher correlation with the Wechsler than did the AGCT.   I doubt that anyone will challenge my maximum estimate on these grounds - for it is based on a correlation of .77.   It would be extraordinary if the Second World War mix correlated with any standard IQ test at that level.   But someone might challenge my realistic estimate by hypothesizing that the above mix correlated with the Wechsler at above the .41 level.   I think that such a hypothesis is very unlikely when applied to blacks.   I would cite not only the black military personnel with very low AGCT scores (there were almost no white personnel with such low scores) but also the incentive factor we discussed some pages ago.   Recall that a significant number of high IQ blacks may have flunked the Second World War tests with intent.   This would have lowered the correlation coefficient between these tests and IQ quite radically.

The objective of the armed forces was to select good soldiers - and not to achieve an elite in terms of IQ. But given the massive programme of mental testing, it may seem odd that the effects on the black population were so minimal.   I can only call the reader's attention to all that we have learned: (1) when alternatives to the AGCT were used as screening devices, these appear to have been even less effective than the AGCT itself;   (2) the content of the AGCT, or the conditions of its administration, or the unusual incentives it brought into play, or all of these, lowered black performance on it half a standard deviation below what is usual;   (3) some or all of these factors added almost 50 per cent to the usual black variance for mental tests - and it is far more likely that the added variance signals unusual environmental factors at work than the existence of a sample of testees who were

atypical genetically;   (4) some or all of these factors
reduced the correlation between black performance on the
AGCT and IQ well below the usual correlation between
mental tests - with a correlation between .30 and .50 as
most likely.   None of these points mean that armed forces
testing made no sense or was valueless.   It may well have
screened the white population of America, and 90 per cent
of those screened were white, quite adequately for the
army's purposes, e.g. by selecting out men who could do
well at Officers Candidate School, or benefit from technical training, and so forth.   And of course the high-
scoring blacks, the small percentage who were in class III
or above, would have been an elite of equal value.

    I regret that so much of this appendix has been devoted
to my 'most realistic' estimate.   Focusing on that estimate necessitates dwelling on ambiguities concerning
method and data and warnings that our conclusions must be
tentative.   Therefore, I wish to emphasize that my main
purpose has been to defend my maximum estimate, that is,
to show that a figure of 89 for black in-service genotypic
IQ is indeed a maximum estimate.   The figure of 89 rests
on two things: a value for the correlation between armed
forces selection criteria and IQ that is very, very generous; a mass of data about AGCT scores that is extensive,
coherent and cumulatively compelling.   Where we have had
to make assumptions, about such things as air force data
and officer's scores, the penalty for being mistaken would
be very minimal in terms of effect.   It just will not do
to speculate about figures above my maximum estimates:
even a point or two would suggest standards of armed forc
forces selection far above what we know to have been the
case.

    It has been a long road to reach this destination, but

in some ways the material in the archives made me feel
closer to the problem of black and white than anything
else done to research this book.   There was much that was
very human in that material: the officer who always referred to blacks as 'our sun-burned brethren';   the war
department official who asserted that the fact that the
army might have more blacks than the air force did not
constitute a national emergency;   the disappointment of
black musicians who were not 'intelligent enough' to
qualify for the band.

JENSEN VERSUS
SANDRA SCARR

After this book had been completed, Sandra Scarr gave
Jensen an opportunity to criticize her blood-group study
(see Chapter 3, pp. 77-9) and her study of black children
adopted by white families (see Chapter 3, pp. 102-8).
Naturally, she has written her own reply but since Jensen's comments contain the only detailed criticism he has
made of the 'direct evidence' on race and IQ, I want to
give my own views.

The reader will recall that I do not believe that
blood genes give a very reliable indication of the extent
to which American blacks have inherited genes for intelligence from white ancestors, and therefore do not give much
weight to the fact that these studies seem to support an
environmental hypothesis about the black-white IQ gap.
Thanks to this I will comment on only one issue raised in
the Jensen-Scarr debate on her blood-group study.   Jensen
points out that there was a positive correlation of .13
between good performance and white blood genes on one of
the cognitive tests the black subjects took, namely,
Ravens Progressive Matrices.   This correlation may seem
very low, but note that it is similar to the correlation
of the white blood genes with one another.   Jensen goes
on to assert that the Ravens test is a better measure of

'g' (general intelligence) than any of the other tests administered and moreover, that it is a better measure than the first principal component of the total battery of five tests. (1)   The implication is that Scarr's study is compatible with the hypothesis that blacks gain an advantage from white ancestry, an advantage in terms of the best measure of general intelligence her study uses.

Scarr reminds Jensen that she did not use the first principal component of all five tests as her measure of 'g'.   One of the tests was merely a paired-associate or rote-learning test, so she used the first principal component of the other four, all of which qualify as genuine cognitive tests (Ravens, Peabody, Columbia Mental Maturity and Revised Figural Memory).   She concedes that Ravens would be the best measure of general intelligence among these four taken one by one, but asserts that the first principal component of the four taken collectively is clearly the best measure of 'g' available, given that the tests are equally intercorrelated. (2)   She insists on this point because the correlation between white blood genes and 'g' measured in this way was virtually nil, allowing her to argue against the notion that blacks gain an advantage from white ancestry.

My view is that Jensen can hope for no better than a stand-off in this debate.   He himself has emphasized that 'g' is a theoretical construct whose very purpose is to explain the positive intercorrelation among a variety of mental tests.   And he says that the first principal component of 'a large number of diverse mental tests' will serve as an operational measure of intelligence. (3)   It is worth noting that whatever its other merits, Ravens has a lower retest reliability than most IQ tests, a very low correlation with verbal tests of intelligence, and a lower

external validity than the usual verbal tests. (4)   Perhaps the most useful thing I can do is give a literal summary of the results of all the blood-group studies done
thus far: the two samples studied by Loehlin, Vandenberg
and Osborne showed no advantage from white ancestry on a
battery of 19 cognitive tests;   the study by Scarr et al.
found no advantage on 3 cognitive tests, an advantage on
Ravens, and a disadvantage on a paired-associate test.
Most of those who hold a strong genetic hypothesis about
the IQ gap will, I suspect, wish to join the author in
classifying these studies as inconclusive thanks to methodological problems.

   Turning to Scarr's adoption study, in Chapter 3 I described it as a study that points in two directions at
once.   The gap between the IQs of the black-black children (both natural parents black) and the black-white children (father black and mother white), a gap of 12 points,
is an embarrassment for the environmentalist, albeit the
only embarrassment found within the category of direct
evidence.   The environmentalist can provide explanations
but he is forced to do some explaining.   Jensen of course
emphasizes the existence of the above gap and I have
nothing new to add about its possible causes. (5)   On the
other hand, taking the results for the black-white children as a separate piece of evidence, I argued that the
study supports a hypothesis of rough equality between the
races.   The black-white children had a mean IQ of 109
after having been reared in white homes.   My interpretation: the black fathers really had a genotypic IQ of 105
despite the fact that, being typical of Minnesota blacks,
they would have tested out at a phenotypic IQ of 90.   Now
clearly if this last is a mistake, if their tested IQs
would have been say 97, the genotypic increment due them

on the face of the evidence would not be as much as 15
points.   The extra 7 points of tested IQ would be worth
something like 4 points in genotypic terms reducing 15 to
11.

Therefore, I was shaken when I read one paragraph of
Jensen's critique of this study.   In it he says that a
majority of the adopted children came from states in which
blacks may have an unusually high mean IQ and he cites
armed forces mental tests to suggest that at least one of
these states has a black population with a mean of approximately 97. (6)   Upon examination, this paragraph was
found to consist almost entirely of a series of mistakes.
First, Jensen misinterpreted Scarr's Table 2 and asserts
that 31 per cent of the adoptees were from Wisconsin and
21 per cent from Massachusetts.   Actually fully 60 per
cent were from Minnesota and the other two states contributed 12.3 per cent and 8.5 per cent respectively.
Second, Jensen asserts that when preinduction tests were
given to draftees in 1968, Wisconsin blacks had the highest average score and Massachusetts was among the top
three states in terms of best black performance.   In
fact, taking the three states that are most relevant,
Wisconsin, Minnesota and Massachusetts ranked either 1st,
4th and 9th or 1st, 9th and 10th (depending on the test)
out of 37 states with sufficient blacks to merit a rank.
Third, when Jensen estimates the mean IQ of blacks from
Wisconsin at 97, he does so on the basis of their failure
rate on the Armed Forces Qualification Test (AFQT), supplemented by the Army Qualification Battery (AQB), as compared to the failure rate of white draftees from the
United States plus Guam and Puerto Rico.   It would have
been better to compare Wisconsin blacks to whites from the
continental United States (the 'Zone of Interior') in that

the data from Puerto Rico is quite atypical and lowers the
white mean.   But more important, Jensen misused his table
of areas under a normal curve: he forgot to subtract from
.5000 before calculating how far Wisconsin blacks were
below the white mean.   With these corrections, he would
have got 93.5 for Wisconsin blacks in 1968 rather than
97.3.

However, all these are mistakes of detail which are
less significant than the overall drift of the paragraph.
Its overall drift might give the reader the following impression: that if we were to analyse the appropriate data
from armed forces mental tests, we would find that the
black population of those states from which most of
Scarr's children come had a mean IQ well above 90, perhaps
as high as 97.   Jensen encourages such an impression by
comparing his estimate of 97 for Wisconsin blacks with the
96.8 achieved by Scarr's black-black adoptees. (7)
Therefore, let us see what a careful and comprehensive
analysis of the armed forces data has to say.   The states
of Massachusetts, Minnesota and Wisconsin contributed
80.8 per cent of Scarr's children and I have provided
estimates of the mean IQ of blacks from those states in
Table XVI. (8)   I have used all the data from 1965-8, the
peak period of testing during the recent Vietnam War.   As
for method: since the AQB is primarily a series of aptitude tests, estimates have been given for both the AFQT
alone and the AFQT supplemented by the AQB;   comparisons
have been made between the relevant states and both the
white mean and the black mean for the continental United
States;   the estimates for the whole period of 1965 to
1968 have been summed up by way of weighted averages;   as
a check I also calculated estimates from Karpinos's data,
which pools the data from the AFQT only for the period of

TABLE XVI   Estimates of mean IQ of blacks from Massachusetts, Minnesota and Wisconsin - based on preinduction
testing of draftees during Vietnam War

Using AFQT and white mean

	1965	1966	1967	1968	Wt. Ave.	Karpinos
Mass.	91.1	88.8	89.1	89.7	89.6	89.2
Minn.	89.6	88.2	91.5	90.3	89.9	89.8
Wisc.	87.0	86.6	87.4	96.0	89.6	89.2

Using AFQT and black mean

	1965	1966	1967	1968	Wt. Ave.	Karpinos
Mass.	92.5	90.0	87.4	90.1	90.3	89.9
Minn.	91.1	89.4	89.5	90.6	89.9	90.4
Wisc.	88.9	88.0	85.9	95.5	90.2	89.9

Using AFQT-AQB and white mean

	1965	1966	1967	1968	Wt. Ave.	Karpinos
Mass.	86.9	88.6	88.3	89.2	88.3	-
Minn.	86.4	84.2	88.9	90.7	87.6	-
Wisc.	83.3	84.7	82.9	93.5	86.7	-

Using AFQT-AQB and black mean

	1965	1966	1967	1968	Wt. Ave.	Karpinos
Mass.	90.7	91.0	87.5	90.4	90.3	-
Minn.	90.4	87.1	88.0	91.7	88.9	-
Wisc.	87.6	87.5	82.8	94.1	88.8	-

Average of the above estimates

	1965	1966	1967	1968	Wt. Ave.	Karpinos
Mass.	90.3	89.6	88.1	89.9	89.6	89.6
Minn.	89.4	87.2	89.5	90.8	89.1	90.1
Wisc.	86.7	86.7	84.8	94.8	88.8	89.6

Note: (1) White mean and black mean based on data from
'Zone of Interior';   (2) failure rates on AFQT assume that
those 'mentally and medically disqualified' failed the
AFQT;   (3) comparisons to white and black means assume
values of 100 (SD = 15) and 85 (SD = 13) respectively.

1966 to 1969.   To aid the reader, the significant estimates in Table XVI are those of the last two vertical
columns.

The overall data suggests estimates for blacks from
these states of 89 or 90 and it does so with a consistency
which I would have thought simply not possible.   Wisconsin is seen to be slightly peculiar from year to year,
going as low as 84.8 in 1967 and as high as 94.8 in 1968,
but even for it, the overall data makes an estimate of 89
to 90 the only possible value.   Although Scarr does not
analyse the armed forces data, she was concerned to refute
Jensen on this point.   Her original estimate of 90 was
based on IQ tests of black school children mainly in Min-
neapolis and St Paul (private communication to the author)
but she now uses data obtained from the 1976 standardiza-
tion of the WISC (Wechsler Intelligence Scale for Children), a study which tested representative samples from the
major geographic regions. (9)   The values for black children from the North Central Region (which contributed 102
of Scarr's 130 children) and the New England Region (which
contributed 14) are 88.1 and 93.0 respectively, which
gives a weighted average of 88.7.   In sum, the evidence
is simply overwhelming that typical blacks in the states
in which Scarr's children were born have a mean IQ of no
more than 90.   (Scarr's data from the 1976 standardiza-
tion of the Wechsler suggests 102 as a value for the white
mothers of the black-white children rather than the 105 I
assumed in Chapter 3.   If the white mothers were below
105, it would favour an environmental hypothesis in that
the black fathers would have to have a genotypic IQ above
105 to explain the high IQ of their children.   But the
gain entailed would amount to only one or two points.)

This poses the next question: whether or not the black

parents of Scarr's children (and the white parents for
that matter) were typical of their larger populations.
Jensen advances several reasons why the natural parents
might be an above-normal group, e.g. that adoption agencies might try to place the brighter black children into
the white homes concerned, or that the adoptive parents
willing to co-operate with the study might have been those
who happened to get brighter children. (10)   As to the
first point, in another place, Scarr and Weinberg have
given strong evidence against selective placement: all
but two black children in foster homes in Minnesota were
placed in white adoptive homes, so there could have been
no pattern of the brighter going to white homes and the
less bright to black homes;   the children were placed
quickly and no prospective adoptive parent was allowed a
choice of child. (11)   If we are to speculate, I can advance reasons why the natural parents of Scarr's children
might be a below-normal group, e.g. it might be below-
normal parents who were inclined to give their children up
for adoption, who felt they could not cope or lacked the
support of relatives, etc.   It is because we can all
think of reasons why the natural parents might not be
typical that we want actual evidence about them, so as to
end speculation in favour of facts.   The only conclusive
evidence would be the tested IQs of the natural parents.
Scarr could not obtain that so she did the next best
thing: she got all the data she could about the years of
schooling of the natural parents, something significantly
correlated with IQ, and compared them to their larger
populations.   As we have seen, in those terms, they were
found to be typical.

I stand by my interpretation of the results for Scarr's
black-white children as expressed in Chapter 3:   taken as

a separate piece of evidence, it offers support to an environmental hypothesis about the IQ gap between the races
and thus tallies with the main drift of the direct evidence.   In addition, I would like to pass on an interesting discovery made while doing the calculations for this
appendix: using essentially the same methods and data as
for Table XVI, the gap between the races within the continental United States is 1.139 SDU or 17.1 points, while
within Puerto Rico it is .329 SDU or 4.9 points.   The environmentalist would like to argue that environmental differences between white and black are less in Puerto Rico
and that this has eliminated fully 70 per cent of the continental IQ gap.   The hereditarian will suspect either
that the whites of Puerto Rico have a lower genetic value
than those within the USA, or that the blacks of Puerto
Rico are superior, or both.   Other possibilities include:
the armed forces tests need a better translation into
idiomatic Spanish and that the present translation acts as
a leveller; racial prejudice is less in Puerto Rico, so
that the population socially classified as white possesses
a significant amount of African ancestry.   It seems
appropriate to end this book on a teasing problem.

NOTES

CHAPTER 1   THE RACIST AND HIS NEED FOR EVIDENCE

1   Adolf Hitler, 'Mein Kampf', trans. Ralph Manheim
    (Boston: Houghton-Mifflin, 1943), pp. 301-2.

2   G.W. Prange (ed.), 'Hitler's Words' (Washington, DC:
    American Council on Public Affairs, 1944), p. 73.

3   Ibid., p. 79.

4   Hitler, op. cit., p. 325.

5   Prange, op. cit., pp. 71 and 77-8.

6   Hitler, op. cit., pp. 285-6 and 430.

7   See Lucy S. Dawidowicz, 'The War Against the Jews:
    1933-1945' (New York: Bantam Books, 1976), pp. 121-2.

8   See R. Hofstadter, 'Social Darwinism in American
    Thought' (New York: Brazillier;   rev. ed., 1959),
    pp. 173-5.

9   Frederick Law Olmstead, 'The Cotton Kingdom' (New
    York: The Modern Library, 1969), pp. 568-9;   cited in
    Thomas Sowell, 'Black Education: Myths and Tragedies'
    (New York: David McKay, 1972), p. 180.

10 Arthur R. Jensen, 'Genetics and Education' (New York:
    Harper & Row, 1972), pp. 57 and 329.

11 Ibid., pp. 57-8.

12 For Jensen's views on how racial differences in intel-
    ligence may have come about and how long they may have

existed, see: 'Educability and Group Differences' (New York: Harper & Row, 1973), pp. 24, 65-6, 130-2 and 159; also 'Educational Differences' (London: Methuen, 1973), pp. 358-61.

13   Jensen, 'Genetics and Education', op. cit., p. 57.

14   Jensen is not alone in oversimplifying the relation between facts and values. He cites a passage from Spuhler and Lindzey with obvious approval: J.N. Spuhler and G. Lindzey, Racial differences in behaviour, in J. Hirsch, ed., 'Behavior-genetic Analysis' (New York: McGraw-Hill, 1967), p. 375.

15   Jensen, 'Genetics and Education', pp. 327-8.

16   Ibid., pp. 21-8 and 45-8.

17   Ibid., pp. 22, 28, 39 and 45.   Also see Ashley Montagu, 'Man's Most Dangerous Myth' (New York: Oxford University Press, 1974; 5th ed. rev. and enlarged), pp. 400-2.

18   Jensen, 'Genetics and Education', pp. 4, 21, 28-9, 38 and 43.   Also see C.L. Brace, Introduction to Jensenism, in C.L. Brace et al., eds, 'Race and Intelligence' (Washington, DC: American Anthropological Association, 1971), pp. 7-8.

19   Jensen, 'Genetics and Education', pp. 51-2, 157, 202-3 and 241; 'Educability and Group Differences', pp. 33 and 39; 'Educational Differences', pp. 83-90, 112-15, 154-5, 168, 178-82, 223-4, 272-3, 316-21, 378-81 and 430-3.   Also see Arthur R. Jensen, The price of inequality, 'Oxford Review of Education', vol. 1, 1975, pp. 61-2 and 67-71; and Equality and diversity in education, in N.F. Ashline, T.R. Pezzullo and C.I. Norris, eds, 'Education, Inequality and National Policy' (Lexington, Mass.: Heath, 1976), pp. 125-36.

20   Jensen, 'Educational Differences', pp. 218-22.

21 Jensen, 'Genetics and Education', pp. 5-10.

CHAPTER 2 JENSEN AND HIS CRITICS
1 Arthur R. Jensen, 'Educability and Group Differences'
   (New York: Harper & Row, 1973), p. 294.
2 Audrey M. Shuey, 'The Testing of Negro Intelligence'
   (New York: Social Science Press, 1966; 2nd ed.), pp.
   32-259.   For Jensen's citations of Shuey, see: 'Genetics and Education' (New York: Harper & Row, 1972),
   pp. 160-1; and 'Educational Differences' (London:
   Methuen, 1973), p. 233.
3 'Educability and Group Differences', p. 363.
4 'Genetics and Education', pp. 77-84, 108, 171, 227-31
   and 281-91; 'Educability and Group Differences', pp.
   34 and 72; 'Educational Differences', pp. 245-6, 344,
   347-9 and 390.
5 'Genetics and Education', pp. 170-1; 'Educability and
   Group Differences', pp. 66-7.   Also Arthur R. Jensen,
   'Bias in Mental Testing' (New York: Free Press,
   197?), p. 114.
6 'Genetics and Education', pp. 171-2 and 196-203;
   'Educability and Group Differences', pp. 89-90 and
   104-5; 'Educational Differences', pp. 83-5, 178-83,
   218-22 and 315-21.   Also Arthur R. Jensen, The nature
   of intelligence and its relation to learning, 'Journal
   of Research and Development in Education', vol. 12,
   no. 2, winter 1979, p. 93.
7 'Genetics and Education', p. 76.
8 'Educational Differences', pp. 245-6 and 345-6.
9 'Genetics and Education', p. 77.
10 N.J. Block and Gerald Dworkin, IQ, heritability, and
   inequality, in N.J. Block and Gerald Dworkin, eds,
   'The IQ Controversy' (New York: Pantheon Books,
   1976), pp. 411-73.

11   'Bias in Mental Testing', chapters 5, 6 and 8;   'The
     nature of intelligence', pp. 82-94;   and Arthur R.
     Jensen, The current status of the IQ controversy,
     'Australian Psychologist', vol. 13, no. 1, March 1978,
     p. 11.

12   'Genetics and Education', pp. 121-30;   'Educability
     and Group Differences', pp. 42-8;   'Educational Dif-
     ferences', pp. 200-12, 349-50 and 391-7.

13   'Educability and Group Differences', pp. 175-86, 345
     and 355;   'Educational Differences', pp. 213-14, 349-
     50, 392, 397 and 415.

14   'Educability and Group Differences', pp. 270, 280,
     291-320 and 360-1;   'Educational Differences', pp.
     257-8 and 421-5;   'Bias in Mental Testing', chapters
     9-12 and 14.   Also Arthur R. Jensen, The differences
     are real, 'Psychology Today', vol. 7, no. 7, December
     1973, pp. 81-2;   The effect of race of examiner on the
     mental test scores of white and black pupils, 'Journal
     of Educational Measurement', vol. 11, no. 1, Spring
     1974, pp. 1-14;   How biased are culture-loaded tests?,
     'Genetic Psychology Monographs', vol. 90, no. 2, Nov-
     ember 1974, pp. 185-244;   and An examination of cul-
     ture bias in the Wonderlic Personnel Test, 'Intelli-
     gence', vol. 1, no. 1, January 1977, pp. 51-64.

15   'Educability and Group Differences', pp. 121-2, 260-
     90, 321-51 and 361-3;   'Educational Differences', pp.
     191, 287-9, 421 and 426-8;   The differences are real,
     pp. 82-6;   'Bias in Mental Testing', chapter 12.

16   'Genetics and Education', pp. 153-6, 161 and 210-14;
     'Educability and Group Differences', pp. 168-71 and
     235-7;   'Educational Differences', pp. 170, 195-6,
     235-6 and 418-20.

17   'Genetics and Education', p. 167;   'Educability and

Group Differences', pp. 243-54, 303-5, 312 and 360;
'Educational Differences', pp. 315, 348 and 421.

18   'Educability and Group Differences', pp. 202-4 and
356-7;   'Educational Differences', pp. 417-20.

19   'Genetics and Education', pp. 15-17;   'Educability and
Group Differences', p. 241;   'Educational Differences', pp. 405-7.

20   'Genetics and Education', pp. 136-8;   'Educability and
Group Differences', p. 178;   'Educational Differences', pp. 94-6 and 404-5.

21   Thomas Sowell, 'Black Education: Myths and Tragedies'
(New York: David McCay, 1972), pp. 275-6.

22   Vera P. John, Whose is the failure?, in C.L. Brace et
al., eds, 'Race and Intelligence' (Washington DC:
American Anthropological Association, 1971), p. 39.

23   Sandra Scarr, Genetic Effects on Human Behavior:
Recent Family Studies (unpublished: A Master Lecture,
delivered at the annual meeting of the American Psychological Association, San Francisco, 26 August
1977), pp. 39-40 and 75.

24   'Educability and Group Differences', p. 170.

25   'Genetics and Education', p. 127;   'Educational Differences', p. 350.

26   Richard C. Lewontin, Race and Intelligence, in Block
and Dworkin, op. cit., pp. 85-90.

27   J.F. Crow, Genetic theories and influences, 'Harvard
Educational Review', vol. 39, no. 2, Spring 1969, p.
308;   T.G. Gregg and P.R. Sanday, Genetic and environ-
mental components of differential intelligence, in
C.L. Brace et al., op. cit., p. 60;   Sandra Scarr-
Salapatek, Unknowns in the IQ equation, 'Science',
vol. 174, no. 4015, 17 December 1971, p. 1226;   W.F.
Bodmer, Race and IQ: the genetic background, in K.

Richardson et al., eds, 'Race and Intelligence' (Bal-
timore: Penguin Books, 1972), pp. 105-6;   Howard F.
Taylor, Playing the dozens with path analysis: methodological pitfalls in Jencks et al., 'Inequality',
'Sociology of Education', vol. 46, Fall 1973, p. 446;
Howard F. Taylor, IQ heritability: a checklist of
methodological fallacies, 'Journal of Afro-American
Issues', vol. 4, no. 1, Winter 1976, p. 41;   S.J.
Gould, Racist arguments and IQ, in Ashley Montagu,
ed., 'Race and IQ' (New York: Oxford University
Press, 1975), p. 149;   Glenys Thomson, More than black
and white, 'Nature', vol. 258, no. 5534, 4 December
1975, p. 462;   David Lazar, Science or superstition?
A physical scientist looks at the IQ controversy, in
Block and Dworkin, op. cit., pp. 201-2;   N.J. Block
and Gerald Dworkin, IQ, heritability, and inequality,
in Block and Dworkin, op. cit., pp. 476-7;   P.R. Ehrlich and S.S. Feldman, 'The Race Bomb' (New York:
Quadrangle, 1977), pp. 132-4 and 178-81.

28   Thomson, More than black and white, p. 462.

29   Ehrlich and Feldman, op. cit., p. 133.

30   A.R. Jensen, Race and the genetics of intelligence: a
reply to Lewontin, in Block and Dworkin, op. cit., pp.
103-5.

31   'Genetics and Education', pp. 29 and 117;   'Educability and Group Differences', pp. 134-5.

32   'Educability and Group Differences', pp. 135-9 and
186-90;   'Educational Differences', p. 351.

33   'Educability and Group Differences', pp. 166-9 and
'Educational Differences', pp. 411-14.

34   'Educability and Group Differences', p. 185.   Also
see ibid., pp. 117-19 and 'Educational Differences',
pp. 416-17.

35   J.M. Thoday, Educability and group differences, in
     Block and Dworkin, op. cit., p. 150.

36   Arthur R. Jensen, Race and mental ability, in A.H.
     Halsey, ed., 'Heredity and Environment' (London:
     Methuen, 1977), pp. 226-7.

37   'Genetics and Education', pp. 164-5; 'Educability and
     Group Differences', pp. 238-40 and 358-9.

38   'Genetics and Education', pp. 29-30 and 162; 'Educa-
     bility and Group Differences', pp. 144-7; 'Education-
     al Differences', pp. 408-11.

39   'Educability and Group Differences', p. 146; 'Educa-
     tional Differences', p. 410.

40   J.C. DeFries, Quantitative aspects of genetics and en-
     vironment in the determination of behavior, in L. Ehr-
     man, G.S. Omenn and E. Caspari, 'Genetics, Environ-
     ment, and Behavior: Implications for Educational
     Policy' (New York: Academic Press, 1972), p. 7.

41   J.C. DeFries, Reply to Professor Fuller, in Ehrman et
     al., op. cit., p. 21.

42   Arthur R. Jensen, Comment, in Ehrman et al., op. cit.,
     p. 23.

43   J.C. DeFries, Reply to Professor Jensen, in Ehrman et
     al., op. cit., p. 25; also see p. 11 of De Fries's
     paper (see note 40 above).

44   For a first attempt, which has run into difficulties,
     see Arthur R. Jensen, A theoretical note on sex link-
     age and race differences in spatial visualization
     ability, 'Behavior Genetics', vol. 5, no. 2, 1975, pp.
     151-64; and Sex linkage and race differences in spa-
     tial ability: a reply, 'Behavior Genetics', vol. 8,
     no. 2, 1978, pp. 213-17.   For a more promising possi-
     bility, see 'Bias in Mental Testing', p. 362.

45   Arthur R. Jensen, The meaning of heritability in the

behavioral sciences, 'Educational Psychologist', vol.
11, no. 3, 1975, pp. 175-7;   Race and mental ability,
in Halsey, op. cit., pp. 228-32;   and The current
status of the IQ controversy, op. cit., p. 21.

CHAPTER 3   DIRECT EVIDENCE AND INDIRECT

1   William Shockley, Dysgenics, geneticity, raciology,
'Phi Delta Kappan', vol. 53, no. 5, January 1972, p.
303.

2   Audrey M. Shuey, 'The Testing of Negro Intelligence'
(New York: Social Science Press;   2nd ed., 1966) p.
466.

3   Arthur R. Jensen, 'Educability and Group Differences'
(New York: Harper & Row, 1973), pp. 223-4.

4   J.C. Loehlin, S.G. Vandenberg and R.T. Osborne, Blood
group genes and Negro-white ability differences, 'Behavior Genetics', vol. 3, no. 3, September 1973, pp.
263-70.

5   S. Scarr, A.J. Pakstis, S.H. Katz and W.B. Barker, Absence of a relationship between degree of white ancestry and intellectual skills within a black population,
'Human Genetics', vol. 39, 1977, pp. 73-7 and 82-3.

6   Loehlin, Vandenberg and Osborne, op. cit.

7   Scarr, Pakstis, Katz and Barker, op. cit., pp. 80-1.

8   P.A. Witty and M.D. Jenkins, The educational achievement of a group of gifted Negro children, 'Journal of
Educational Psychology', vol. 25, no. 7, October 1934,
p. 586.

9   M.J. Herskovits, 'The Anthropometry of the American
Negro' (New York: AMS Press;   1930, reprinted 1969),
pp. 4-18 and 270.

10   P.A. Witty and M.D. Jenkins, Inter-race testing and
Negro intelligence, 'Journal of Psychology', vol. 1,
second half, 1936, pp. 188-91.

11 J.C. Loehlin, G. Lindzey and J.N. Spuhler, 'Race Dif-
    ferences in Intelligence' (San Francisco: W.H. Free-
    man, 1975), pp. 129-30.

12 See: L.M. Terman and M.A. Merrill, 'Measuring Intel-
    ligence' (Boston: Houghton Mifflin, 1937), pp. 14 and
    48; and P.M. Johnson, Applications of the standard-
    score IQ to social statistics, 'Journal of Social Psy-
    chology', vol. 27, second half, May 1948, p. 223.

13 Klaus Eyferth, Eine Untersuchung der Neger-Mischings-
    kinder in Westdeutschland, 'Vita Humana', 1959, no. 2,
    pp. 104-5.

14 Ibid., p. 105.

15 K. Eyferth, U. Brandt and W. Hawel, 'Farbige Kinder in
    Deutschland' (Munich: Juventa Verlag, 1960), p. 15.

16 Klaus Eyferth, Leistungen verschiedener Gruppen von
    Besatzungskindern im Hamburg-Wechsler Intelligenztest
    für Kinder (HAWIK), 'Archiv für die gesamte Psycholo-
    gie', 1961, no. 113, p. 223.

17 Eyferth, 'Vita Humana', p. 105.

18 Eyferth et al., p. 13.

19 Ibid., pp. 26-7 and 30-1.

20 Ibid., pp. 28-9.

21 Ibid., pp. 16-17.

22 See K.H. Wolff, German attempts at picturing Germany:
    texts (Columbus: Ohio State University, 1955), p. 32.

23 Eyferth, 'Archiv ... Psychologie', pp. 230-1.

24 Data in the author's possession, compliments of the
    Military Attache, French Embassy, Washington DC.

25 Private letter to the author from General Porret,
    Chief of the Office of Military History, French Army,
    dated 12 July 1978.

26 Eyferth, 'Archiv ... Psychologie', p. 222.   Also see
    my Appendix A.

27   Ibid., pp. 229 and 231.

28   The sources are numerous. First, Marcus H. Ray, Re-
      port of tour of European installations (directed to
      the Secretary of War), December 1946, pp. 3-4.   On
      file at National Archives and Records Service, located
      at Washington National Records Center, Suitland, Mary-
      land: Record Group No. 165, Decimal No. 291.2.
      Second, the Occupation Forces in Europe Series: Negro
      Personnel in The European Command, 1 January 1946-30
      June 1950.   Unpublished manuscript housed at US Army
      Center of Military History, Historical Records Branch,
      Forrestal Building, Washington DC.   The theme runs
      throughout but see pp. 61-78, 110 and 140-8, p. 61 in
      particular.   Also see the chronological volumes in
      the Occupation Forces in Europe Series, particularly
      The First Year (Part V), The Second Year (Vol. II),
      The Third Year (Vols I-III), and the volume entitled
      Manpower Problems of the Occupation, 1 July 1946-30
      June 1947.

29   See Negro Personnel in the European Command, pp. 148-9.

30   Harold Zink, 'The United States in Germany 1944-1955'
      (Princeton: Van Nostrand, 1957), pp. 137-8.

31   Ibid., p. 132.

32   Leona E. Tyler, 'The Psychology of Human Differences'
      (New York: Appleton-Century-Crofts, 3rd ed., 1965),
      pp. 340-1.   Also see pp. 333-40.

33   Loehlin et al., 'Race Differences in Intelligence',
      pp. 131-2.

34   Sandra Scarr and R.A. Weinberg, IQ test performance of
      black children adopted by white families, 'American
      Psychologist', vol. 31, no. 10, October 1976, pp. 726-
      39.

35   R.F. Harrell, E. Woodyard and A.I. Gates, The influ-

ence of vitamin supplementation of the diets of pregnant and lactating women on the intelligence of their offspring, 'Metabolism', vol. 5, 1956, pp. 555-62.

36 See US Department of Health, Education and Welfare, 'Ten-State Nutrition Survey 1968-1970' (Washington: Government Printing Office, 1972).

37 Scarr and Weinberg, op. cit., pp. 729-32.

38 B. Tizard, O. Cooperman, A. Joseph and J. Tizard, 'Environmental effects on language development: a study of young children in long-stay residential nurseries, 'Child Development', vol. 43, no. 2, June 1972, pp. 342-3.

39 Barbara Tizard, IQ and race, 'Nature', vol. 247, no. 5439, 1 February 1974, p. 316.

40 Tizard et al., Environmental effects, p. 343.

41 Tizard, IQ and race, p. 316.

42 B. Tizard and J. Rees, A comparison of the effects of adoption, restoration to the natural mother, and continued institutionalization on the cognitive development of four-year-old children, 'Child Development', vol. 45, no. 1, March 1974, p. 94.

43 E.J.B. Rose, 'Colour and Citizenship' (London: Oxford University Press, 1969), pp. 173-4.

44 J.J.D. Greenwood, IQ and race, 'Nature', vol. 249, no. 5457, 7 June 1974, p. 594.

45 S. Patterson, 'Immigration and Race Relations in Britain 1960-1967' (London: Oxford University Press, 1969), pp. 146-7; also S. Patterson, 'Dark Strangers' (Bloomington: Indiana University Press, 1964), pp. 75-6.

46 Rose, op. cit., p. 51. Also: Ruth Glass, 'London's Newcomers' (Cambridge: Harvard University Press, 1961), p. 24.

47 Tyler, op. cit., p. 341.   My calculation is based on
    the following assumption: that 50 per cent of the
    population with a mean IQ four points below the popu-
    lation mean has been eliminated.   Evidence that
    elimination of 50 per cent of Jamaica's population,
    all from the class of unskilled farm workers, would
    give an accurate estimate of the effect of selective
    migration available on request.
48 Tizard et al., Environmental effects, p. 343.
49 Ibid., pp. 338 and 356.
50 Ibid., p. 355.

CHAPTER 4   A PROBLEM FOR THE SOCIAL SCIENCES
1 Arthur R. Jensen, 'Genetics and Education' (New York:
   Harper & Row, 1972), pp. 127 and 301;   and 'Educational Differences' (London: Methuen, 1973), pp. 200,
   349-50 and 396.
2 'Genetics and Education', p. 322.
3 Arthur R. Jensen, Cumulative deficit in IQ of blacks
   in the rural South, 'Developmental Psychology', vol.
   13, no. 3, May 1977, pp. 185-7 and 190-1.
4 Arthur R. Jensen, Cumulative deficit: a testable
   hypothesis?, 'Developmental Psychology', vol. 10, no.
   6, November 1974, p. 1018.
5 'Educational Differences', p. 411.
6 Ibid., pp. 411-13 and 'Educability and Group Differences' (New York: Harper & Row, 1973), pp. 163-7.
7 'Educability and Group Differences', p. 166 and 'Educational Differences', pp. 413-14.
8 'Educability and Group Differences', p. 165.
9 'Educability and Group Differences', p. 172;   and
   Arthur R. Jensen, Race and mental ability, in A.H.
   Halsey, ed., 'Heredity and Environment' (London:
   Methuen, 1977), pp. 232-3.

10   Source for screening towns and counties: '1978 Com-
     mercial Atlas and Marketing Guide' (Chicago: Rand
     McNally, 1978).

11   Source for median family income of blacks: US Bureau
     of the Census, 'County and City Data Book' (Washing-
     ton, DC: Government Printing Office, 1972).

12   'Genetics and Education', p. 205.

13   Ibid., pp. 136-8.

14   Ibid., p. 137 and 'Educability and Group Differences',
     p. 175.

15   'Educability and Group Differences', pp. 332-4.

16   Ibid., pp. 335-6 and 362.

17   Ibid., pp. 302 and 314.

18   'Genetics and Education', pp. 143-4.

19   N.C. Myrianthopoulos, P.L. Nichols, S.H. Broman and
     V.E. Anderson, Intellectual development of a prospec-
     tively studied population of twins and comparison with
     singletons, in J. de Grouchy, F.J.G. Ebling and I.W.
     Henderson, eds, 'Human Genetics' (Amsterdam: Excerpta
     Medica, 1972), p. 250.

20   R.G. Record, T. McKeown and J.H. Edwards, An investi-
     gation of the difference in measured intelligence be-
     tween twins and single births, 'Annals of Human Gene-
     tics', vol. 34, no. 1, July 1970, pp. 11-18.

21   Ibid., p. 18.

22   Thomas McKeown and R.G. Record, Early environmental
     influences on the development of intelligence, 'Brit-
     ish Medical Bulletin', vol. 27, no. 1, 1971, pp. 51-2.

23   Myrianthopoulos et al., op. cit., pp. 244-8.

24   Ibid., pp. 250-1.

25   'Genetics and Education', pp. 324-5.

26   'Educability and Group Differences', pp. 203-4 and
     357.

27   Ibid., p. 165.

28   J.C. Loehlin, G. Lindzey and J.N. Spuhler, 'Race Dif-
     ferences in Intelligence' (San Francisco: W.H. Free-
     man, 1975), p. 289.

29   Oliver Gillie, Sir Cyril Burt and the great IQ fraud,
     'New Statesman', 24 November 1978, pp. 688-94.

30   James Shields, 'Monozygotic Twins' (London: Oxford
     University Press, 1962), p. 61.

31   Ibid., p. 144.

32   Ibid., pp. 101 (table 21), 102 and 48.

33   Leon J. Kamin, 'The Science and Politics of IQ' (Poto-
     mac, Maryland: Lawrence Erlbaum Associates, 1974),
     p. 51.

34   Shields, op. cit., p. 193.

35   James Shields, MZA twins: their use and abuse, in
     W.E. Nance, ed., 'Twin Research: Psychology and Meth-
     odology' (New York: Alan R. Liss, 1978), pp. 83-8.

36   'Genetics and Education', p. 313.   I am ignoring
     Burt's study on the grounds that it has been dis-
     credited.

37   Shields, op. cit., pp. 163-245.

38   Ibid., p. 221.

39   Howard F. Taylor, The IQ Game: a Methodological In-
     quiry (unpublished manuscript, Dept of Sociology,
     Princeton University, 1977), table 4.1.

40   Kamin, op. cit., pp. 52-6.

41   Taylor, op. cit., table 4.1.

42   Ibid., chapters 2-4.   Also Howard F. Taylor, Quanti-
     tative racism: a partial documentation, 'Journal of
     Afro-American Issues', vol. 1, no. 1, Summer 1972, pp.
     1-20; Playing the dozens with path analysis: metho-
     dological pitfalls, in Jencks et al., 'Inequality',
     'Sociology of Education', vol. 46, Fall 1973, pp. 433-

50; IQ heritability: a checklist of methodological fallacies, 'Journal of Afro-American Issues', vol. 4, no. 1, Winter 1976, pp. 35-49.

43   Loehlin, Lindzey and Spuhler, op. cit., p. 288.

44   J.C. Loehlin and R.C. Nichols, 'Heredity, Environment, and Personality: a Study of 850 Sets of Twins' (Austin: University of Texas Press, 1976), p. 40.

45   Loehlin and Nichols, op. cit., pp. 39-40.

46   'Genetics and Education', p. 300.

47   In other words, given his data and assumptions, Jensen is guilty of no mathematical error. Other scholars, Loehlin et al., Roubertoux and Carlier and D.W. Fulker, have analysed essentially the same data and arrived at h^2 estimates of .70 and above. See: Loehlin, Lindzey and Spuhler, op. cit., pp. 83-4; and H.J. Eysenck, 'The Structure and Measurement of Intelligence' (Berlin: Springer-Verlag, 1979), pp. 102-32 and 227-8.   The estimate in Eysenck was actually calculated by Fulker - for Roubertoux and Carlier's estimate, see p. 117 of Eysenck.

48   Compare Fulker's data and analysis in Eysenck, op. cit., pp. 111-12.

49   Loehlin and Nichols, op. cit., pp. 51-2.

50   Ibid., pp. 80-2.

51   Christopher Jencks, 'Inequality' (New York: Basic Books, 1972), pp. 69-72 and Appendix A, particularly pp. 315-16.

52   See: Loehlin, Lindzey and Spuhler, op. cit., pp. 300-2; and J.M. Horn, J.C. Loehlin and L. Willerman, Intellectual resemblance from adoptive and biological relatives: the Texas adoption project, 'Behavior Genetics', vol. 9, no. 3, 1979, pp. 177-9, 183 and 194-200.

53   D.C. Rao, N.E. Morton and S. Yee, Resolution of cultural and biological inheritance by path analysis, 'American Journal of Human Genetics', vol. 28, no. 3, May 1976, p. 238.

54   Arthur S. Goldberger, Pitfalls in the Resolution of IQ Inheritance (unpublished manuscript, Institute for Research on Poverty Discussion Papers, University of Wisconsin, Madison, November 1977), pp. 7-13.

55   N.E. Morton, 'Human behavioral genetics' in L. Ehrman, G.S. Omenn and E. Caspari, 'Genetics, Environment, and Behavior: Implications for Educational Policy' (New York: Academic Press, 1972), p. 262.   At this earlier time, Morton had less faith in the potency of path analysis.

CHAPTER 5   A PROBLEM FOR BLACKS

1   Elizabeth W. Reed and Sheldon C. Reed, 'Mental Retardation: a Family Study' (Philadelphia: Saunders, 1965), pp. 2 and 77.

2   Ibid., p. 40.

3   Following Lemkau and Imre's data as presented by Jensen and assuming a roughly normal distribution. See Arthur R. Jensen, The race × sex × ability interaction, in Robert Cancro, ed., 'Intelligence: Genetic and Environmental Influences' (New York: Greene & Stratton, 1971), pp. 153 and 154 - Table 23.

4   Reed and Reed, op. cit., p. 41.

5   L. Willerman, A.F. Naylor and N.C. Myrianthopoulos, Intellectual development of children from interracial matings: performance in infancy and at 4 years, 'Behavior Genetics', vol. 4, no. 1, 1974, pp. 84-8.

6   US Department of Commerce, Bureau of the Census, 'Historical Statistics of the United States: Colonial

Times to 1970', Part 1 (Washington: Government Printing Office, 1975), p. 381.

7 Census data from the 'Washington Post', Thursday 4 May
1978, Section A, pp. 1 and 5.

8 Paul E. Meehl, Nuisance variables and the ex post
facto design, in M. Radner and S. Winokur, eds, 'Minnesota Studies in the Philosophy of Science' (Minnea-
polis: University of Minnesota Press, 1970), vol. IV,
pp. 373-402.

9 Willerman et al., op. cit., p. 83.

10 R.F. Harrell, E.R. Woodyard and A.I. Gates, The influence of vitamin supplementation of the diets of pregnant and lactating women on the intelligence of their
offspring, 'Metabolism', vol. 5, 1956, pp. 555-60.
Also Harrell et al., 'The Effects of Mothers' Diets on
the Intelligence of Offspring' (New York: Teachers
College, Columbia University, 1955).

11 Harrell et al., The influence of vitamin supplementation, pp. 556-8 and 560-1.

12 Census data from the 'Washington Post', op. cit.

13 J.C. Loehlin, G. Lindzey and J.N. Spuhler, 'Race Differences in Intelligence' (San Francisco: Freeman,
1975), pp. 200-1.

14 B. Tizard, O. Cooperman, A. Joseph and J. Tizard, Environmental effects on language development: a study
of young children in long-stay residential nurseries,
'Child Development', vol. 43, no. 2, June 1972, pp.
337-40, 342 and 355-6.

15 Ibid., pp. 340-2 and 347.

16 Ibid., pp. 342-3, 345-6 and 355. Also Barbara
Tizard, IQ and race, 'Nature', vol. 247, no. 5439,
1 February 1974, p. 316.

17 Tizard et al., op. cit., p. 352.

18   Ibid., p. 351 - Table 5.

19   Ibid., pp. 338-9 and 343-53.

20   Ibid., pp. 350 and 356-8.

21   Martin Deutsch, Minority groups and class status as
     related to social and personality factors in scholas-
     tic achievement, 'Monographs of the Society for
     Applied Anthropology', no. 2, 1960, pp. 4-5.

22   Martin Deutsch and Bert R. Brown, Social influences in
     Negro-White intelligence differences, in Martin
     Deutsch et al., 'The Disadvantaged Child' (New York:
     Basic Books, 1967), pp. 301-5.

23   J.M. Hunt and G.E. Kirk, Social aspects of intelli-
     gence: evidence and issues, in Robert Cancro, ed.,
     'Intelligence: Genetic and Environmental Influences'
     (New York: Greene & Stratton, 1971), pp. 279-81.
     Also see Bernard Brown, ed., 'Found: Long-Term Gains
     from Early Intervention' (Boulder, Colorado: Westview
     Press, 1978).

24   Rick Heber and Howard Garber, The Milwaukee Project:
     a study of the use of family intervention to prevent
     cultural-familial mental retardation, in B.Z. Fried-
     lander, G.M. Sterritt and G.E. Kirk, eds, 'Exceptional
     Infant 3: Assessment and Intervention' (New York:
     Brunner/Mazel, 1975), pp. 399-403 and 406-17.

25   Ibid., pp. 405-6, 416-17 and 430-1.   Also: R. Heber
     and H. Garber, Progress Report II: an experiment in
     the prevention of cultural-familial retardation, in
     D.A.A. Primrose, ed., 'Proceedings of the Third Con-
     gress of the International Association for the Scien-
     tific Study of Mental Deficiency' (Warsaw: Polish
     Medical Publishers, 1975), vol. 1, pp. 35-7.

26   Table 5.1 compiled from: Heber and Garber in Fried-
     lander, op. cit., pp. 428-31 (using the text and

Figure 5, not Figure 4);   H. Garber and F.R. Heber,
The Milwaukee Project: indications of the effectiveness of early intervention in preventing mental retardation, in Peter Mittler, ed., 'Research to Practice
in Mental Retardation', vol. 1, 'Care and Intervention' (Baltimore: University Park Press, 1977), p.
125 (using Figure 1);   and Howard Garber and Rick
Heber, The Efficacy of Early Intervention with Family
Rehabilitation (unpublished draft: Paper delivered at
Conference on Prevention of Retarded Development in
Psychosocially Disadvantaged Children, Madison, Wisconsin, 23-26 July 1978), pp. 18 and '19 plus' (Figure
4) - note that the early Control Group scores in
Figure 4 are Stanford-Binet rather than Wechsler.

27   R.F. Heber, H.L. Garber, C. Hoffman and S. Harrington,
Establishment of the High-Risk Population Laboratory
(unpublished research project report, Dept of Psychology, University of Wisconsin, undated - but circa
early 1977), pp. 6-7 and 10-11.

28   Ibid., pp. 5-6 and 10.

29   See Ellis B. Page, Miracle in Milwaukee: raising the
IQ, in Friedlander, op. cit., pp. 438-9.

30   Thomas Sowell, 'Black Education: Myths and Tragedies'
(New York: David McKay, 1972), pp. 186-7.

31   Arthur R. Jensen, 'Educational Differences' (London:
Methuen, 1973), pp. 236-42.

32   Martin D. Jenkins, A socio-psychological study of
Negro children of superior intelligence, 'Journal of
Negro Education', vol. 5, 1936, pp. 175-6 and 180;
and Martin D. Jenkins, A Socio-psychological Study of
Negro Children of Superior Intelligence (unpublished
PhD dissertation, Northwestern University, 1935), p.
44.

33 Jenkins, A Socio-psychological Study (1936), pp. 180
    and 189.

34 Edelbert G. Rodgers, The relationship of certain meas-
    urable factors in the personal and educational back-
    grounds of two groups of Baltimore Negroes, identified
    as superior and average in intelligence as fourth
    grade children, to their educational, social and eco-
    nomic achievement in adulthood (unpublished PhD dis-
    sertation, New York University, 1956), Introduction
    (unpaged), plus pp. 28 and 74-5.

35 See: Lillian S. Proctor, A case study of thirty
    superior colored children in Washington, DC (unpub-
    lished Master's thesis, University of Chicago, 1929),
    pp. 6-15; H.H. Long, Test results of third-grade
    children selected on the basis of socio-economic
    status, 'Journal of Negro Education', vol. 4, 1935,
    pp. 192-212; and Audrey M. Shuey, 'The Testing of
    Negro Intelligence' (2nd ed.; New York: Social Sci-
    ence Press, 1966), pp. 35 and 377.

36 Table 5.2 compiled from: Proctor, op. cit., pp. 252-
    81; Long - see Jenkins, A Socio-psychological Study
    (1936), p. 180; Jenkins, A Socio-psychological Study
    (dissertation), p. 44; and Rodgers, op. cit., pp. 28
    and 74-5.

37 M.D. Jenkins and C.M. Randall, Differential character-
    istics of superior and unselected Negro college stu-
    dents, 'Journal of Social Psychology', vol. 27, 1948,
    pp. 188-90 and 200.   In calculating the IQ equiva-
    lents to percentiles on the ACE, I have used Traxler's
    estimate that the median of all entering freshmen was
    equivalent to a Stanford-Binet IQ of 109.   See: Lee
    J. Cronbach, 'Essentials of Psychological Testing'
    (New York: Harper, 1949), p. 123.

38   Shuey, op. cit., p. 267.

39   Anne Anastasi, 'Psychological Testing' (2nd ed.;   New
     York: Macmillan, 1961), p. 227.

40   L. Rainwater and W.L. Yancey, eds, 'The Moynihan Re-
     port and the Politics of Controversy' (Cambridge,
     Mass.:   MIT Press, 1967), pp. 77-9 and 119.

41   Jensen, The race × sex × ability interaction, p. 145 -
     Table 18.

42   Jensen, 'Educational Differences', p. 242.

43   Jenkins, A Socio-psychological Study (dissertation),
     p. 44.   In his dissertation, Jenkins speculates that
     his data was less reliable within the IQ range of 120-
     129 than at the higher levels (pp. 38-40).   If so,
     and if we used his ratios (p. 40) to adjust the rele-
     vant table (p. 44 - Table VII), the 10-point decrement
     for black boys would begin at 130 rather than 120.
     He is also more cautious about the sex ratios in his
     data (pp. 41-3) than he was in the published version
     (see my note no. 34).   The need for further research
     is clear!

44   Jensen, in Cancro, op. cit., p. 155.

45   Arthur R. Jensen, Cumulative deficit: a testable
     hypothesis?, 'Developmental Psychology', vol. 10, no.
     6, November 1974, pp. 1000 and 1018.

46   See: R.O. Blood and D.M. Wolfe, 'Husbands and Wives:
     The Dynamics of Married Living' (Chicago: Free Press,
     1960), pp. 34-5;   R.M. Williams, 'Strangers Next Door'
     (Englewood Cliffs, New Jersey: Prentice-Hall, 1964),
     p. 240;   T.F. Pettigrew, 'A Profile of the Negro Amer-
     ican' (Princeton, New Jersey: Van Nostrand, 1964),
     pp. 14-18;   and Martin Deutsch, Minority groups and
     class status as related to social and personality fac-
     tors in scholastic achievement, in Martin Deutsch et

al., 'The Disadvantaged Child' (New York: Basic Books, 1967), pp. 107-8 and 110-11.

47   Ibid., pp. 93-5, 101 and 106.

48   Ibid., pp. 98, 101 and 109.

49   Ibid., p. 106.

50   K.B. Clark and M.P. Clark, Skin color as a factor in racial identification of Negro preschool children, 'Journal of Social Psychology', vol. 11, 1940, pp. 159-69.

51   R. Coles, It's the same, but it's different, 'Daedalus', vol. 94, 1965.

52   K.J. Morland, Racial recognition by nursery school children in Lynchburg, Virginia, 'Social Forces', vol. 37, 1958, pp. 132-7.

53   Pettigrew, op. cit., p. 8.

54   J. Hraba and G. Grant, Black is beautiful: a re-examination of racial preferences and identification, 'Journal of Personality and Social Psychology', vol. 16, 1970, pp. 398-402.

55   H.J. Greenwald and D.B. Oppenheim, Reported magnitude of self-misidentification among Negro children - artifact?, 'Journal of Personality and Social Psychology', vol. 8, no. 1, January 1968, pp. 51-2.

56   E.S. Brand, R.A. Ruiz and A.M. Padilla, Ethnic identification and preference: a review, 'Psychological Bulletin', vol. 81, no. 11, November 1974, pp. 863-6. On p. 866, the authors mention 4 studies which contradict Clark and Clark. However, one of these (Kline) I have discarded because the questions asked were different and another (Greenwald and Oppenheim) did not contradict Clark and Clark on preferences.

57   Greenwald and Oppenheim, op. cit., pp. 50-2.

58   P. Harrison-Ross and B. Wyden, 'The Black Child: a

Parents' Guide' (New York: Wyden, 1973), pp. 23-41,
particularly pp. 23-5.

59 Jane R. Mercer, 'Labeling the Mentally Retarded'
(Berkeley: University of California Press, 1973), pp.
185-96, particularly Table 12; also pp. 144-54 and
Appendix B.

60 Arthur R. Jensen, 'Genetics and Education' (London:
Methuen, 1972), pp. 204-93; Jensen, 'Educational Differences', op. cit., pp. 19-85.

61 B.J. Guinagh, An experimental study of basic learning
ability and intelligence in low socioeconomic populations (unpublished PhD dissertation, Michigan State
University, 1969).

62 Heber et al., Establishment of the ... Laboratory,
pp. 8-10.

63 R.L. Green et al., The educational status of children
in a district without public schools (Washington, DC:
Department of Health, Education and Welfare, Office of
Education, 1964).

64 S.B. Sarason, Jewishness, Blackishness, and the
nature-nurture controversy, 'American Psychologist',
vol. 28, no. 11, November 1973, pp. 963-4.

65 Sowell, op. cit., pp. 26 and 228-30.   Also see pp.
28, 40, 184, 234-5, 253-4 and 305.

66 Census data from the 'Washington Post', op. cit.

67 Deutsch in 'The Disadvantaged Child', pp. 99, 110 and
117-18.   Also see Sowell, 'Black Education', pp. 6
and 10.

68 B. Levy, An urban teacher speaks out, in S.W. Webster,
ed., 'The Disadvantaged Learner' (San Francisco:
Chandler, 1966), pp. 430-1.

69 James S. Coleman et al., 'Equality of Educational
Opportunity' (Washington, DC: US Department of

Health, Education and Welfare, 1966), p. 27 - cited in
Sowell, op. cit., p. 231.

70 The author is in a difficult position here because of
the confidentiality of his sources. But I urge the
reader to scan carefully the 'letters to the editor'
column of, say, the major newspapers of Washington,
DC, particularly those where the teacher who writes in
is protected by anonymity.

71 S.S. Baratz and J.C. Baratz, Early childhood intervention: the social science base of institutional
racism, 'Harvard Educational Review', vol. 40, 1970,
pp. 34-6.

APPENDIX A   BLACK SOLDIERS AND WHITE SOLDIERS

1 B.D. Karpinos, The mental qualification of American
youths for military service and its relationship to
educational attainment, 'Proceedings of the 126th Annual Meeting of the American Statistical Association,
Social Statistics Section', 1966, p. 96.

2 Joseph D. Matarazzo, 'Wechsler's Measurement and Appraisal of Adult Intelligence' (Baltimore: Williams &
Wilkins; 5th and enlarged ed., 1972), pp. 245 and 246.

3 Ibid., p. 257.

4 For an indication of the content of the AGCT, see Anne
Anastasi, 'Psychological Testing' (New York: Macmil-
lan; 2nd ed., 1961), pp. 224-6.

5 A.W. Tamminen, A comparison of the Army General Classification Test and the Wechsler Bellevue Intelligence
Scales, 'Educational and Psychological Measurement',
vol. 11, no. 4, Winter 1951, p. 650.

6 US Department of Commerce, Bureau of the Census, 'Historical Statistics of the United States: Colonial
Times to 1970', Part 1 (Washington: Government Printing Office, 1975), p. 381.

7 Tamminen, op. cit., p. 651.

8 W.D. Altus, A note on group differences in intelligence and the type of test employed, 'Journal of Consulting Psychology', vol. 12, no. 3, May-June 1948, pp. 194-5.

9 Charles Fahy, Chairman President's Committee on Equity of Treatment and Opportunity in the Armed Forces - Memo for the Secretary of the Army, 8 September 1949, Table III (see Tab J for the rough data on which the final table is based - the rough data is entitled as 'Table I'). On file at National Archives and Records Service, located at Washington National Records Center, Suitland, Maryland: Record Group No. 319, Decimal No. 291.1 to 291.2.

10 B.E. Fulk and T.W. Harrell, Negro-white test scores and last school grade, 'Journal of Applied Psychology', 1952, vol. 36, p. 34.

11 ORO Staff, Draft copy of A Preliminary Report on Utilization of Negro Manpower, 30 June 1951, vol. III (Appendix for Part II, chapter I), p. 95. At National Archives, Suitland: Record Group No. 319, Decimal No. 291.2.

12 Marcus H. Ray, Report of tour of European installations (directed to the Secretary of War), December 1946, pp. 3-4. At National Archives, Suitland: Record Group No. 165, Decimal No. 291.2.

13 US Forces European Theatre (USFET), G-4 Periodic Report, 1 July-30 September 1946, p. 33. At National Archives, Suitland: Record Group No. 407, Decimal No. 97-USF5-4.1.

14 Maj.-Gen. E.F. Witsell - Report to Division of Personnel and Administration, US Army General Staff, 24 March 1948. At National Archives, Suitland: Record Group No. 165, Decimal No. 291.2.

15   Charles Fahy, op. cit., Table IV (see Tab J for rough data - which is entitled 'Table II').

16   ORO Staff, Draft copy of Report: Utilization of Negro Manpower in the Army, 1 November 1951, vol. I, p. 28. At National Archives, Suitland: Record Group No. 319, Decimal No. 291.2. Here the data used in my Table IX is dated June 1950, but in the final published draft of this material it is dated January 1950. See ORO Staff, 'The Utilization of Negro Manpower in the Army' (Chevy Chase, Md.: Johns Hopkins University, 1955), p. 10. Whichever data is accurate makes no difference to my calculations.

17   'U.S. Air Force Statistical Digest', 1 January 1949-30 June 1950, pp. 57-8. Housed at Office of Air Force History, Forrestal Building, Washington DC.

18   ORO Staff, op. cit., 1 November 1951, vol. I, p. 37.

19   B.D. Karpinos, 'Male Chargeable Accessions, Evaluation by Mental Categories, 1953-1973' (Alexandria, Virginia: HUMRRO, Eastern Division, 1977).

20   Ibid.

21   The Occupation Forces in Europe Series: 'Negro Personnel in the European Command, 1 January 1946-30 June 1950', p. 133. Unpublished manuscript housed at US Army Center of Military History, Historical Records Branch, Forrestal Building, Washington DC.

22   Roy K. Davenport, Implications of military selection and classification in relation to University Military Training, 'Journal of Negro Education', vol. 15, no. 4, Fall 1946, p. 592 - see Table III.

23   Ibid. Note Davenport's footnote and the drop in class V accessions between his first and second periods.

24   Samuel A. Stouffer et al., 'The American Soldier'

(Princeton, New Jersey: Princeton University Press,
1949), vol. I, p. 501 - Table 7.

25   The figure of 68 per cent is a compromise between (1)
Stouffer et al., op. cit., p. 234 - who estimates 66.7
per cent; and (2) my own estimate of 69.6 per cent
based on computer printout (in author's possession)
made available by Department of the Army, Adjutant
General's Office, Statistical Clearance Section,
Washington DC.

26   The rates for the period up to June 1943 are based on
Rowntree et al. (1943) plus Smith (1948) as reported
in: A.M. Shuey, 'The Testing of Negro Intelligence'
(New York: Social Science Press, 2nd ed., 1966), pp.
329 and 330.   The rates for the period thereafter are
based on Davenport, op. cit., pp. 587-8.

27   Karpinos, The mental qualifications of American
youths, p. 96.

28   'The 4th Report of the Director of Selective Service',
1944-5, with a Supplement for 1946-7 (Washington: US
Government Printing Office, 1948), pp. 52 and 73 - see
figure 1.

29   Based on Stouffer et al., op. cit., pp. 246 and 501.
Details of calculations available upon request.

30   The figure of 72 per cent is an estimate of the percentage of officers who came up through the ranks
during the appropriate period - based on computer
printout (in author's possession) made available by
Department of the Army, Adjutant General's Office, op.
cit.   It was assumed that 11 per cent of white armed
forces personnel and .87 per cent of black were
officers.

31   Stouffer et al., op. cit., p. 246; and L.J. Cronback,
'Essentials of Psychological Testing' (New York:
Harper, 2nd ed., 1960), p. 174.

32   Fulk and Harrell, op. cit., p. 34.

33   ORO Staff, op. cit., 30 June 1951, vol. III (Appendix
     for Part II, chapter I), p. 95.

34   Fulk and Harrell, op. cit., p. 34 - Table 1.   As evi-
     dence of the presence of blacks with AGCT scores below
     50, note that seven of the black cells have means in
     the 50s and standard deviations ranging from 11.6 to
     20.0   The distribution within cells entailed by the
     last two columns make it clear that there was consid-
     erable variance below the means, enough to take some
     scores into the 30s and a few into the 20s.

35   See Klaus Eyferth, Leistungen verschiedener Gruppen
     von Besatzungskindern in Hamburg-Wechsler Intelligenz-
     test für Kinder (HAWIK), 'Archiv für die gesamte Psy-
     chologie', 1961, no. 113, p. 222.   Table 1 gives the
     division of the five groups of children by age.   As
     for when the oldest were conceived, they were a 5 per
     cent sample of occupation children born from November
     1945 to late 1953 - see: Klaus Eyferth, Eine Unter-
     suchung der Neger-Mischlingskinder in Westdeutschland,
     'Vita Humana', 1959, no. 2, p. 105.   I have assumed,
     with evidence on my side I think, that they were con-
     ceived nine months before birth.

36   Compare: ORO Staff, op. cit., 30 June 1951, vol. III
     (Appendix for Part II, chapter I), p. 95; and Stouf-
     fer et al., op. cit., p. 246.

37   'Strength of the Army', 1 February 1945 through 1 Sep-
     tember 1946 - relevant tables.   Housed at US Army
     Center of Military History, Historical Records Branch,
     Forrestal Building, Washington DC.   This source con-
     tains data for both the Army and Air Force until the
     two were separated in 1948.

38   Ibid., 1 April 1945 (pp. 24 and 48) and 1 April 1946
     (pp. 25 and 45).

39 Ibid., 1 September 1946 through 1 April 1948 - rele-
    vant tables.

40 The Occupation Forces in Europe Series, op. cit., 'The
    First Year', Part V, pp. 30-1; also Ray, op. cit.,
    pp. 3-4.

41 The Occupation Forces in Europe Series, op. cit., The
    First Year, section on Manpower, p. 106.   If the
    reader scans the above series, he will at times find
    the historians telling him that 70 was the cutting
    line between classes IV and V.   This is simply incor-
    rect - they made the mistake of assuming that the
    army's minimum standard was the cutting line.
    Throughout the period that concerns us, whenever we
    have the rough data of those who actually compiled the
    statistics, they used 60 as the cutting line.

42 The Occupation Forces in Europe Series, op. cit., Man-
    power Problems of the Occupation, 1 July 1946-30 June
    1947, p. 58.

43 Lt.-Gen. C.P. Hall and Brig.-Gen. G.L. Eberle, Memo-
    randum for the Director of Personnel and Administra-
    tion, War Department General Staff, 4 December 1946,
    p. 1.   At National Archives, Suitland: Record Group
    No. 165, Decimal No. 291.2.

44 See the references to Ray and his office in The Occu-
    pation Forces in Europe Series, op. cit., Negro Per-
    sonnel in the European Command, pp. 61, 79 and 110.

45 Based on: 'Strength of the Army', op. cit., 1 January
    1948 through 1 January 1953; and 'U.S. Air Force
    Statistical Digest', op. cit., 1 January 1948 through
    30 June 1953.

46 Ibid.   The calculation for the Air Force assumes that
    the ratio between the races in Germany was similar to
    that in overseas commands in general.

47   'Strength of the Army', op. cit., 1 September 1946
     (pp. 11 and 35) and 1 February 1948 (pp. 28 and 30).

48   Ibid., 1 April 1948 through 1 November 1949, 'U.S. Air
     Force Statistical Digest', op. cit., 1 January 1948
     through 31 December 1949 - relevant tables.

49   See Charles Fahy, op. cit. for a discussion of army
     minimum standards during this period.

50   Ibid., Tab J - the data entitled 'Table II'.

51   'Strength of the Army', op. cit., 1 April 1949 (pp. 30
     and 32).

52   Ibid., 1 November 1949 through 1 June 1951; 'U.S. Air
     Force Statistical Digest', op. cit., 31 December 1949
     through 30 June 1951 - relevant tables.

53   Table IX officer percentages: 'Strength of the Army',
     op. cit., 1 February 1950 (pp. 29 and 31).   Table XI
     officer percentages before deductions: ibid., 1 Sep-
     tember 1951 (pp. 29 and 37).   Table XI deductions for
     overlap: computer printout (in author's possession)
     made available by Department of Army, Adjutant Gene-
     ral's Office, op. cit.

54   ORO Staff, op. cit., 1 November 1951, vol. I, p. 37.

55   'Strength of the Army', op. cit., 1 June 1951 through
     1 January 1953; 'U.S. Air Force Statistical Digest',
     op. cit., 30 June 1951 through 30 June 1953 - relevant
     tables.

56   Table XI - see note 53 above.   Table XII officer per-
     centages before deductions: 'Strength of the Army',
     op. cit., 31 December 1953 (pp. 9 and 16).   Table XII
     deductions for overlap: computer printout (in
     author's possession) made available by Department of
     Army, Adjutant General's Office, op. cit.

57   Anastasi, op. cit., p. 129.

58   Altus, op. cit., p. 194.

59   Fulk and Harrell, op. cit., p. 34 - Table 1.

60   Altus, op. cit., p. 194.

61   Matarazzo, op. cit., pp. 245 and 246.

62   Davenport, op. cit., pp. 585-7.

63   See Ray, op. cit., pp. 3-5 and the following volumes
     from The Occupation Forces in Europe Series, op. cit.:
     'The First Year', section on Manpower, p. 106;   Negro
     Personnel in the European Command, pp. 60-5;   and
     Manpower Problems of the Occupation, pp. 58-60.   Also
     see the warning to the reader appended to my note 41
     above.

APPENDIX B   JENSEN VERSUS SANDRA SCARR

1   Arthur R. Jensen, Obstacles, problems, and pitfalls in
    differential psychology (unpublished draft: comments
    for forthcoming book by Sandra Scarr, 'IQ: Race,
    Social Class, and Individual Differences'), pp. 60-1.

2   Sandra Scarr, A reply to some of Professor Jensen's
    commentary (unpublished draft: intended for forthcom-
    ing book by Scarr, op. cit.), pp. 7-8.

3   Arthur R. Jensen, 'Bias in Mental Testing' (New York:
    Free Press, 1979), p. 249.   Also: The nature of in-
    telligence and its relation to learning, 'Journal of
    Research and Development in Education', vol. 12, no.
    2, Winter 1979, p. 82.

4   Ann Anastasi, 'Psychological Testing' (New York: Mac-
    millan;   2nd ed., 1961), p. 262.

5   Jensen, Obstacles, problems and pitfalls, pp. 57-9.

6   Ibid., p. 55.

7   Ibid., p. 55.

8   Table XVI compiled from Bernard D. Karpinos: Results
    of the examination of youths for military service,
    1965, complementary analysis, 'Supplement to Health of

the Army', vol. 21, September 1966, pp. 4-7;   Results of the examination of youths for military service, 1966, 'Supplement to Health of the Army', vol. 22, March 1967, pp. 28-31;   Results of the examination of youths for military service, 1967, 'Supplement to Health of the Army', vol. 23, December 1968, pp. 40-3; Results of the examination of youths for military service, 1968, 'Supplement to Health of the Army', vol. 24, June 1969, pp. 46-9;   and 'Draftees: AFQT Failures, 1953-1971' (Alexandria, Virginia: Human Resources Research Organization, February 1973), pp. 5-8.

9   Scarr, A reply to Jensen, op. cit., pp. 3 and 15.

10   Jensen, Obstacles, problems, and pitfalls, op. cit., pp. 54-5.

11   See the comments by Sandra Scarr and Richard A. Weinberg in 'American Psychologist', vol. 32, no. 8, August 1977, p. 683.

AUTHOR INDEX

303

SUBJECT INDEX

abstract-conceptual thinking, 27, 205-6, 210-12,
263
ACE Psychological Examination, 190, 192
adoptions: interracial,
102-8, 262, 264-70,
black-black children,
104-6, 264, 266, black-
white children, 106-8,
264, 268-70, and Jensen
vs Scarr, 262, 264-70,
methodological problems,
103-6, and quality of
homes, 107-8, relevant
data, 102-3; Texas adop-
tion project, 157
American Indians, 7, 48, 52
American occupation of Germany, see Germany
anxiety, see test anxiety
armed forces mental tests:
AGCT-AFQT, 89, 94-5, 219-
28, 233-4, 236-7, 239-44,
247, 252, 254-60, 265-7,
294; army qualification
battery (AQB), 265-7;
correlation with Wechsler,
94, 221-3, 225, 254-60;
effect on inservice AGCT
scores, effect on means,
94-5, 222, 236, 253,
effect on SDs, 243-4,
methodological problem,

220, 228, 237-45, 253;
effect on inservice IQs,
effect on means, 88-9,
92-4, 112, 222-3, 225,
232-3, 254-5, 260, effect
on 'IQ gap', 88, 92, 94-
5, 219, 233, 255, metho-
dological problem, 220-5,
254-60; and Eyferth's
chronology, 245-53; and
h^2 narrow, 222, 233, 254-
5; and illiterates, 226-
7, 258; inservice data,
229-32, 245-53; and
Jensen vs Scarr, 265-8;
mobilization populations,
229, 234-6, 242-4; and
officers, 234-5, 239,
253, 260; and Puerto
Rico, 265-6, 270; and
racial differences, 224-
8, 252
ascorbic acid, 105, 171, 173
associative learning, 27,
205, 210, 263
assortive mating, 39, 76-7,
84, 138

Bayley Mental Scale/Infant
Scale, 167, 171
between-families environ-
ment, see h^2 estimates
between-group heritability,
see heritability